Body Politics and the Fictional Double

BODY POLITICS

and the

FICTIONAL DOUBLE

Edited by Debra Walker King

INDIANA UNIVERSITY PRESS   BLOOMINGTON & INDIANAPOLIS

THIS BOOK IS A PUBLICATION OF

INDIANA UNIVERSITY PRESS
601 NORTH MORTON STREET
BLOOMINGTON, IN 47404-3797 USA

HTTP://WWW.INDIANA.EDU/~IUPRESS

Telephone orders   800-842-6796
Fax orders   812-855-7931
Orders by e-mail   IUPORDER@INDIANA.EDU

THE PAPER USED IN THIS PUBLICATION MEETS THE MINIMUM
REQUIREMENTS OF AMERICAN NATIONAL STANDARD FOR INFORMA-
TION SCIENCES—PERMANENCE OF PAPER FOR PRINTED LIBRARY
MATERIALS, ANSI Z39.48-1984.

MANUFACTURED IN THE UNITED STATES OF AMERICA

LIBRARY OF CONGRESS CATALOGING-IN-PUBLICATION DATA

BODY POLITICS AND THE FICTIONAL DOUBLE/EDITED BY DEBRA
WALKER KING.
P.   CM.
INCLUDES BIBLIOGRAPHICAL REFERENCES AND INDEX.
ISBN 0-253-33779-8 (ALK. PAPER)—ISBN 0-253-21409-2 (PBK. :
ALK. PAPER)
1. AMERICAN FICTION—WOMEN AUTHORS—HISTORY AND CRITICISM.
2. BODY, HUMAN, IN LITERATURE.   3. WOMEN AND LITERATURE—
UNITED STATES—HISTORY—20TH CENTURY.   4. AMERICAN
FICTION—MINORITY AUTHORS—HISTORY AND CRITICISM.
5. AMERICAN FICTION—20TH CENTURY—HISTORY AND CRITICISM.
6. BODY IMAGE IN LITERATURE.   7. DOUBLES IN LITERATURE.
8. ARTS, AMERICAN.   I. KING, DEBRA WALKER, DATE

PS374.B64 B64 2000
810'.509352042—dc21

00-035046

1   2   3   4   5   05   04   03   02   01   00

CONTENTS

INTRODUCTION: BODY FICTIONS DEBRA WALKER KING

> Seeing the dead body of Mrs. Walker there on the enamel table, I
> realized that indeed, she might have been my own mother and
> that perhaps in relation to men she was also symbolic of all wom-
> en, not only including my husband's grandmother and mother,
> who were as different from my own, I had thought, as possible,
> but also of me. That is why she is named Mem, in the novel, after
> the French *la meme*, meaning "the same."
>
> Alice Walker[1]

In recent years, discussions concerning the materiality of the body and its place in postmodern discourses have taken center stage in academic conferences and publications across disciplines. This volume was conceived as a result of my encounter with a collection of personal stories titled *Minding the Body*[2] and two academic events: Duke University's 1996 interdisciplinary symposium "African American Women: The Body Politic," and the 1997 Ford Fellows Conference panel "The Body Politics of Race, Class, Gender, and Sexuality." Each of these venues involved women from various disciplinary backgrounds and, with the exception of the Duke symposium, of different ethnicities exchanging information about the ways in which our bodies are written, read, and interpreted. As I listened to discussions and read stories about the cultural manipulation and exploitation of women's bodies, it occurred to me that they all had one thing in common. The lives recounted, the situations problematized, and the histories revealed were in some way influenced by body fictions. I wanted to hear more and share more. The result is a volume of essays that contributes to the ongoing discussion of body politics by highlighting the challenges women face when their externally defined identities and representations as bodies—their *body fictions*—speak louder than what they know to be their lived experiences. In other words, this collection of essays is about the collision

vii

between real bodies and an unfriendly informant: a fictional double whose aim is to mask individuality and mute the voice of personal agency.

Although this double is created and maintained most often by forces beyond ourselves (television, magazines, cultural mandates and myths), we bear its markers on our bodies, particularly those of age, race, and gender. In this way the fictional double is always with us, constantly speaking, telling, misinforming—determined to be heard and heard first. When we enter a room, it enters with us. Those we meet see it and listen to its story before they ever speak to us. Unfortunately the informant they see, and to whom they are willing to listen, lies. Instead of telling a story of individuals living in social reality, this cultural construction of racialized, gendered, or sexual body fictions disfigures or conceals women beneath a veil of invisibility, threatening economic, political, emotional, and spiritual suffocation.

The lives and relationships affected by the stories that body fictions tell are frequently female and "of color" while the interpreters and empowered authorities are not. As the object of interpretation, "female bodies" in search of health care, legal assistance, professional respect, identity confirmation, and financial security must first confront their fictional doubles in a collision that, in many cases, ends in feelings of isolation, disappointment, distress, and even suicide. It is for these reasons that *Body Politics* concerns itself with women's bodies as well as the difference race, sexual orientation, class, age, and ethnicity make.

In the following pages female scholars and artists of various ethnicities and from various disciplines who have made an impact in their area of specialization, as well as their newly emerging colleagues, enter into a dialogue that theorizes the layered effects and expectations of gendered, sexualized, and racialized bodies. *Body Politics* brings this material together in an attempt to demonstrate how the boundaries of difference and the limits of universality converge upon women's bodies. The ultimate goal of this volume, however, is to suggest, through its structure and dialogues, the need for women's cross-cultural and cross-racial alliance building.

All women share an equal responsibility for rewriting the stories our bodies tell in a manner that gives presence and respect to the living beings body fictions often camouflage. The essays presented here explore what a few of these fictions are, how they are constructed, how they function, and how they are manipulated—both by the women they attempt to camouflage and by others. It is my hope that this volume will bring heightened awareness of the oppressive nature of our obsession with *"the" body*—a phrase used here to signify a stereotyped identity and singularity—as an object of cultural consumption and the locus of sociopolitical negotiations.

Much used phrases like *the body* and *the female body* prefigure a paradigmatic construction that emphasizes categorization of bodies, all bodies, as immutable and externally defined, though fundamentally similar. Through the use of phrases such as these, individuality remains quarantined, while corporeal mechanisms of representational control become agents of perception and corporeal colonization. The primary identity differentiators available within this limiting ideological structure are the subcategories of race, gender, and sexuality. Even the identifying markers and performance of class (from perfectly manicured nails, designer costumes, and expensive cars to standard English usage and Ivy League educations) lose their persuasive power when one is seen foremost as a female of a particular race or sexual orientation. Within this framework of public or popular perception there is little or no space for affirming multiple identities such as Black woman intellectual and healer or White lesbian mother and scientist. Such identity constructions, though a common occurrence in contemporary culture, are considered oxymoronic and socially incongruous. Within the artificial lexicon of "the" body, nothing is allowed to exist but culturally prescribed fictions.

Society's unquestioning reliance upon stereotyped constructions of "the" body as a vehicle for recognizing and knowing the other quietly undermines self-determination, while dominant systems of masculine privilege and cultural commodification alienate and silence individual agency with a roar. The negating force of body fictions is even more destructive to women's alliance building and women's lives than masculine privilege. In fact, the privileges of masculinity depend upon the quiet deterioration of female power, influence, and unity for their continuance. As long as body fictions and the factional relationships they ensure function as the molding rules of bonding and trust among women, the sometimes vicious (and always profitless) female infighting of the past will continue to offer itself as an invisible pillar of masculine privilege in the future.

Not only does the constant bombardment of fictionalized female body images, externally conceived personas, and rules of body play (such as "black women do this" or "older women don't do that") alienate women from each other, it also fragments minds. This I call *conceptual violation*— a violation so severe that it can kill. I use the term to suggest how body fictions produce overwhelming confrontations that act out violence against the mind and spirit of the individual whose body is gazed upon. We all react in some way when doors of opportunity shut tight before us, lines of communication break down, or we find ourselves victims of professional and social "type-casting" because *we* have been made invisible by a body fiction. Some of us simply ignore the attempted assault and move forward. Others stand and fight, while still others internalize the residue of their encounter until that residue erupts in the form of rage, fear, insanity, or death. It is through internalization of the negative that conceptual violation does its most damaging work.

Fear of being defeated or undermined by the fictional double, for instance, can transform an individual's behavior. It is, on one level, akin to what Robin West calls ethical fear—"a fear [of being labeled inappropriately] so pervasive that it forces [those who experience it] to adapt continually to its pressures and begins actually to determine their personality and character."[3] The fear of being misjudged or misunderstood can lead an individual to allow externally constructed body fictions, operating as a threat that resists reinterpretation, to invade or usurp the influencing power of an internally defined and conceptualized self, rendering identities of self-determination ineffectual within certain public spheres. As a result, the subject of the conceptual violation, like the subject of ethical fear, readjusts, transforms, or shifts through multiple actions of self-presentation in order to conform to or challenge the stories body fictions tell. In a move similar to that of cultural assimilation, that which exists prior to the encounter, no matter how beautiful or socially beneficial, dies or is otherwise mutated and denied. Eventually, the "authentic" self is silenced, lost.

Admittedly, the sense of authenticity referred to here is itself a construction, but one each of us creates, owns, and celebrates within herself (or himself). It is cut from the fabric of our experiences (without being controlled by those experiences), sewed with threads of a cultural heritage untainted by derogatory ethnic and racial stereotypes, and laced with dreams unobstructed by hierarchical limitations, social mandates, fear, and powerlessness. At its best, "authenticity," as conceived here, is an understanding of self supported by introspective awareness, honest self-evaluation, personal integrity, and self-avowed worth. It is not constructed through alien (that is, external) concepts of the authentic.

Worse than the death of the authentic or the mutating effects of ethical fear is the failure to overcome the assaults of conceptual violation that result in silence and spiritual (if not also physical) illness and death. In 1996, an assistant English professor at a California university sat down in her home office, wrote a letter revealing the conceptual violence she felt she had suffered while seeking tenure, and then committed suicide. Having grown depressed and alienated beneath the strain of body fictions and racial prejudices, she laid down her battle gear and left us. Her loss is our loss; her defeat, our defeat.

For the sake of all women who have been silenced, turned away, disrespected, and devalued because their bodies inform against them, I offer *Body Politics*. It includes critical essays, personal meditations, and an interview, all of which bring into clear and dramatic focus the persons, the cultures, and the beauty hidden behind the fictions our bodies tell. While many of the contributors to this volume celebrate the defeat of the fictional double by what I describe above as the self-conceived "authentic," others work from a methodology that questions recourse to any notion of authenticity—an original self subject to subsequent distortions. These contributors maintain a sharp critique of the destructive aspects of images imposed on women by cultural forces beyond their control.

Essays such as Maude Hines's "Body Language," Maureen Turim's "Women Singing, Women Gesturing," S. Yumiko Hulvey's "Myths and Monsters," and Stephanie Smith's "Bombshell" (among others) discuss the creation, appropriations, and reinterpretations of body fictions and resistance to them, and theorize the discursive forms this "informant" takes. Instead of focusing on notions of authenticity, these essayists record the historical and traditional make-up of body fictions while theorizing how they are manipulated politically, expressively, communally, and individually.

Maude Hines, for instance, questions the idea of an immutable original self that stands above the fictions our bodies tell by arguing the multiplicity of selves we all possess and manipulate as we confront essentialist body readings daily. In other chapters, such as the interview with Coco Fusco and Nao Bustamante, authors denounce Western concepts of authenticity as a self-serving manipulation of individuals through ideologies that meet the expectations of outsiders and circumscribe a "comfort zone" for those who colonize. Still others, like Gloria Wade-Gayles and myself, discuss the battles of the authentic against body fictions that threaten to stifle self-defined identities with imposed social mandates, myths, and negating stereotypes.

Body Politics brings diverse approaches such as these together in order to offer a methodological synthesis that leads to coalition. Each approach demonstrates that when women's bodies are viewed through the lens of culturally constructed fictions the material existence of those bodies becomes the stimuli of misinterpretation and violation. In many instances they open a space for interpretive moments that allow vicious lies and destructive gazes to jeopardize, manipulate, and bar individual and group access to resources, institutions, privilege, and power. With this in mind, the moments of collision examined in this volume include not only those defined by the interpretive performance and influences of body fictions but the cultural productions, icons, and myths that give these fictions their power as agents of distortion and destruction.

In the first two essays, contributors speak from personal experience and offer counter-narratives which challenge or revise distorted gazes and destructive images. Gloria Wade-Gayles takes on the issue of aging and the commands of body fictions that restrict or attempt to control both the self-images and the activities of women over fifty. In defiance of what I identified earlier as the "rules of body play," Wade-Gayles extends an invitation to women of all ages to forget the restrictions society and "ageism" instruct "older" women to honor. Forget them and *dance*. In a similar vein, Sue V. Rosser examines the impact body fictions have when partial identifications infringe upon our ability to see and hear multiple identities, such as middle class, white, fifty-year-old, lesbian mother, program director, and scientist. For Rosser, when those in the academy hear the voice of only one part of her they do not hear her. They do not see the full context of her work, nor can they appreciate that work fully.

While Rosser uses personal experience to survey how body politics influence curriculum, professional behavior (including research behavior), and collegiality within the academy, Maude Hines uses Black women's literature as the primary focus of an essay that offers a similar discussion of multicultural studies. Hines examines two novels, Alice Walker's *Possessing the Secret of Joy* and Paule Marshall's *Praisesong for the Widow,* to demonstrate our social understanding of bodies as texts and to elaborate on the academy's use of texts as bodies. Ultimately, Hines exposes the relationship between the surface "diversity" that results when texts are read as bodies and the reality of diverse representation in the political machinery of academia.

Body Politics continues its discussion of institutionalized body politics as constructed and manipulated through literature in the following two chapters. Each offers critical assessments of the literary creation and subversion of body fictions by focusing the reader's attention on elements of the text that, at first glance, appear counterproductive of a positive development and presentation of female bodies. Each demonstrates how the use of perverse or grotesque body images and myths in women's literature subverts and critiques problems surrounding the conflation of real bodies with fictional doubles in interpersonal and social relationships, politics, and culture.

"Writing in Red Ink" examines the function of the horrific bodily mutilations and bloody scenes that appear in Black women's fiction. Revising the phrase "writing in white ink," used by Hélène Cixous to describe how women write, this essay suggests that black women write with the blood-stained pen of a historical past drenched in bodily sacrifice and pain. By giving voice and presence to that past, Black women writers offer their readers a path of willfulness that leads beyond the pain of adverse body politics and body injury—a path supported by memory, constructed in blood, and sustained by audacity.

S. Yumiko Hulvey's "Myths and Monsters" traces the origins of Japanese myths that designate women's bodies as the source of defilement and death. She questions the function of *yamauba* myths that characterize women as devouring or destructive monsters, especially when modernized versions of these myths appear in fiction written by women. According to Hulvey, Japanese women writers "prefer to be feared as agents of death, as decreed by myth, rather than bow down meekly as the oppressed Other." In a bold move of defiance and subversion, they appropriate negative images of women, images whose literary history is bordered by the grotesque, to expose the political enterprise of these images (and the body fictions they support) as one that limits and controls the lives and influence of women.

This theme of appropriation and subversion appears briefly in each essay presented in *Body Politics,* but it becomes the primary focus of the essays and interview that follow. Chapters 6 through 9 explore what happens to the fictional body when its appropriation becomes the subject of performance or the overwhelming influence on not only a performer's career but also her life and relationships.

Caroline Vercoe's "Agency and Ambivalence" and Rosemary Weatherston's interview "Performing Bodies" spotlight the performance artists Coco Fusco and Nao Bustamante. The work of these women exposes the play between the colonized and the colonizer, as dangerous body fictions are appropriated and performed by the subjects they attempt to control. Together these chapters ask (among other questions), what results when women "wear" images that usually circumscribe antithetical identities? In addressing this question the authors and performers uncover and problematize the matrix of desires, secrets, and silences that hold our bodies captive. We continue this discussion with Maureen Turim's "Women Singing, Women Gesturing." This essay interrogates the historical nexus of gendered and racialized bodily commodification, body coding, and systems of desire—particularly those that give value to normalized or exoticized images of "the" female body. Turim explores re-signification of body image, as well as the problems women engaged in acts of re-signification face. This dialogue on bodies asks, for instance, have women's representations of their bodies on MTV been successful in exposing the mendacity of the fictional double, or have their attempts to defy body fictions contributed to the maintenance of structures that mask self-determination and fuel moments of collision?

Stephanie Smith's "Bombshell" answers a similar question by presenting an analysis of a dangerous body fiction—one performed by Marilyn Monroe, a woman whose fame and whose destruction can in many ways be attributed to it. Smith examines the image and the word *bombshell* for their historical and political importance. She also probes the image's ability to "reveal and reveil" the instruments of a culturally manipulated bodily (and mental) distortion that masks justice and intelligence. In this essay, the life of Marilyn Monroe emerges as an example of, and a statement about, our society's obsession with the artificial lexicon of "the body" as an element of "common sense" that maintains culturally prescribed fictions while shadowing (and ignoring) "a traumatic knowledge of the Real."

This volume challenges the ideological priority our society gives the fictional double. Both the personal and the critical meditations presented reveal the limits of individual agency, coalition building, fair treatment, and justice by focusing on what happens when the tales told by hostile or essentialized bodily informants are privileged by those who police our professional or personal lives and govern our institutions. Most importantly, as this volume's diverse approaches to its subject matter attests, it celebrates the value and importance of difference while taking the "I" of insulated cultural, sexual, and racial concerns and merging it with "We." By doing so, *Body Politics* reveals the shared stake all women have in the stories our bodies tell. Without being overbearing or demanding, it asks for coalition and offers insights and comments on how a few problems resulting from oppressive body reading can be rectified or, at least, aggressively challenged.

That challenge begins with each of us, acting as individuals empowered with an appreciation for the deliciously distinct human experiences that we each bring to the table of diversity. There, informed by knowledge of something with the ability to reshape and silence the influence of fictional doubles, we celebrate each other. To paraphrase Alice Walker and Gloria Wade-Gayles, that *something*, the secret, is resistance, continual subversion, and the nerve to *DANCE*—even when the music is not intended for you.

Body Politics and the Fictional Double

[1]

WHO SAYS AN OLDER
WOMAN CAN'T/SHOULDN'T DANCE? **GLORIA
WADE-GAYLES**

When you are fifty and over, people seem to feel the need to tell you how well you are physically wearing/weathering your age. Their evaluations are compliments, or perhaps I should say "condiments"—thick catsup, sweet jellies, creamy sauces, and brown gravy needed for meals we did not order and do not relish. In other words, they are intended to make palatable the unappetizing reality of growing older. "Don't let this go to your head," they caution, "but you really look good for your age." The compliments, so unoriginal, so tired, so cliché-ish, so focused exclusively on the physical, are, I suppose, the answers women want to hear when they ask, "Mirror, mirror on the wall, who's the best preserved of them all?" Those who hold the mirror for me have no idea that I am turning away in irritation. I mean, who gave them the right to assume that I need to be reassured about the good fight I am waging against the scarring hand of time? They compliment, and I talk back to them with my inside voice:

"How do you do it? You just don't look your age."
[Do what? Look how?]

From *Rooted against the Wind,* by Gloria Wade-Gayles. Copyright 1996 by Gloria Wade-Gayles. Reprinted by permission of Beacon Press, Boston.

"You're so playful so . . . so much fun. You don't act your age."
[I came out of my mother's womb playful, and pray tell me why I can't remain so at my age, and says who?]

"No gray hair? Come on now. I know you are using a rinse."
[Are you asking me or telling me?]

"It's the natural! That's the magic. People do say a natural takes years off a black woman's face. When I see how young it makes you look, I seriously consider giving up my perm."
[Give up your perm! You wouldn't go natural if guidelines for the crowning of Miss America required that the tiara be placed only on top of peppercorn.]

"You're the kind of older woman who could drive a young man crazy."
[That's supposed to be a compliment? All he needs to be is young, but I have to be some kind of special-old! Exactly what bait am I using to get this so-called catch?]

"It's amazing. You still look sexy."
[You need a crash course in sexuality after fifty.]

"Me. Personally, I prefer older women, unless they're fat. Now that, even in a young woman, turns me off."
[When was the last time you stepped on the scale, I wonder.]

"Girl, you're lucky. You don't have to worry about lying on top."
[Lying on top? What in the world is *that* about?]
"You know. When we lean over our sag really sags."

When a woman reaches fifty, her age becomes "the talk of the town," and most of the people doing the talking are other women, not men. To be sure, men are curious about our age, but they express their curiosity in ways allowed only to their gender. Some of them are bold enough to ask directly, "How old are you?" We need not answer, for as the eyes undress us they say, "You couldn't be more than . . . but it really won't matter when the lights are out." In other words, men flirt. Women, however, pry, and understandably so because we know that asking a woman her age can be as invasive as a gynecological exam. Consequently, we are forced, as men are not, to use search-and-find techniques which would be offensive if they weren't so transparent and silly.

We measure the number and length of wrinkles on a woman's face as if, like rings around a tree, they indicate the exact number of years lived. Laughter however throws off our computation, turning parallels into a thicket of lines we can neither count nor measure.

We conduct clandestine research on her life which aids us with our math. "Let's see now. Her children are —— and that would make her at least ——, and since she graduated college ——, . . ." Or, "She was in the class with ——, maybe a year ahead or behind, but definitely around the same time, and since —— is ——, she would have to be at least ——."

We disclose in order to get a disclosure. For example, we share our disappointment in having been "done in" on our driver's license. Showing the unbecoming mug shot, but really the year beneath it, we ask, "Did they do you in, too?" I don't play show-'n-tell: "Worse, girl. Mine is so bad I won't let anyone see it, not even traffic cops."

Am I running from my age?

Can we accept our age and at the same time reject assumptions about age? Really, what is a woman over fifty supposed to do? Go silent? 'Fess up? Cop an attitude? Be coquettish? Or lie? As in—shave a year or two? "Yes, lie," I think to myself because even if we tell the truth, the assumption is that we always lie. That is what we hear in recycled material for sexist jokes about older women and in beauty myth commercials. The former fills clubs with loud laughter; the latter fills already fat pockets with profit. Since I stopped going to clubs (it's an age thing, you see), I don't know the latest old woman joke, but beauty myth commercials? That's a different story altogether. I can close my eyes and see a flawless face attached to flowing hair (fragmented woman) whispering seductively, "Don't lie about your age, defy it." In all things, women are expected to be pure like driven snow—gotta find another image!—but when it comes to age, we are al-lowed the transgression of a lie. This being the case, if/when we lie, we can say, in truth, "The culture made me do it."

Am I running from my age?

This culture-induced shaving goes well with the American sport of guess-ing a woman's age, and the playing field is wherever we find ourselves. I find that the sport brings out the mischief in me. When my friends play backcourt, aiming for my birth year, I play net, foiling their attempts to know. That is what I did in Mississippi (state changed to protect the not-innocent) when a friend attempted to *see* the age on my driver's license. I was on tour at the time and splurging a bit in a department store which was offering end-of-the-season sales prices that made Filene's Basement seem like Saks or Nieman Marcus. I mean, these were *incredible* bargains. With my friend's assistance (because I am color blind and style ignorant), I selected several outfits, the total price of which exceeded the amount of cash I could spend on something not included in my budget. Having decided that plastic is the root of all evil, I reached into my purse for my checkbook.

"Do you take out-of-town checks?" I asked the saleslady, looking with envy at her manicured nails and rethinking (but only for a second) my decision not to wear acrylic.

From rote memory, she recited responses learned in training. "We take Visa, MasterCard, Discover, American Express. . . ."

"Not credit cards," I said. "Checks. Do you take out-of-town checks?"

"Sure," she said. "All you need is a driver's license and a major credit card."

A driver's license? Eureka! My absolute age was within reach of my friend's eyes. I could feel her breathing hard, almost salivating over the find, when I laid the license on the counter, face up, teasing her. At the very second her contorted neck goosed its way over the plastic square, her breathing increasing in tempo, I mischievously turned my birth year face down in the cashier's hand. And why not? My age did not reduce the price of the clothes or improve the quality of our friendship.

Each time I hear "you look good," I hear the loud follow-up silence that is actually a blank I have to fill in with my age, which, in my over-fifty way of thinking, proves that my friends are sleuthing rather than compliment-ing. And since they are so very serious about their work, "over fifty," cannot fill in the blank. That's only a clue, not the real find. They want to know how *much* over fifty, down to the month, the week, the day, the minute, the second, perhaps, that I came out of my mother's womb and screamed that I was a live birth. Sometimes I think true-false would be more creative than fill-in-the-blank, or, if not more creative, certainly easier for those of us who do not feel compelled to say or write our exact age. Just think about it. "You are fifty-five. True or false?" All we need do is circle a word. We can tell the truth without disclosing our exact age.

Am I running from my age?

"Girl, if I looked as good as you, I would tell the whole world how old I am," a friend says. I want to tell her (perhaps I did) that "good" strains at being a compliment. I learned this four years ago in a chance meeting with an old friend (old as in, I had known him for many years, rather than his life totaled many years) in a bank parking lot on a sunny July afternoon. I had not seen him for at least five years and there he was, directly in front of me, rushing to the bank, at 3:55, to get inside before the guard locked out late-comers like us. When last I saw him, he was a smooth voice emanat-ing from the pulpit of a black Baptist church and a warm smile signaling me out of a group of visitors for a special embrace. What delight to see him indistinguishable among laypeople, without his black robe and his word of

God. I rushed toward him and gave him an embrace I know now was much too tight. "Bill, you look *so* good!" I said. He returned the embrace and then directed me, politely, to the back door through which my compliment had entered: "*Good,* Gloria, is what we say to people who are growing old."

Good. Yes, that's an age-word! How surprised (and delighted?) I am that my children never say, "Mom, you look good." Instead, they say, "Mom, you look great," never adding "for your age." They can fill in the blank, for my birth year is face up in their hands, but without any coaching from me, they protect it as much as I do. There must be something in my demeanor that prevents them from using any form of the word "old," which is a radical departure from their obsession with the word during their preteen years. Then "old" was the word they seemed to have coined all by themselves, with the help of their peers, to stake out a claim for some kind of autonomy in a world peopled with "adults" who were agents of interference they could not shake. Then "old" seemed to connote authority more than calendar years, unless it was preceded by "real," which was used to describe adults who, as elders, could do whatever they wished almost with impunity. Now in their early twenties, my children describe *things* rather than *people* as "old," giving the word new definitions: frayed, too small, outdated, or in serious need of repair, as in "old" sweater, "old" coat, "old" typewriter, or the "old" car I drive.

I have no doubt they used "pretty" when I and they were younger, an expression of their love for me rather than a statement of fact about my appearance. They internalized the be-pretty requirement for mothers. "Pretty" mothers, our children learn in this culture, can greatly improve their social status. "Your mama is pretty!" means she's the one peers choose as chauffeur for a field trip, giving them a sense of importance they might not otherwise have; and "I bet you're gonna look like your mother when you get old" polishes the mirror in which they see themselves. While having a pretty mother (pretty here for black women meaning not overweight, not too dark, attractively coiffeured, well-dressed, and young-looking) might not protect them from Mama-insulting jokes (that is, the "dozens"), it might dull or shorten the cutting knife. There are no dozens for fathers. There is no be-pretty requirement for men.

I didn't attempt to meet the be-pretty requirement—perhaps because I thought I couldn't but mainly because I didn't think it gave my statement on self the right punctuation. For whatever the reason, I chose, as my mother did (But *she* was pretty!) to be a plain woman. I wore very little makeup, did not perm my hair, and had a blind spot when it came to fashion. Among a community of mothers, I probably stood out as a "hippie." I know it is foolish of me now to wonder how I looked then, but "re-winds," I have come to realize, go with the territory of fifty. Reclaim, recapture, recollect, remember, we are taught, because fifty begins the quick slide into forgetfulness. I rewind to my thirties and, yes, there I am, an unforgivably plain woman.

Choosing to be plain when I was younger was an act of defiance with few if any consequences, but choosing to be plain now that I am older could be much too risky. After all, makeup, hairstyles, and dress can do wonders for an older woman. Is that what my neighbor in Talladega, Alabama, was trying to tell me when she advised me to wear makeup, even arch my eyebrows? A woman past thirty who refuses to beautify herself, she said, is either crazy or incredibly vain. Years later, I tried to follow her advice, only to learn that not every woman looks good arched.

I expected a gloriously improved Gloria after my dear friend, Ann-Rebecca, the children's godmother, made me over when I was in my late thirties. She worked lovingly (more important, carefully) with the sharp razor blade, removing thick brows and, with perfection, arching the remaining hair. She worked in front of the mirror in the master bathroom while the children sat in front of the television in the den. "Are you ready yet, Mommie?" Monica asked more than once. Finally, I had a new face! "Come see how pretty Mommie looks," I called to them. I will never forget the look of fear on my daughter's face or the tears. "Mommie, you look like a witch." That was the last time I went down that avenue of beauty. I entered fifty bushy-eyed, and plain.

"Did you ever have to defend me?" I want to ask my children now that I am older. "Did anybody ever play the dozens on you? Back when I was young, did you ever wish I looked different? Did you . . . ?" But why ask when their eyes say "You look great, Mom," but "No more years, please." It is that look all of us have when we see our parents becoming older. It is concern. It is fear. Addition of years eventually brings us frighteningly close to our mortality.

How fast the years went. Only yesterday, it seems, I was the young mother whose two-piece bathing suit my children held onto in swimming lessons at the neighborhood YMCA or whose legs in short shorts they saw racing toward them when they crossed the finish line in a high school track meet. Only yesterday, I was skipping rope with them, banging backboards, climbing over rocks in a tame Georgia pond, beating them to the door on a summer's day, and cheering with them at their high school football games. Of course, they don't do those things themselves any longer. They, too, are older, but they are older-young. According to our reading of age in America, I am older on my way to being old.

The big *Five O* is the culprit. It doesn't matter that the graying of America has changed the line of demarcation between still-capable and over-the-hill, making fifty a young age as it was not in the past. I mean, is fifty still the stopping age for being alive and active and not-yet old? Nor does it matter that women have challenged the nonsense by claiming and celebrating their arrival at fifty. Our culture is so stuck in patriarchal mire about so many things, most especially age, that the big *Five O* remains the culprit, and when we reach it, according to the assumption, the decline begins. That is what we are taught in America. At fifty, the decline begins.

Maturity, the magazine published by the Association of Retired Persons, features the faces and brief bios of women and men who have reached "the big Five O!" Not Five O, but Five "Oh" as in, it seems, "Oh no!"

"Many people fifty and over," Ed McMahon says, the premiums moving on the screen beneath the policy he holds, "don't think they can qualify for health insurance without having to answer embarrassing questions about . . . ," but there is hope in a policy that will bleed our blood. At fifty we are a risk even for those who never take risks with money.

A national leader reaches her fiftieth birthday and it becomes national news. People respond: "I didn't know she was that old." Or, a friend discloses that she is forty-five and people respond, "I didn't know she was that close to fifty."

Articles entitled "Women Who Are Young After Fifty" flood magazines, some of which are not tabloids.

Books on how to enjoy sex after fifty constitute a large market in our nation (though many of the readers stealing a look in mall bookstores are in their teens).

Outfits for the "mature woman" are outfits for women who are at least fifty. Mature is not attractive.

In our obsession with age, fifty—*half a century!*—means as we add years, we subtract capabilities. Fifty-something (even if it is fifty-plus-one) means being close to sixty; which begins the terrifying move to seventy, which traumatizes many of us because everyone knows—since the Bible told us so—that God promised us only seventy-plus years on this earth. Even forty-something now frightens us, and thirty-something is not far behind. How young they are, and yet my children and their friends and my former students lament in their early and mid twenties, "I'm almost thirty!" To be "thirty-something," we learned from the popular television show by that name, is to be close to the problem arena of middle age. And now there is "Twenty-Something." Age is a national obsession.

Correction: *Aging*. That is the politically correct word for the addition of years to our lives, but I find it a sterile word, and therefore appropriate, I suppose, for the kind of reality women are supposed to have as we become older. It is flat like our breasts which (without implants) sag, cold like our feet, which we must cover with socks or risk "turning off" the man with whom we sleep, and colorless like the lives we are supposed to live. It lacks poetry, color, and movement. It is a neutering word that places us in clinical categories: premenopausal, menopausal, postmenopausal, losing this and needing that. Like a cold stethoscope pressed against our bosom, *"aging"* listens for a weaker heartbeat; or like an unfeeling gloved hand, it enters those parts of ourselves where we are most vulnerable. How much like "ailing" it sounds. Was *aging* always the naming word?, I wonder. What was the word for my mother's generation and her mother's? Has anyone conducted research on the different words for this "affliction" and examined them in a political context? Always, there is a political context.

What about "senior citizen"? Well, it *is* a kinder term, but, unfortunately, it does not always mean "senior" in ability or position. It directs our attention to retirement and to residence in senior citizen high-rises, and, in the minds of many people, that means diminution of capabilities.

"It's a shame," my mother said, "the way we retire people before we should." We give legal clout to the myth that "mind damage" comes by an age arbitrarily determined and applied to everyone. Without a paper trail on poor performance, we put people "out to pasture" automatically at sixty-five, or seventy; My God did I wish when I was forty to have the analytic ability, the sharpness, and the retention of vital information my mother had at seventy! And how I do envy today the mind, the energy, and the clarity of friends decades older than I. How foolish we are to use calendar years as the measurement of anyone's talents, capabilities, or value in society.

Instead of saying that people are aging, or growing old, why don't we say that years have been added to their lives? Yes, why not describe/name the process as "the addition of years"? That is benign and precise. It makes a statement of fact *objectively and quantitatively* reached, predicting no absolutes as to resultant limitations and crippling restrictions of an arbitrary but definite age.

Am I running from my age?

A friend accused me of going the route of euphemism ("the addition of years") in order to avoid the path my age is furrowing for me. She had a good argument: euphemisms might keep us in denial, but they don't alter that which we deny. I understood her point and even helped her develop it. "I know that using 'resting place' rather than 'cemetery,'" I said, "does not change what we experience when we lose a loved one. Everyone knows that! And I know that no matter what we call it, we get older every single day that we breathe." But in my defense, I emphasized the importance of naming-words; they carry nuances, attitudes, assumptions, and expectations, and ultimately they shape behavior. They can liberate or imprison. The word "aging," in my opinion, imprisons.

And double standards shaped by gender throw away the key. To wit: being male in patriarchy is an advantage and being female, a disadvantage, in *everything*, even in the God-decreed process of adding years to your life.

A man in his seventies, deep wrinkles and all, can become president of the nation. If a woman could jump the gender hurdle (and that would require wings), she would see a higher hurdle of age. In other words, if a woman ever becomes president, it is doubtful that she will wear deep wrinkles.

A man in his fifties or sixties (even early seventies) sits at the anchor desk, dispensing news and analysis often "decorated" by a woman younger than he in years. A woman in her fifties who wears even faint signs of age roves from crisis to crisis, standing rather than sitting in front of the camera. (If she is slightly "overweight" and not so "pretty" she will rove even at pre-fifty; if she is all of this and black, she probably won't rove at all.)

Age-and-gender biases are invisible particles in the air we breathe; they get into our bloodstream and change the chemistry of our attitudes toward other people and, if we are women, toward ourselves. In the media, they are the stark and seductive images that turn on the projector, amplify the sound, color the scenes, and write scripts that give leading lines to women who are young and only a nod to women who are older. To men, however, they give the enviable ability to be more attractive, more sexy, more suave, more everything desired precisely because they are older, even if age walks in deep crevices on their face. Like aged wine, older men, mellowed and smooth, become a desired vintage. Older women, on the other hand, are the tasteless wine, rendered flat from having been open so many years. Proof is the saying that older men are sexy, so much so that young women sometimes choose older men—graying temples and all—for their sex fantasies. There is no such saying for older women, and if they, by chance, enter the fantasies of younger men, we charge, "Oedipal!"

A dramatic example of media rendering of age and sexuality is the recent box-office hit *The Bridges of Madison County*, which received, and deserved, accolades for its departure from media commodification of lovemaking as hard sex that bones, bangs, and knocks, and therefore sells. It contains no rough gymnastics, no full nudity, no hint of dominance, no on-top/on-bottom positioning, only sweet ecstasy. The lovers are one body oiled satin by hypnotic and seductive intimacy. They perform the love dance, vertically and horizontally, slowly and gently, with pleasure giving pleasure. And when the dance ends, satisfied, they love again, this time with light strokes and color-painting words.

But the film stops short of challenging gender assumptions about age which patriarchy creates and perpetuates. Both characters are middle-aged, but only Clint Eastwood is visibly so. His wrinkles are deep, promising passion. Meryl Streep's wrinkles, by contrast, are faint, lying like pencil marks on her epidermis. Only a hair ribbon is missing from the image of a middle-aged woman looking younger than her years. Visible age on women is a sexual turn-off rather than a sexual turn-on.

Racism ensures that there be no Eastwood versions of sexual passion colored black. Black men as gentle lovers capable of magical intimacy rarely, if ever, appear on the silver screen, and our affected minds lead many of us to doubt that they appear in our bedrooms. It is all bump-and-grind with/for us, rumor has it, and songs sing it, even popular songs written and performed by us. "Ain't nothing wrong with a little bump and grind" and "Pump it up" are two mild examples of this vinegar taste of hard black sex packaged for a good sell.

Nor are there Streep versions of older black women. Down through the centuries, we have been the "darker berry" (an *object!*) that gives "sweeter" juice, and recently we have become "freaks, superfreaks" no man would dare "take home to Mama." The "berry" and the "freak," like the pumping-grinding brother, are young. When we become older, we are neither berries nor freaks. We are, instead, neutered uncles and mammies. Bandannas, not ribbons, and aprons of asexuality, not dresses that catch the wind, are our media costumes. And how appropriate this is for a nation that created the asexual mammy in order to conceal the very sexual requirements of her role in the big house.

To be black, woman, and older is to be plunged whole into toxic waters from head to torso to heel, and we must find creative ways to prevent the damage from being consummate, for this triple jeopardy removes us from what this culture values: being white, being male, and being young. This is the case in the white world outside our communities, and no less so within our communities, for we have yet to develop immunities to the ailments white America suffers. We love young as much as we love white and we continue to privilege male over female.

Of course, we put the problem squarely on the shoulders of "the man." Before we were assimilated into white America, we say, or before we were Europeanized, we say, we valued the wisdom and beauty of older women. Like syphilis, we say, obsession with age is a disease we contracted from "them." My over-fifty way of thinking tells me that knowing who gave us the disease (as if we actually contracted it from "them" in particular rather than from human beings in general) does not remove it from our bloodstream. Once we have it, the search for a cure cannot take us away from ourselves. And a cure we *do* need. Older black women are the butt of offensive jokes in the black community. "Ain't nothing an *old* black woman can do for me" is a common punch line in comic routines, as is "Ain't nothing a *real* black woman can do for me" ("real" meaning very or "too").

Moms Mabley turned the age punch line on its head. Donning dress and mannerisms that accentuated assumed limitations of her race and her age, and using a mop and bucket as props, she pulled audiences from their seats with her gummed recitation of the uselessness of old men. Maybe they could bring her a cup of coffee, but even that was questionable. What "Moms wants, children" is a "*young* man." But that is not what a black "Moms" will get. The truth is, black men as a group are less likely than white men as a group to become involved with older women (publicly, that is). Denied manhood in white America, they, more than white men, need a young woman to give proof of their undiminished sexuality. I do not mean to indict all black men or even most of them, as my wording "as a group" indicates, but I believe we are in denial if we do not admit the difficulty black men as a group have marrying dark, marrying "not pretty," and marrying not young.

Women, too, breathe in the toxicity. Let's face it, we have internalized double standards about age. Albeit with some difficulty, we are more likely to accept an older man (though not too old) for our daughters than an older woman for our sons. And while we don't think twice about a male friend who has taken up with a younger woman, we look with disfavor at a woman friend who is involved with a younger man.

A FRIEND: "Did you hear about _____? She's living with a man ten years her junior."

ME: "Really?" Wondering why the issue is his age rather than their cohabitation, or any other issue at all.

THE FRIEND: "I guess that's a sign of the times. There aren't many available men and . . . (a pause) we are once again imitating white women."

ME: "Frankly, I prefer older men. Actually get excited over graying temples and a smile topped by bald. But I think women should be free to do their own thing. With whomever."

I think becoming fifty made a "new woman" out of me. Shock treatment. That's what it was. I saw "Five O," I heard "half a century"; and I became determined to fight the demons that frighten us about age. My retina worked better than it ever had and my ear canal became long enough to be written up in the *Guinness Book of Records*. I began to see and to hear age biases I missed in my younger years. Sometimes I wish I didn't have this worrisome thing called awareness because it critiques the very pleasure out of a movie and jangles the chord of a song. It was that way with my awareness of misogyny ("Can't you just see the movie," my children used to ask, "and forget what's gender-wrong with it?"); and it has always been that way with my awareness of racism ("Don't you think you are being racially hypersensitive?" white friends ask). Sometimes when I am weary of the weight of awareness, I tell myself, "Just forget the lyrics, girl, and go on and dance to the beat." That is what I said when I recently bought a discounted CD containing the best hits by Ray Charles. I danced, as I had many years ago, to "Smack Dab in the Middle," a favorite of mine because it is Charles at his gospel-funk best, accompanied by his talking piano rather than symphonic strings which can't talk the way only Charles can. I danced, trying to ignore that the song objectifies women, putting us in a list of things Charles desires. I danced, trying to ignore a message I was hearing for the first time: that the women are desired only if they are young. Charles sings that he wants:

> *Ten Cadillacs.*
> *A diamond mill.*
> *Ten suits of clothes*
> *To dress to kill.*
> *A ten-room house.*
> *Some barbecue.*
> *And twenty chicks*
> *Not over twenty-two.*

Am I jealous that I am not in the middle with the Cadillacs, the suits of clothes, the house, and barbecue? Naw! I don't take well to being an object. Would I like to be twenty-two again? Now *that* is a different question. I am not one of those women over fifty who have been known to say,

"You couldn't pay me to be in my twenties again, what with drugs, violence, AIDS, the shortage of men! I feel sorry for this generation." They might "feel sorry for this generation," but I think they lie when they say they wouldn't like to be younger. No one welcomes the addition of years to their life. I think they lie because being in our twenties is a far greater distance from retirement, nursing homes, and the cessation of life than being in our fifties. I think they lie because being in our twenties means our parents are actively involved in our lives and we in their lives; there are no all-night prayers for their recovery from illness attributed to age. I know they lie because the loss of a parent is a trauma none of us wants to experience and from which none of us ever fully recovers. Preferring to be fifty rather than twenty-two flies in the face of logic.

I would prefer to be younger. Correction and confession: I wish I were younger and sometimes the wish brings on sadness. But on my fiftieth birthday, I accepted that numbers don't lie. "And now, Gloria," I told myself, "you are what is called an older woman." But I did not feel that the addition of years to my life had resulted in a subtraction of joys, goals, or even energy. In fact, I felt young, even more exuberant than I had been in years, and alive with passion for projects that only recently I have claimed as my own. I had reached fifty; and yet I still played tennis. I still ran up and down my steps. I still danced to fast rhythms. And I knew I was capable of marching again, facing billy clubs again, and singing from jail cells again in a new movement I believe we so desperately need. I know that I can because I am the racial kin of Septima Clark, Ella Jo Baker, and, before them and others like them, Harriet and Sojourner and the thousands unnamed. They were not twentyish when they were on the battlefield. My age, then, was a year on my driver's license, not an albatross around my neck.

That did not mean, however, that I wanted anyone to give a party; I had the breath to extinguish fifty candles, but not the desire. Gratitude, not happiness, was the emotion I experienced. I remembered better women than I—high school and college classmates, neighbors, and friends—who did not live to be fifty, forty, and, in several cases, thirty. To lament reaching fifty would have been the ultimate in vanity and ingratitude.

When gratitude quieted my sadness, a different emotion came into play. Fear. I actually began to worry about dying. This is an understandable response, I think, given the plethora of after-fifty problems for women that saturate the media. *After fifty,* a woman must go for mammograms more frequently, and mammograms, some people believe, increase the risk of breast cancer. *After fifty,* many women must make a difficult decision: to do estrogen replacement and live with the fear of breast cancer, or not do it

13

and live with the fear of a heart attack, as well as, though not life-threatening, the absence of pleasurable—or possible—sex. And *after fifty*, a woman must exercise her vaginal muscles in order to strengthen the bladder in order to ward off incontinence. Most advertisements for Depend feature women. Our minds can become so inundated with these reminders of how vulnerable we are to everything bad that paranoia invites them to enter our bodies which are older, but not yet afflicted.

Which is why, by fifty-two—or was it fifty-three—I became fanatical about vitamins, enzymes, and herbs that, according to books increasing daily in numbers, prevent everything from loss of memory (B-12) to high cholesterol (niacinamide), cancer (the antioxidants A, C, and E), dry skin (E), heart disease (garlic), thickened arteries (lecithin), osteoporosis (calcium plus D), or whatever (a teaspoon of apple vinegar every day). Not until I reached my mid fifties (fortunate never to have flashed hot once) did I learn to love the taste of tasteless tofu and add yams to every meal because, so say the experts, both are good estrogen-replacement foods. Where once the only magazines stuffed in my mailbox were news and scholarly ones, *Prevention* appeared, and I confess, there were days when it assumed greater importance for me than the others. (Alas, *Prevention* has gone the way of commodification.)

Where once I went directly to sections marked "Women's Studies," "African-American Studies," or "Classics," I entered bookstores with my eyes searching for sections containing how-to manuals, inspirational writings, and books on aging. Ask me about passages and tunnels and fountains and I can give you salient quotes from the experts.

Unfortunately, all of the experts are white women. I wonder why we are not writing books about us and the addition of years? As with everything else, in this, too, we are unique. We can complain that we are not in *Passages, The Fountain of Age, Salty Old Women,* and *The Beauty Myth* (which is, in its own way, about age since beauty requires youth), but we don't have a varicosed leg to stand on if we do. The way that racism exacerbates ageism, which is further exacerbated by class, is our project and nobody else's. To paraphrase Langston Hughes, somebody oughta write a book about black women coping with the addition of years, and I guess it oughta be us.

We oughta look with our own eyes at the clever ways American culture has caused all eyes to turn away from the prevention of illness and become fixed on the elimination of visible signs of aging. The inside can be collapsing, but all is well if the outside looks good. Ours is a culture of denial and fantasy, programming and profit. America sells vanity at a high cost. A billion-dollar industry (which makes the rich richer) bombards us with happy jingles, talking jars, and non-greasy liquids that, before our very eyes (on television, that is) perform miracles. They remove wrinkles, they tighten the skin, they lighten dark spots, they smooth away cellulite, they keep us dry or prevent us from becoming dry. They are miracle workers, these products, and the people who tell us so are women, pretty women, wearing just-right colors and sitting with their legs angled just right for the unseen cameras that are meant to give these infomercials. All the women have teeth filed down and capped for the perfect smile. All the women smile, for all the women are happy that they have found the elixir of youth, and they know how to pose happy having been trained in modeling schools to do so. But they are not all the same, these women, in their skin care needs. Some have dry skin; others, oily skin; and still others, dry and oily. How amazing, they tell us, that one cream works for all types of skin. Most of the women are white, though occasionally one is black, but not too Africanic; or Asian, but not too Asian.

Beauty commercials get into our psyche and direct us down this aisle and up that one, delivering us to the very place where the product, expecting our arrival, jumps from the shelf into our waiting hands. Me? Spend money for a product that makes being pretty synonymous with being young, and white (or, in black magazines, white-looking), and that can't deliver on its promise of a miracle! No way! I was too self-respecting for that and, besides, I didn't need a miracle. I had no wrinkles, no graying hair, no dark age spots, no drawn neck, no dry hands, and no ravaging cellulite.

Arrogant and judgmental, I criticized women who lined their dressers with age-defying moisturizers, but when I reached my mid fifties, I had to "eat crow." Age did what age does for most of us; it crept up on me. While I was sleeping, it walked all over my face. I'd swear I went to bed one night without a wrinkle and awoke the next morning to what I thought was the imprint of the mattress on my face. Wrinkles! Not prescription creams or expensive name-brand creams, but plain old ordinary you-buy-at-a-drug-store creams appeared on my dresser. I rationalized, there is no need to let too many wrinkles come too early if, at a small cost and without injury to my health, I can put on a little dab of cream every night and keep my face smooth. You know, it's like using Vaseline Intensive Care Lotion on my hands. I don't want dry hands; I don't want a dry face. Actually, it's a health thing, isn't it? There's nothing obsessive about that, is there? I am not trying to look young, am I?

Is that what people think, I wonder, when they see my over-fifty body wrapped in blue jeans? But I love my blue jeans, the plain ones, I mean, not the designer jeans that turn our broad hips into billboards for a white woman named Gloria or a white man named Calvin. Not the designer ones that cost a fortune. Not the designer ones that are used to sell a woman's body. Not the designer ones that are stretched tight on women's open legs (yes, ours are always open; men's are usually closed) in magazine ads. Not those jeans, but rather the ordinary, plain, and reasonably priced ones. I wear them for the same reason men have worn them for decades—they are the *only* clothing that needs limited care. You can wear a pair of blue jeans for a week (if you shower daily) and still be clean and look clean. You can dress a pair of blue jeans down or, with a colorful jacket, dress them up. You can lie on the grass in blue jeans without worrying about grass stains or work on the car without being concerned about oil stains because the amazing thing about blue jeans is that they convert a stain into a design. The more stains, the more authentic the blue jeans. I was okay with my love for blue jeans until

I heard them talk about her when she passed. "She's some fine," one of them said. "Phat," the other said. She was an older woman. In her mid fifties I would guess, her body wrapped well in a pair of blue jeans. They talked about her. "She's some fine," and then they "undressed" her. "Yeah, but wonder how she look with her pants off?" They laughed.

I felt a lump forming in my throat. Had men ever "undressed" me?, I wondered. Had they "taken off" my blue jeans and "touched" flaccid skin and sagging breasts? Did anyone, stranger or friend, think my preference for the easy-go/nonprofessional look—jeans, denim skirts, loose-fitting dresses, turtlenecks, vests with Aztec designs, blouses made for rolled-up sleeves, dangling earrings, sandals, flats—was my attempt to deny the truth about my body, my age? Should I care?

Should I care that as a black woman in her fifties, I am consigned emotionally to one of three groups? Women who are depressed, made so by loneliness, regrets, and fear of a speedy decline into emptiness. Women who are angry, made so by remembering too well who did them wrong, including themselves in the group. Women who are saintly, though I can't for the life of me understand what made this group, except perhaps the prescription that we begin preparing early for the afterlife to ensure that we walk on streets of gold rather than burn in furnaces. Saintly. Translation: bland and blind. We see no evil, speak no evil, do no evil, and for that matter, remember no past evil seen, spoken, or done. By us, that is. Saintly? Translation: asexual.

I am sometimes sad about being no longer young, but I am not depressed. Busy women usually aren't. I'm certainly not angry. Blessed women rarely are. And though I am hopelessly tied to old-fashioned notions of morality; that is, I am a "good girl," and I work hard at speaking no evil and doing no evil, I am nobody's saint. I am as human in my fifties as I was in my twenties, and, therefore, flawed.

If I am not depressed, angry, or saintly, what am I? Myself. Just an ordinary woman who, having decided not to be too concerned about this age thing, will dance to her own rhythm. Like a college administrator who was the "belle" of one of our annual Christmas parties, I am going to be myself. Regardless.

The band was playing, and we were dancing—men with women, women with women, men alone, and women alone. Just dancing. Having a ball. I sat down to get my second wind, having danced continuously to three numbers, when I heard someone at a nearby table say, "Can you believe the way she is dressed?" I looked at the center floor and saw her whirling. She was in another world. What daring, I thought to myself noticing for the first time that she was dressed in a black micro-miniskirt and in black semisheer tights. "That outfit is what the students wear," I heard the critic say. I said nothing. Instead, I bounded up from my table and bopped my way to the dance floor. I made my statement in my dance. I danced wildly, knowing that people might think I was competing with her when all along I was affirming her, and myself.

Coming from a culture, or a community, or perhaps an era, that passed censure on women over fifty who acted or dressed too young for their age, I have to forgive myself at the end of each day for the way I am. I rewind the tape of my memories and hear women from my youth excoriating one among them who broke the rules about age-behavior and dress:

"Look at her wearing clothes like that. At her age. She's fifty if she's a day. I know it. And just look at her trying to catch a man. It's pitiful. Real sad. She better learn to look her age 'cause men don't want you even if you do dress young."

This is an early lesson in what a woman actually loses when she gets older—not her youth, but men, and since men are needed to validate a woman she also loses her worth.

I understand the reaction black women of my mother's generation had to dressing young. It signified dignity and a noble resignation to the unerring hand of time, but, more importantly, it offered proof that they had more character than white women. They were devoted to keeping their children looking good, not to keeping themselves looking good. They were anchored in family rather than propped up in front of a mirror. Unlike them, white women were incredibly vain, given to fighting age in various ways, the women said, layering on the foundation, wearing low-cut dresses, putting flat hips (ethnicity makes ours broad) into painted-on pants, and, if they had money, going under the knife. No, they did not want to be like vain white women.

But other rewinds suggest they would try to be like vain white women if doing so would give them what black women are programmed to believe white women receive from white men, even when they reach fifty: attention and affection.

"You know white women are something else. They put on bikinis and let all those wrinkles show. And you know, they think they are looking good. They can be old and ugly but they strut around as if they're young and beautiful."

"That's what they're told from the time they're born. That they're beautiful. And don't let them be a blonde or a redhead! Then they're really ruined."

"But you know, the thing that gets me is the way white men treat them with wrinkles and all."

"I know what you mean."

"Holding their hands and sitting in department stores while they shop. It's something else."

Silence.
Pain.

Perhaps I dance because many of our mothers could not, or did not. Perhaps I dance because I am celebrating the liberation they did not experience, but wanted so desperately for their daughters. Perhaps I dance because their struggles and their sacrifices have blessed me with good-life rhythms they never heard. Perhaps I dance as a way of screaming against the dirges poor black women hear every day of their lives. Dirges are for death, not life. I want to live. I want to live as fully at fifty-plus, at sixty, and at seventy as I lived at twenty, thirty, and forty. I want to live and therefore I must dance. I dance, then, in spite of my age and because of my age.

I know I am no longer young because in my night dreams and day fantasies I am holding an infant nestled against sagging breasts that give the aroma of love, not milk. That I am ready and anxious to become a grandmother is the most joyous age-music to which I now dance.

I know I am no longer young because my day visions of tomorrow show junior faculty with whom I work at Spelman College directing programs, chairing departments, writing books, winning awards, and heading institutions. Such joy there is in witnessing their becoming! We should not put ourselves on a shelf when we reach a certain age, but we must make way, prepare the way and clear the way, for younger women when their time arrives.

I know I am no longer young because my financial planning focuses on retirement, yes, but more on the future of my children and my grandchildren yet unborn. I want to leave them enough memories to last a lifetime and enough money to get them through difficult periods today's conservative politics suggest will surely come.

I know I am older when I stand naked before my mirror and see my brown, older woman's body with discerning/non-rejecting eyes. I see my hands. As I move fast toward sixty, they are designed with a network of tiny lines. They are my hands and with them I can hold myself and others.

I see my face. The lines around my mouth are deeper now than they were last year and the dark hollows beneath the eyes, a genetic trait, are darker. It is my face, and it wears the smile I give myself and others.

I see my neck. It asks for high-neck blouses and scarves that accentuate as they cover, but it rests on shoulders sturdy enough for my weight and the weight of others.

I am not depressed about being older, and yet sometimes it is my voice I hear when Nina Simone, in the deep dark chocolate of her alto, sings, "I live alone. . . . The walls talk back to me and they seem to say, 'Wasn't yesterday a better day?'" Sometimes yesterday haunts me. It is the train whistle I hear when a litany of regrets disturbs my sleep, or the train itself, grander, perhaps, than in reality, moving to places once filled with my breath and shaped by my desires. I want to board yesterday, so much do I miss the texture of the life I lived then, the joys that are now then-joys. I miss yesterday, sometimes with an ache that defies description. If only I could relive my life, so much I would say and not say, feel and not feel, think and not think, do and not do, accept and reject, learn and unlearn, struggle to keep and find the courage to release. I would be different, I tell myself in my revelry, and therefore I would come different to this new place.

But only on rare cloudy days does yesterday as longing enter my new space, slowing the rhythm of my dance, but not for long because I will not permit it to linger, not in that way. As knowledge and insight, however, it is always with me, an almanac for my now-life. This will bring rain, it tells me. That, sunshine. This will affirm. That, alienate. This will confuse. That, clarify. This advises pull back. That, hang on. This cautions, "Be still." That says, "Dance!"

We are always in the process of becoming, philosophers tell us, moving through one stage in preparation for the next, each stage having its own purpose, our understanding of which ends delusional longing for previous stages. As with nature, so, too, with humankind. There are seasons in our lives we cannot bypass. We enter them when we are supposed to and, once there, we do what we are supposed to do.

The first half-century of my life was the "yes" season. I could not shape my lips to answer "no" to others' needs or remember how to say "yes" to my own. I was always interruptible, always accessible and available, always willing to get out of a document that bore my name and pull up, on my own computer no less, someone else's document. I was like a plant from which one takes cuttings. A piece for this one. A piece for that one. A piece for those over there and these over here. Although there were times when I could feel the blade, I did not regret the cuttings. They strengthened my roots.

But there is a time when a plant should be left still, when the number of cuttings should be reduced, when it should be left undisturbed in the light of its own nourishing suns. Now is that time for me, and I am content in accepting that only now could the me-time have arrived. I believe I entered this season when I was supposed to. What remains is for me to do what I believe I am supposed to do: pick up the pen, or turn on the computer, and attempt to write.

When friends tell me that I should have tried to write years ago, planting seeds of regret in the earth of my feelings, I add rather than subtract, and the result is a full life of memories and experiences that form words and images I was not supposed to know, until now. Becoming older is a gift, not a curse, for it is that season when we have long and passionate conversations with the self we spoke to only briefly in our younger years. It could be argued that if gender politics changed, that is, if women in patriarchy weren't conditioned to be other-oriented, we could reach this season earlier in life. Perhaps that is true for some women, but not for me. Patriarchy did not force me to be maternal, and that is what I was, and am. Maternal. I chafe at the very idea that anyone would attribute this joy to patriarchy, to sexism, to restrictions on my life. If all the rules had been different, I know that my longer conversations would have been with my loved ones, my students, and others. That was my choice, and that was my joy. It was not so much that I held the joy of writing in suspension as that the season for writing had not yet arrived.

"I can't talk to you now," I say in this season. "I'm writing."

"This is not a good weekend for a visit," I am able now to tell friends. "I am driving up to the mountains to meditate and to write."

And to my own children, "Let me call you back later. I don't want to lose the words."

20

Those who love me are delighted rather than offended by the new Gloria. They call and begin their conversation with, "I'm not going to talk long. I can hear in your voice you're busy." But they are certain enough of the availability of cuttings to feel comfortable saying, "I must talk to you now." "Hold on," I tell them. I leave the phone for the second it takes me to push Fro, directing the computer to save my document, and I return, the clock for the day turned face down in my heart.

Who or what I will become in this season is beyond my knowing, but I feel pregnant with the promise of new joys. I do not think they could equal the joys from my past, but they will be joys nonetheless, for as a woman thinketh, so is she in her heart. I think joy. I *choose* to think joy, and by so doing, I bring joy into my life.

I am calmer now. More introspective. More tolerant. More thoughtful. More observant. More expectant of success than fearful of failure. More aware of what I once called small details but which I now know are not small at all. I am different.

Here, I see in sharp/clear lines the primacy of every thought, every act, every person, every experience to my becoming and to my health. In my earlier life, I understood this intellectually. Here I experience it spiritually.

I always felt a sense of urgency about achievement, about getting things done, about finding all the answers and bringing closure to all the conflicts, but here I measure achievement differently; it is less what someone says I should achieve and more what I want to achieve.

Here, I get things done, but in fuller appreciation of the process of doing them and the self that evolves thereby/therefrom.

Here, I search for answers, but with the understanding that each answer leads me to new questions. Indeed, having arrived here, I understand that living is the experience human beings have with questions. The nature of the questions we ask and the answers we offer is the statement we make on who we are in relation to ourselves, to others, and to the world in which we live. The questions end only when life ends—if either does.

Here, I have learned that closure is an act of the heart opening, not of the mind clarifying.

Here, I want no toxins in my heart or in my mind.

Here is the place for purging, for filtering, for distilling.

Here, I know that any diminishing of who I am will not result from the addition of years to my life, but rather from the senseless waste of self and talents, time and breath, that hatred, lack of forgiveness, selfishness, and materialism make of all lives, regardless of age. My heart has aged, but it has grown stronger. It loves with greater care, locking out no one and trying to beat with a fast and defensive pulse when it senses the approach of negative energy. It directs my hands to move in circles continuously in front of my face, protecting my spirit from harm. As smoke in African rituals that wards off evil spirits, so are my circling hands.

Here, I have discovered the beauty of taking time to enjoy the time I give, with mindfulness the Buddhists say, to ordinary joys of life which are, in fact, our blessings.

Here, I feel a magical and inexplicable zest for life. Show me the mountain and if it interests me, I think I would dare try to climb it.

As I sing a soon-sixty song, I hear the same chords of meaning I have sung all of my singing life. They instruct me in how to work at living an examined life and how to *choose joy*. But of course *joy*, because sadness has no rhythm to which wrinkled hands can clap and to which varicosed legs can dance. Dance. *DANCE!*

[2]

WHEN BODY POLITICS OF PARTIAL IDENTIFICATIONS COLLIDE WITH MULTIPLE IDENTITIES OF REAL ACADEMICS: LIMITED UNDERSTANDINGS OF RESEARCH AND TRUNCATED COLLEGIAL INTERACTIONS **SUE V. ROSSER**

White, fifty years old, middle-class, lesbian, mother, formerly married for eleven years, French major, Ph.D., scientist, director of women's studies, interdisciplinary—all are descriptors of me. Some, such as my race, stand as immutable markers known from the time of my birth. Others, such as motherhood, became biological and psychological constants after a particular moment in my life. Another may have been set since birth, but only became evident to me over time as I struggled against prevailing social expectations and norms to realize my lesbian identity. My marital status changed from single to married to divorced, although these categories signify markers available only for heterosexual relationships, which apply to part of my adult life. Despite my desire to slow it down, my age changes at a constant rate over time. Some of these other descriptors and identities I have worked to obtain, acquire, or achieve. I worked hard to obtain my academic credentials of a double undergraduate major in French and zoology and M.S. and Ph.D. degrees in zoology. These credentials laid the groundwork for my deep-rooted interest in interdisciplinary studies. When coupled with additional hard work and some luck, they provided an entree to my professional identities as a full professor and as director of women's studies. These latter titles suggest, but do not fully document, my strong identities as a scholar and as an administrator.

All of these descriptors are accurate. In accepting, working to achieve, and struggling to understand each of them. I have attempted to weave a coherent identity that I think of as me. Some descriptors identify my body and politics more strongly in the way I perceive myself and try to project myself to others. Depending upon the situation and the person, some remain invisible, ignored, or misunderstood by others.

Since some of these body inscriptions, such as my white race, my female gender, my middle age, and perhaps my class, become evident the moment I am seen or heard to speak, I have difficulty deciding how they affect my academic status, relationships with colleagues, and work. From my academic backgrounds in both a nontraditional area for women (science) and a field in which the expectation is that the person will embody the identity (women's studies), I can glean some insights into reactions to my female body and gender. In women's studies, my female body and gender fit the professional expectations for the field; others in the profession assume that we will have shared experiences, reactions, and treatment, which predispose them to accept my scholarship and me. I would have to do something to warrant exclusion from this insider status. If anything, some colleagues in women's studies may assume that our ideas, opinions, and interests are more similar than they actually are, because we share the same sex and gender.

In contrast, colleagues in the sciences tend to cast me in the role of outsider. In recent years I have attributed their assumption to my introduction as director of women's studies; since much feminist scholarship originated from the humanities and social sciences, they imagine that I have no background in science. Previously, I believed that my gender caused this outsider designation. When I received my Ph.D. in zoology, the sciences, even the life sciences, included very few women. Unless my scientific identity had been revealed, I was ignored or treated as a spouse, a secretary, or possibly a lab technician at any scientific gathering, because science was a nontraditional area for women. These experiences began to open my eyes to how professional colleagues might make assumptions and see only parts of me and my academic knowledge because of expectations they held based upon my body.

As a young scientist, I experienced these partial understandings as a form of discrimination. I wondered how I could ever be accepted as a scientist, since my female body and gender socialization meant that I did not look and act like them (male and masculine). When I had my first child, shortly after I received my master's degree, my colleagues appeared to perceive me as a less-than-serious scientist. They seemed to write me off as not a genuine graduate student, although I had already passed my qualifying examinations for the Ph.D. My major professor did not demonstrate these perceptions in any overt manner, and in fact he was one of the few faculty in this all-male department who took women as graduate students. But I did notice that he suggested a dissertation topic for me that could be pursued in the United States, with minimal time in the field. Typically his students went to Africa for several months to complete their research. Although my initial reaction was to attribute the changed attitude of my peers and major professor to my new bodily identity as a mother because of my pregnancy and childbirth, the next thoughts I had centered on whether what I did was real science, measured up to what they did, and focused on the important questions. I desperately sought women scientists as role models, as proof that it was possible to be a woman, do good science, and be accepted.

Perhaps my fears of not being taken seriously spurred me to work especially hard and prove myself. Despite having the baby, I finished my Ph.D. four years after receiving my bachelor's degree; seven years was the departmental average. Then I took a postdoctoral position at the same institution. This was generally viewed as a professional mistake, particularly since I had also obtained my undergraduate degree there and would now be working in a distantly related field, and it provided further proof that I must not be serious about my career. As my colleagues perceived, my gender undergirded this unorthodox career move. Since I was married with a child and my husband had not yet completed his Ph.D., I wanted to stay in town.

After I had spent two years learning a new area of biology, my postdoctoral research finally appeared to be on track. When I became pregnant with my second child, the professor supervising my research suggested that I get an abortion, since it was "the wrong time in the research" and we needed to obtain more data to have the grant renewed. I did not have the abortion. I rationalized that taking minimal time off for childbirth meant that everything would be fine in the lab and with my scientific career. One day when I was out at noon to breast-feed the baby, a call came which focused on my area of research. Although many of the other postdocs and graduate students (all males) used their lunch hour to play squash, I later learned that the professor had made comments to others in the lab about my being off nursing again. Those comments, coupled with related incidents, made me decide to accept the offer of the new women's studies program to teach a course on the biology of women.

Women's studies gave me new space, perceptions, knowledge, and connections to understand my bodily identity and the reactions it invoked. It was the mid-1970s, the program's first year, and only women were involved in it then; they welcomed me because I was a woman and even encouraged me to bring the baby to some meetings. From the stories of the more senior women in the academy, I learned that much of the discrimination I had experienced was not unique, but resulted from being a woman in a patriarchal university which only the previous year, under court order, had dropped its official quotas for women medical students and nepotism rules against women faculty. Because I was teaching the biology of women, I began to read the evolving critiques revealing bias in research developed by men, using only males as subjects, and with theories and conclusions extrapolated inappropriately to the entire population of both men and women. While developing a new course in women's health, I recognized that, despite my Ph.D. in zoology and having given birth to two children, I knew almost nothing about my own body and its functioning. When I sought materials to fill this knowledge gap, I learned that very little research had focused on women and their bodies in health and disease. Recognizing this dearth and that any research that existed had been undertaken by men from their perspective, I began to work to create materials that reflected women's experience of their biology and bodily identity. Suddenly, I felt a connection with teaching this research and with my search for materials, from medical textbooks through scientific journals to fiction, to convey the information to students. Trained in the humanities, social sciences, and fine arts, my colleagues in women's studies helped me to uncover the interdisciplinary resources needed to understand the components of women's health.

Integrating biology and women's studies into my teaching using interdisciplinary methods and materials seemed exciting and natural to me. This evolution of new curricular content and new teaching methods interwove the threads of my undergraduate humanities background with my years of training in the sciences. I saw inclusion of material about women in science courses as a way to attract women to the sciences; introductory biology stood as an important opportunity because it often serves as the gateway to other science courses and determines a student's decision to pursue work in science or abandon it.

In 1986, I described my efforts to teach a transformed introductory biology course:

> Teaching science from a feminist perspective should make young women realize that science is open to them. . . . The question for the introductory biology teacher then becomes how—at the present time—does one incorporate the nascent scholarship on women and science into the biology curriculum in a manner that will inspire further critiques and theoretical changes? How can one integrate into the standard biology curriculum the considerable, but diffuse, information constituting the contemporary feminist perspective; the critique of biological determinism and androcentric "objectivity," the substantial information about famous and lesser-known women scientists and their discoveries, some remarks about the obvious influence of masculine thinking on the descriptive language of biology, the feminist theoretical changes that have already taken place, and those areas where the theoretical changes are still needed?[1]

In addition to attracting women to science, incorporation of feminist perspectives would create better science:

> Taken together, it becomes evident that the inclusion of a feminist perspective leads to changes in models, experimental subjects, and interpretations of the data. Not only should these changes attract more women to science, but the changes entail more inclusive, enriched theories compared to the traditional, restrictive, unicausal theories. These alternative, multidimensional theories generally provide a more accurate description of the realities of our complex biological world which should be integrated into the standard biology curriculum, even and perhaps especially at the introductory level. (*Teaching Science,* 30)

Changing the science curriculum to include women constituted a difficult task. Seen as an innovator in this area, I became involved in a number of curriculum transformation projects at institutions throughout the nation that were working to integrate women's studies into traditional disciplines. But it took several years for me to realize the more positive side coming from the different bodily identity in my own research. My male colleagues had partially ignored me because of my female body, my different experiences, and my interdisciplinary interests and because I considered alternative approaches and asked questions different from theirs. Eventually I recognized that their male bodies and masculine identities had limited them to partial understanding of the world they studied.

Gender bias pervaded a science developed almost exclusively by men, whose bodily experiences provided them with a masculine perspective on the physical, natural world. They had given only partial, cursory examination to females of other species and had looked at the human female body primarily to ask how it suited their needs and interests. For example, Robert M. Yerkees, in his early primatology work, indicated that he chose the baboon and chimpanzee as ideal for study primarily because observers saw their social organization as closely resembling that of human primates in its male dominance. However, subsequent researchers forgot the limitations imposed by such selection of species and proceeded to generalize their data to universal behavior patterns for all primates. It was not until a significant number of women entered primatology (including J. Lancaster, R. R. Leavitt, L. Leibowitz, and Thelma Rowell) that the concepts of the universality and male leadership of dominance hierarchies among primates were questioned and shown to be inaccurate for many primate species. Women uncovered cooperative patterns and even female dominance in other primate species.[2]

In addition to the problems of selective use of species, anthropomorphic and vague language, and universalization and extrapolation beyond the limits of the data, feminist scientists revealed another significant flaw in much animal behavior research: failure to study females. When females were studied, it was usually only in their interaction with (and usually their reaction to) males or infants. Presumably the fact that until then most animal behavior researchers had been male resulted in an androcentric bias in the way observation of animal behavior was designed and conceptualized. Because male researchers had only *experienced* male-male and male-female interactions themselves, their male worldview prohibited them from realizing that female-female interaction might be *observed* in their own species and others.

As it did nonhuman primates, male bias excluded women from medical research. When I and others first began to discuss the exclusion of women from clinical drug trials, most people tended to doubt us and question whether we weren't carrying feminism too far. They assumed that an objective science could not encompass such exclusions. But a study published in September 1992 in the *Journal of the American Medical Association* surveyed the literature from 1960 to 1991 on studies of clinical trials of drugs used to treat myocardial infarction. Women were included in only about 20 percent of those studies; elderly people (over seventy-five years) were included in only 40 percent. Some diseases which affect both sexes have been defined as male diseases. Heart disease has been so designated because at younger ages it occurs more frequently in men than women. Most of the funding for research on heart disease has been appropriated for research on predisposing factors that takes the male body as norm. This has led to diagnoses and treatments more appropriate for the male body. Extrapolation of these to the female body is less successful. This male perspective in research bias is the primary reason why women's death rate during treatment for heart attack is ten times that of men, and why angioplasty and coronary bypass are less successful in the female body.[3]

These insights into the limitations and biases introduced by male bodies and masculine identities as a result of the virtual nonexistence of women scientists proved significant for me. I began to feel whole as I understood that my female body and the perspectives gleaned from experiences as a woman provided new understandings of questions asked, research design, and theories and conclusions drawn from data in both science and health. Scientific colleagues grudgingly admitted that perhaps feminist perspectives could be useful in science, at least in revealing gender bias. Concerns over shortages of scientists and lack of diversity in the pool of scientists sparked interest in the potential of feminist pedagogical methods and theories of women's studies to attract men of color and women to science. Both science faculty and administrators responded well to the pedagogical techniques and models for integrating race and gender into the science curriculum which I presented in *Female-Friendly Science*.[4]

Women's studies colleagues, in addition to having substantial interest in women's health because of their own bodily experiences with the health care system, recognized the necessity of including science in this interdisciplinary field. The opportunity to obtain grants and to interact with faculty from the sciences, engineering, and medicine also piqued the interest of women's studies faculty in having feminist scientists in the program. Pioneering the uncharted territory, creating new vocabularies to bridge the disciplines, and using methodologies from one field to explore questions in another fused body, research, academia, and identity. I could envision an integrated identity symbolized by a positive, upward spiral, in which work on feminist critiques of science, curricular transformation, pedagogy, and women's health, nourished by theoretical changes and methodological applications from the humanities and social sciences, would fuel new ideas. Colleagues from the humanities, social sciences, and sciences, recognizing the benefits for science, health, and women's studies, would eagerly pursue these ideas and other interdisciplinary projects.

The vision of integration faded rapidly, as colleagues revealed their willingness to include only part of this identity. Although initially many scientists considered feminism too radical and women's studies just a passing fad, most eventually agreed that feminists had pointed out sources of gender bias, whose correction led to better science. Most scientists found feminists and their insights acceptable, as long as they remained within the liberal feminist theoretical perspective. Since both liberal feminism and the scientific method accept positivism as the theory of knowledge and assume that human beings are highly individualistic and obtain knowledge in a rational manner that may be separated from their social conditions, they share a belief in the possibility of obtaining knowledge that is both objective and value-free. Liberal feminism reaffirms the idea that it is possible to find a perspective from which to observe that is truly impartial, rational, and detached. Bias and lack of objectivity occur because of human failure to properly follow the scientific method and avoid bias due to situation or condition. Attempts to become more value-neutral by pointing out the bias due to the absence of females or to focus on female perspectives revealed androcentrism in scientific research. Since liberal feminism does not question the integrity of the scientific method itself or of its supporting corollaries of objectivity and value neutrality, my work and identity as a feminist remained acceptable to most of my scientific colleagues, as long as I stayed within a liberal feminist theoretical framework.

Although most scientists lack understanding of the variety of feminist perspectives and could not define distinctions between postmodern, essentialist, and other feminisms, they have encountered individuals who hold or espouse different feminist theoretical positions. Many scientists have difficulty with theories which question positivism and the possibility of objectivity obtained by value neutrality, with social constructivist views of knowledge, and with theories that imply gender differences in the conduct of scientific research. Perceiving that these theories call into question the fundamental assumptions which underpin the scientific method and its corollaries of objectivity and value neutrality, they reject them and feminists who espouse them.

I found that most scientific colleagues could accept my feminist ideas and my identity as a feminist until they learned that I thought most feminist theories, including radical, postmodern, and postcolonial feminism, provided interesting insights for science and scientists.[5] Many colleagues yield the point made by socialist feminists that scientific knowledge revealed through funded research under capitalism reflects the interests of the dominant class, yet few will question the notion of objectivity, as such a social-constructivist stance requires. Some colleagues agree that male domination of the sciences has led to the exclusion of women and to an androcentric bias in research, while almost none support women-only research institutes: a mechanism that might be envisioned under radical feminism as a way to generate innovative ideas in a patriarchal society. Frequently, colleagues involved with international projects puzzle over the ways that different developing countries have accepted, rejected, or adapted new technologies; few will consider postcolonial feminist critiques to analyze the impact of the technologies on the population of those countries. I risk losing credibility when, misjudging a colleague's willingness to understand more aspects of my feminist identity, I suggest that an insight gleaned from postmodern feminism might be useful in solving a problem.

Colleagues from the humanities and social sciences in women's studies exhibit different, but equally constraining, limits to their acceptance of my academic identities. Very familiar with critiques of objectivity and the advantages of trying a variety of theoretical positions, these colleagues dismiss scientists as naïve and inflexible; they cannot imagine that scientists really believe in logical positivism and objectivity. Simultaneously, because they know very little science, they fail to understand the true strengths of the scientific method, including verifiability and reliability, and that much of science really "works." Because of demonstrated gender bias, poor research design, and extrapolation beyond the limits warranted by the data in some studies, they dismiss all studies as invalid or flawed. Although they live with many of the practical benefits of science and technology, their relatively low level of scientific knowledge makes them vulnerable to throwing out the baby with the bathwater at their first encounter with feminist critiques of science.

Shortly after I realized that many of my colleagues could only acknowledge parts of my academic identity, I began to recognize a part of my identity that I had hidden from myself. Although I had known lesbians as both colleagues and friends, and had taught courses in human sexuality in both zoology and women's studies, I had no inkling that I was a lesbian. When I was thirty, married, with two children, my lesbian identity became evident to me.

Perhaps some of the heated debates surfacing in women's studies over diversity among women facilitated my realization. In their eagerness to make women visible and to define them as a category in traditional academic disciplines, many scholars in the early days of women's studies, in the late 1960s and early 1970s, made a mistake that paralleled the error of which we accused our male colleagues. Just as women's studies scholars revealed that the assumption that male experience coincided with human experience constituted a form of androcentric bias which rendered women invisible, these same scholars learned that the experience of all women was not the same. Women of color, working-class women, and lesbian women pointed out that their experiences as women were not identical to those depicted by many women's studies scholars, which appeared to emanate from a white, middle-class, heterosexual perspective.

My own coming out made me extremely aware of some of the many ways that dominant groups hold privilege. Negotiating divorce, including custody and property issues, brought home *whose* race, class, and sexual orientation, as well as gender, dominated in the Virginia legal system of the 1970s. Daily experience revealed how much I had taken for granted, and I understood heterosexual privilege on different levels as my new identity as a lesbian unfolded.

Gender does not represent a homogeneous category of analysis and must be studied in relationship to other oppressions of race, class, nationalism, and sexual orientation, and I incorporated my recognition of this relatively quickly into curricular content and approaches to teaching. In 1986, I described courses I had taught in the biology of women during the previous nine years:

> Unfortunately, some women's studies classes tend to present sexuality and reproduction only from the perspective of white, middle-class heterosexual women. Many of the facts were gathered from this group, and most of the research is based on them. Quite frequently, given the structure of academia, the instructor is also from the group. As a result, the experiences of only one group of women are held up as the "fact" and models for sexuality. At best, this leaves nonwhite women, lesbians, women of other socioeconomic classes or religions, and physically challenged women feeling that the model does not describe their experiences. They may discount the course as taught from an oppressive, normative viewpoint (Dill, 1983). At worst, women who are not white, middle-class, and heterosexual may instead discount their own experiences. They again realize that they deviate from the standards and wonder why they fail to conform in this area, too.[6] (*Teaching Science*, 52)

Later in that same chapter, I specified, using a particular example, how I had redesigned the course:

> Including perspectives other than that of majority-group women involves rethinking all the issues of the course, not simply adding additional material to what is already said. For example, many instructors approach the birth control issues as if all women came from a heterosexual, white, middle class, able-bodied perspective; it is as an accepted or desired given for all women of reproductive age. This approach also reflects the extent to which the ethos of "compulsory heterosexuality" pervades our patriarchal culture (Rich, 1980). The focus of the discussion thus becomes the advantages and disadvantages of the different methods and the choice of which one to use.

A wider focus means more than including discussion of possible complications of birth control methods for different ethnic or religious groups,
such as the particular health risks to a black woman with sickle cell ane-
mia of taking the birth control pill (Ammer, 1983) or the newer methods
of using the cervical mucus to determine the exact time of ovulation to
aid in rhythm or natural birth control. The very issue of birth control
must become the central focus of the discussion, since it presents itself
differently to different groups of women. To many women of color, the
testing and forced use of birth control may represent a genocidal attempt of whites to limit other racial groups. Puerto Rican women recall
that over one-third of the women on their island were sterilized during
the last thirty years without their consent (Vazquez-Calzadar, 1973) and
that the pill was tested there before it was considered safe to market in
mainland United States (Zimmerman, 1980). Black women, American
Indian women, and Chicanas may feel torn between what their ethnic
liberation movements and the women's movement advocate about con-
traception. To some lower-income women, birth control and forced ster-
ilization represent further humiliations, suggested to them to 'help'
them decrease their government support (Rodgers, 1973). To many
women of Roman Catholic or fundamentalist religions, birth control
may raise a conflict between religious belief and what the "dominant"
culture suggests as ideal. To most lesbians, birth control may be a non-
issue, except when gynecologists assume the heterosexual norm (Darty
and Potter, 1984) and insist on prescribing a method. Thus, the central
focus of the birth control presentation must be a thorough discussion of
the complications of the use and misuse of birth control for women in
different situations. After that, the issues concerning particular methods
can be addressed.[7] (*Teaching Science,* 53–54)

Most of my colleagues appeared relieved when they perceived that in my
teaching, as well as my personal interactions. I remained inclusive, despite
my new identity in terms of sexual orientation. Obviously angry and unable to accept my lesbian identity, a very few colleagues began to interact
with me only when necessary to carry out perfunctory or required professional obligations. Many colleagues, straight and gay, went out of their way
to ensure that I understood that they were "more than okay" with my new
identity as a lesbian. Of course, I formed new bonds with other lesbian
scientists and women's studies colleagues. Some, not completely out of the
closet to their colleagues, surprised me when they revealed their orientation; we passed significant time discussing successful strategies for coming
out in our profession.

If and when to come out continue to be major issues, despite my having
been a lesbian for more than two decades now. Initially, I worried, and with
good reason, about experiencing the pain of rejection from those who had
appeared to respect my work and like me when they thought I was straight.

Now the question has become whether I should tell someone initially, shortly after meeting, even if it doesn't appear relevant (e.g., if we probably will only see each other a few times throughout our professional lives and it has no bearing upon the work or professional task we are undertaking). On some occasions when I have elected not to tell someone for those reasons, it has later turned out to be relevant. For example, when my partner of many years died, it was awkward to receive condolences from some colleagues in front of others to whom I had never come out, although I had been acquainted with them for many years. I wondered whether they thought that I had hidden or deceived them about other aspects of my work and my self.

Possibly because I had been married and have children and perhaps because of my position as director of women's studies, straight faculty frequently perceived me (and still do) as someone with whom they could talk about useful ways to make gay and lesbian students feel comfortable in the classroom. Many sought curricular materials from me or wanted to discuss research on homosexuality. Often the scientists wanted my perspective as a feminist, lesbian, and scientist to help them critique the burgeoning research on "gay genes" and "causes of homosexuality"; puzzled by the shoddy science, they wondered why this line of research continues to be funded. Colleagues in women's studies understood the political motivations and social construction of knowledge which underpinned the funding decisions; they wanted help with critiques of the science. Eventually the questions from colleagues, coupled with experiences I accumulated as a result of my lesbian identity, spurred me to transfer these perspectives to my research. Building upon my earlier work on gender bias in research, I explored the bias resulting from failure to consider diversity among women, particularly women of color, elderly women, and lesbians.

Failure to identify and fund separate studies of lesbian health issues usually results in lesbians' being lumped together with heterosexual women in studies of women's health issues. Combining lesbians and heterosexual women may obscure not only the true incidence but also the cause of a disease. For example, lesbians have a much lower incidence of certain diseases, such as cervical cancer, gonorrhea, syphilis, herpes, and chlamydia, because heterosexual intercourse facilitates transmission of these diseases, while transmission via lesbian sexual contact remains rare. In contrast, lesbians may be at higher risk for certain other diseases, such as breast and uterine cancer.[8] Lumping lesbians together with heterosexual women for research on "women's health" makes both lesbians and nonlesbians suffer. The general population and some health care workers believe that lesbians are at risk for diseases that they in fact are less likely to contract, because they do not engage in heterosexual intercourse, while the risk to heterosexual women appears lower than it actually is.

Lumping lesbians in with male homosexuals also leads to inappropriate results. Most current funding for research on homosexual health care is directed toward the study of AIDS. As a group, lesbians engage in behaviors that put them at the lowest risk for contracting AIDS, although IV drug use, sex with bisexual males, and previous heterosexual history places some lesbians in high-risk categories. Often lesbians are not listed as a separate statistical category in analyses of the incidence of disease. The Centers for Disease Control and Prevention does not include a separate category for lesbians in reports of HIV infection; but homosexual, bisexual, and heterosexual men are listed separately.[9] Listed not only by sexual orientation, men with HIV are also categorized by race and intravenous drug use.

In the few instances when lesbian health is recognized as an issue, sexual orientation becomes the sole identifying characteristic. Bodily characteristics assumed to go with the identity of lesbian, such as neither having had sex with men nor having breast-fed children, obscure genuine health risks for formerly heterosexually active lesbians who nursed their biological children and thus do not match the body politics associated with lesbian identity.

Recognizing that these biases in research led to misdiagnoses and inappropriate treatments for all women in general and lesbians in particular, I advocated health research based in lesbian experience:

> Previously defined by the male, heterosexual norm, both women in general and male homosexuals have struggled for their own health agendas and should be understanding of the need for lesbians to define their own health needs. Lesbian health needs cannot be defined exclusively by either women's health needs or homosexual health needs. Overlapping both groups in many respects, but separate from each in some respects, lesbians are women with a homosexual orientation. Lesbian health issues deserve study and definition based on lesbian experience. (*Women's Health*, 116–17)

Just as these multiple and different, evident and less evident identities derived from my body fueled my research insights, they also attracted people to my scholarly work. My unusual perspective and training made journals and book publishers interested in my work. The many books and articles I published led to invitations to speak at conferences and institutions both nationally and internationally. Women's studies and science departments often cosponsored my lectures to universities; colleagues occasionally revealed that my visit opened dialogues and exchanges among departments and parts of the campus that had not previously experienced positive interaction. All of this helped to make me successful in academia. My rank as a tenured full professor, my track record in receiving grants, and my twenty years as an administrator directing women's studies established my reputation, especially within women's studies circles. An invitation from the National Science Foundation to serve as senior program officer for women's programs signaled the legitimacy necessary for scientists to accept my work. Speaking and consulting at more than 120 universities and colleges provided me with opportunities to understand some of the issues facing women in science and with occasions to hone my skills in talking with chairs, deans, provosts, and presidents about them.

Different colleagues relate to one or more parts of my identity which they share; often because they share some parts of my identity, they willingly attempt to understand parts with which they do not identify. Since other women scientists understand the discrimination I have experienced because of being a woman in a male-dominated field, they listen to my critiques of gender bias in science. Heterosexual women and mothers, who appreciate my revelation of women's exclusion from clinical trials of drugs and lack of attention to women's diseases, attempt to understand my critiques of lesbophobia within medicine. Trusting my training as a scientist and my rank as a female who has achieved some professional status, male science faculty and administrators give some credence to what I say about women's studies and interdisciplinary work. Because of my French degree and feminist credentials, some women faculty in the humanities heed my plea that they read and understand some science.

This understanding of my work because of partially shared identities through body politics builds fragile, tenuous coalitions and limited comprehension of the implications of the research. I fear and have experienced the problems that result when other aspects of my identity conflict with the body politics expected by some individuals who share some parts of my identity: women scientists who, when they learn that I am a lesbian, reject feminist critiques of science and pedagogical techniques, stemming from women's studies, in which they had shown considerable interest; postmodern lesbians who begin to doubt my work on feminist theoretical perspectives on science and health because they view all that can be known from science as simply a cultural construct; male scientists who seek my advice about how to attract and retain women students in science until they learn I am in women's studies; bisexual women who are fascinated with scientific critiques of the recent work on "gay genes" until they realize that I am not only a lesbian but also committed to a monogamous relationship.

When the limits of our shared identity are perceived in these situations, colleagues may truncate interactions and explorations of scholarly work. Failure to share complete identity or failure to hold the scholarly or theoretical perspective expected because of a bodily identity leads to limited understandings of research. Opportunities for interdisciplinary cooperation, learning, and collegial interaction in teaching and research are missed when the body politics of partial identifications collide with the multiple identities of real academics.

[3]

BODY LANGUAGE: CORPOREAL SEMIOTICS, LITERARY RESISTANCE MAUDE HINES

This essay represents an attempt to grapple with the silent and unacknowledged language of corporeal semiotics, that system of signification that our bodies represent to others who read them as texts unauthored by ourselves. I first became interested in (or, more accurately, frustrated by) the ways in which our bodies *mean,* whether we mean them to or not, long before I was able to put a name to it, or even articulate the source of the frustration to myself. I remember one moment in particular (very likely because it was relatively safe, having nothing to do with my own body) in which the awareness that bodies speak came to the surface enough that it registered for me as an uncomfortable confusion. The moment was many years ago, at a party in New York City. I was eavesdropping on a conversation in which a (white) man was talking to a group of (white) men, telling the following story:

> We just moved to 109th Street and Central Park West, and the neighborhood can get pretty hairy. The first night, we were walking to the car, and we saw five black guys coming toward us. We got in in time, though.

His audience responded with appreciative nods and gasps.

Later, in graduate school, I witnessed another party conversation, this time between two graduate students: one was drunkenly announcing that he wouldn't have been admitted into a fraternity while at college (a college where fraternities do not exist) even if he had wanted to be, because he wasn't a "white middle-class male subject." His female interlocutor nodded appreciatively. It may surprise you that the speaker was not only male but white and middle-class. Although he didn't deny it, he was also heterosexual.

Granted, I shouldn't have been eavesdropping, but I was confused and outraged (and confused *by* my outrage) after both of these incidents. The first made me wonder (and hypothesize about) what the speaker meant by "black"; the second made me wonder what the speaker meant by "white," and together they led to a chain of questions that ultimately resulted in this essay. The night of the first party, I realized that the word "black" in the story had almost nothing to do with pigmentation. To make sense, the word, or the color it represented, had to stand for "huge" and "strong" and "evil" and "misanthropic" and, most of all, "existing primarily to do violence to white men." Although none of these descriptions were used, the "five black guys" were clearly not elderly, or peaceful, or small; when these adjectives are substituted, the story doesn't make sense.

That blackness means more in the American imagination than the color with which the dictionary defines it is no news to anyone who's read Toni Morrison's *Playing in the Dark,* or even Leslie Fiedler's *Love and Death,* for that matter. I've now come to think about the incident in different terms: the sense of the story relies on an association with the body marker "black" that is shared among the members of an interpretive community, represented at this party by the group that included the storyteller and his audience. Assigning significance (and thereby creating a sign) is a reading process; attempting to read a body (or five bodies) as an empty text, covering, blurring, or otherwise dismissing subjectivity in order to project meaning onto bodily "markings," is a specifically essentialist reading. An essentialist reading requires a dictionary, a table of equivalence, where certain signs (secondary sex characteristics, skin color, bone structure, hair texture, hair color, etc.) are read as gender, race, age, and so on, and these in turn are associated with specific meanings, which change depending on the bodily presentation—the sentence, so to speak—in which they are read. For example, in the corporeal semiotics of essentialism, the word "black" would signify differently if it had modified the word "women."

In *The Alchemy of Race and Rights,* Patricia Williams tells the story of her attempt to publish an article about being denied admission to a Benetton store by a young white male clerk. In Williams's narrative, the clerk sees her through the window, and decides, based on a visual assessment, not to admit her: the clerk "glared out, *evaluating me for signs* that would pit me against the limits of his social understanding."[1] Williams is fully aware that the clerk is looking for "signs," evaluating her body, deciding from that text that she should be denied admission. The clerk then inserts the "signs" into "the limits of his social understanding." The clerk has a "social" dictionary with which to translate the corporeal text; in this dictionary, skin color—imputed race—is an essential signifier.

When Williams is denied access to the Benetton, she infers that the clerk (whom she refers to as the "saleschild") read her body as belonging to "one who would take his money and therefore could not conceive that I was there to give him money." This reading is publicly supported, and often purports not to be racist at all. Williams writes that

> even civil-rights organizations backed down in the face of arguments that the buzzer system is a "necessary evil," that it is a "mere inconvenience" in comparison to the risks of being murdered . . . and that in any event it is not all blacks who are barred, just "17-year-old black males wearing running shoes and hooded sweatshirts." (44)

Of course, the gum-cracking white "saleschild" is also a "teenager wearing running shoes"; the shoes exacerbate the criminal reading in the former text, functioning as an adjective to the black sign, while signifying nothing, or functioning as a different adjective (perhaps "young"?), to the white sign.

Williams's attempt to publish the story was frustrated by the removal of her race from the narrative. Such an omission changes the story completely: without the important racial signifier, the corporeal text is changed, and the clerk is not reading Williams's race to make his decision. The publisher decides that her race is insignificant. She is certain that it signifies. Williams's account demonstrates the frustration of the known yet unprovable. Williams is not able to prove what we all know the clerk was thinking.

Through free indirect discourse and other narrative means of demonstrating thought processes, fiction provides a forum for representing and articulating the ways in which race and other bodily markers are significant—and signifying. As a case study, I look at two works of fiction by African American women, Paule Marshall's *Praisesong for the Widow* and Alice Walker's *Possessing the Secret of Joy*.[2] The semiotic model of essentialism that I have begun to outline above provides a framework for understanding the ways in which Marshall and Walker use fiction both to articulate the corporeal semiotics of essentialism and to describe resistance to it. *Praisesong* tells the story of Avey Johnson, an African American woman who goes on a cruise and ends up in Grenada, finding the culture (and the self) she has long ago forgotten. *Possessing* tells the story of Tashi, an Olinkan woman who undergoes circumcision to celebrate her culture, then marries an American man and moves to the United States. Both novels show their protagonists in cultural transition. Attention to the treatment of corporeal semiotics in the two novels reveals that these transitions also provide a space of resistance to dominant readings of the body. Through scenes in which the bodies of their characters are read as texts, *Praisesong* and *Possessing* detail the processes of readings that are objectifying and essentializing. However, both Marshall and Walker also provide fictive models of alternative readings that suggest other possibilities. Both authors describe the way (racial) identity is "figured"—both in terms of being "figured out" and in terms of its relation to the corporeal, to a "figure," to a physical manifestation of the self in the world.

Interestingly, both *Praisesong* and *Possessing* subject mixed-race bodies to corporeal readings by black characters. Marshall's Thomasina Moore has "the color to have qualified [as a dancer at the Cotton Club]: black that was the near-white of a blanched almond or the best of ivory. A color both sacred—for wasn't it a witness?—and profane: '*he forced my mother/late/One night/What do they call me?*'" (19). Thomasina Moore's body is read by Avey as a historical repository. Walker's Tashi, on the other hand, in her description of Pierre (her husband's son by a white French woman), reads his skin as an erasure of history:

> I study his face seeking signs of Adam, signs of Lisette. He seems a completely blended person and, as such, new. In him "black" has disappeared; so has "white." His eyes are a dark, lightfilled brown; his forehead is high and tan; his nose broad, a little flat. He has told me he likes men as well as he likes women, which seems only natural, he says, since he is the offspring of two sexes as well as two races. No one is surprised he is biracial; why should they be surprised he is bisexual? This is an explanation I have never heard and cannot entirely grasp. (174)

It is an explanation that I cannot entirely grasp, either. Pierre's "new" identity relies on the simultaneous conflation of sex and sexuality, sexuality and race, and, by some transitive property, race and sex. In addition, while Tashi might see that both "black" and "white" have disappeared, it is unlikely that his classmates at Harvard will read Pierre's body as she does.

Naomi Zack, in *Race and Mixed Race,* attempts to see the mixed-race body as containing an identity in itself, without recourse to the erasure of history:

> It is important to note that when the acknowledgment of a mixed-race individual does not go beyond a reference to the racial diversity of that individual's forebears, the individual is called "of mixed race." But if the individual is acknowledged to be a racial mixture *in himself* then he would be called "mixed race," without the "of." The use of the word "of" in the designation "of mixed race" leaves open the question of what the mixed-race individual *is* racially, and this "of" is compatible with the American one-drop rule.[3]

Zack's position bridges the gap between the erasure of the body of the mixed-race individual and its replacement by ancestral bodies in Marshall's historical reading, and the erasure of history and its replacement by a completely "new" identity in Walker's description of Pierre. Zack calls for an individual identity that does not rely on historical amnesia.

Readings of the body in Marshall's and Williams's texts attempt to uncover either the interior or the ancestral history of their object/text, using the same logic of corporeal semiotics we saw in Williams's Benetton episode and in the party conversations that I overheard years ago. This type of (racist or sexist) corporeal reading, while equally concerned with history, attempts to cover, blur, or deny interiority. In this reading, the body is used as an empty text.[4]

Unlike Williams's publisher, both Walker and Marshall understand the importance of racial signifiers in depicting the frustrations of corporeal semiotics. Marshall's Avey remembers witnessing a scene of police brutality: "*the pale meaty hand repeatedly* [brought the nightstick down until] *the man finally sank screaming to his knees, his blood a lurid red against his blackness. . . .* " (56, Marshall's italics). Avey assumes that the man was stopped "*for what might have been a minor traffic violation*" (56, Marshall's italics). The description registers the whiteness of the reader, together with the blackness of the text. Like many of Marshall's readers, Avey understands the logic of corporeal semiotics: the red blood is at least as likely to result from the "pale" policeman's reading of the victim's "blackness" as it is from criminality. Marshall does not need to describe the actual scene of reading.

In *Possessing the Secret of Joy,* Tashi's black skin is (mis)read by her psychiatrist as having only one possible meaning. She feels

> negated by the realization that even my psychiatrist could not see I was African. That to him all black people were Negroes. . . . He'd been taken aback by the fact that I had only one child. He thought this unusual for

a colored woman, married or unmarried. Your people like lots of kids, he allowed. But how could I talk to this stranger of my lost children? And of how they were lost? One was left speechless by all such a person couldn't know. (18)

Tashi is "left speechless" by the epistemological limitations of essentializing and objectifying corporeal readings.[5] The limitation seems particularly American here. Tashi's husband is "shock[ed] at being constantly harassed because he was black" once he arrives back home, but explains to Tashi, "They behave this way not because I'm black but because they are white" (38). The distinction, then, is between locating meaning in the corporeal text and describing the construction of meaning through essentializing reading practices, with their concomitant epistemological limitations. In other words, it's not the text, it's the reader—or at least the dictionary.

According to existential philosophy, we define ourselves negatively, as that which is not something (or an objectified someone) else. In saying "I am not what you are," I am defining you; I am "realizing" a definition of the other.[6] In doing so, I necessarily make an object of the other. The other side of this is the notion of "being-for-others," the idea of becoming an object when confronted by the presence of another consciousness. As Simone de Beauvoir writes in *The Second Sex,* "man never succeeds in abolishing his separate ego, but at least he wants to attain the solidity of the in-himself, the *en-soi,* to be petrified into a thing. *It is especially when he is fixed by the gaze of other persons that he appears to himself as being one*" (italics added).[7]

Walker's Tashi imagines herself and Adam this way after she has confronted American racism. She begins to see herself and Adam as objects: "There we sat, in the shade of a linden tree, two rotund black people in advanced middle age, our hair graying, our faces glistening with sweat. We might have been models for a painting by Horace Pippin" (39). This realization of the gaze from outside is apparent at her trial, too, when she refers to "the curious onlookers for whom my trial is entertainment" (35), and at the birth of her son, when she realizes that her body is a "sideshow" (61). Tashi's interiority is denied, and she is reduced to her body, which in turn registers as performance. The notion of a black woman's body as a performance is a familiar one. bell hooks writes about a dinner party she attended at which "only one other black person was present . . . speaking in the presence of a group of white onlookers, staring at us *as though this encounter were staged for their benefit,* we engaged in a passionate discussion about black experience."[8] In *Praisesong for the Widow,* Avey has a nightmare that she is having a public "bruising fistfight" with her Aunt Cuney, in which a similar fear of performance, of spectacle, is represented:

> Avey Johnson saw to her horror [that the fight] had brought her neighbors in North White Plains out on their lawns. *Worse,* among the black faces looking on scandalized, there could be seen the Archers with their blue-eyed, tow-headed children, and the Weinsteins. The only ones for blocks around who had not sold and fled. Could it be they had stayed in the hope of one day being *treated to a spectacle* such as this[?] (45, italics added)

In each of these scenes, a black woman feels herself made into an object. She is a "spectacle," a "performance," or a "sideshow." bell hooks has suggested that "we may be seen by white others as 'spectacle'" when we "give expression to multiple aspects of our identity"; she seeks to counter this problem by "decentering the oppressive other" in order to de-objectify the self:[9]

> Often when black subjects give expression to multiple aspects of our identity, which emerge from a different location, we may be seen by white others as "spectacle." For example, when I give an academic talk without reading a paper, using a popular, performative, black story-telling mode, I risk being seen by the dominating white other as unprepared, as just entertainment. Yet their mode of seeing cannot be the factor which determines style of representation or the content of one's work. Fundamental to the process of decentering the oppressive other and claiming our right to subjectivity is the insistence that we must determine how we will be and not rely on colonizing responses to determine our legitimacy. (22)

I propose that this "spectacularization" is produced by the spectator in order to recontain, as performance, the possibility of varied and complex subjectivity. In the literary texts by Walker and Marshall, the clash, or friction, between multifarious subjectivities and their reduction to fixity— mathematically, into "identity," in the sense of a one-to-one correspondence—either by essentializing readings or by the conformity of the women themselves, give birth to a series of reactions and strategies.

Walker and Marshall deliberately and carefully give their main characters unusually multiplex and complicated identities. In *Possessing the Secret of Joy,* there is a connection between multiple aspects of identity and multiple names. The main character's perspective is divided into chapters that are alternately called "Tashi," "Evelyn," "Tashi-Evelyn," and "Evelyn-Tashi." This breaking up of her nominal identity mirrors the fragmentation of her psyche; each chapter describes a piece. The first chapter, titled "Tashi," begins, "I did not realize for a long time that I was dead" (3). The character's identity as "Tashi" is dead; it died with her near-simultaneous circumcision and transport to America. She takes refuge in her "fantasy life. Without it I'm afraid to exist. Who am I, Tashi, renamed in America 'Evelyn,' Johnson?" (36). Tashi, as she resists a surge of memory, feels "as if the greater half of my being were trying to murder the lesser half" (74). For Tashi, these selves have lives; she claims that "I myself have lived and died—in and out of Waverly, in and out of my mind—many times" (155).

Characters in *Praisesong for the Widow*, too, have a multiplicity of identities. Jay has both a private "self that . . . was open, witty, playful, even outrageous at times" and a "carefully protected public self" (95). When Avey has an orgasm, she gives "the slip to her ordinary, everyday self" (128). Once she goes to Carriacou, Avey's "mind continu[es] to swing like a pendulum gone amok from one end of her life to the other, she felt to be dwelling in any number of places at once and in a score of different time frames" (232). The "pendulum gone amok" recalls the head motion of the trickster Lebert Joseph; the simultaneity of place and time suggests that Avey has finally begun to accept her different selves and her ancestral past, to heal. Although both Avey and Tashi have multifarious and dynamic selves, they each have one body that changes only slowly. Their multiple and complex subjectivities are at odds with the monolithic and essentializing readings to which their bodies are subjected throughout the texts.

Marshall plays with the impossible idea of a dynamic body, whose changing presentation can represent different "personas," in her trickster figure, Lebert Joseph. One of the things that makes Lebert Joseph a trickster is his ability to change his physical appearance significantly, in terms of age, gender, and size—categories basic to the corporeal semiotics of essentialism I am describing here.[10] He is able to separate his projected identity from his physical manifestation in the world:

> Where was the walking stick? It had not reappeared since he had abandoned it to sing the beg pardon on his knees. And what of the crippled dwarf of a thousand years she had seen or perhaps not seen at the crossroads earlier? Not a trace of him was evident. *He had been packed away for another time in the trunk containing the man's endless array of personas.* Another self had been chosen for the fete, one familiar to her, because he was once again the Lebert Joseph she remembered from the rum shop, who had amazed her by dancing the Juba over in the sunlit doorway with the force and agility of someone half his age. *Out of his stooped and winnowed body had come the illusion of height, femininity and power.* Even his foreshortened left leg had *appeared to straighten itself out and grow longer* as he danced. (243, italics added)

The trickster's body relies on "illusion," "appear[ances]," and an "endless array of personas" to make it impossible to fix his identity. He becomes alternately male and female, stooped and tall, winnowed and powerful. Any reading of his body as text is immediately contradicted.[11] Lebert Joseph plays with Avey's "social dictionary" as Marshall plays with ours.

The main characters in the novels, both women, are not able to change their appearances. The metaphors the authors use, such as the "lid" of the brain, and the "container" of the mind, present models of interiority that show multiple identities being contained within a single body, a body that presents a text for readers who deny the characters' multiple ways of seeing themselves. The metaphor of the body as container illustrates the confinement created by social pressure to deny multiplicity. This is the confinement described by Williams when she writes,

> While being black has been the most powerful social attribution in my life, it is only one of a number of governing narratives or presiding fictions by which I am constantly reconfiguring myself in the world. Gender is another, along with ecology, pacifism, my peculiar brand of colloquial English, and Roxbury, Massachusetts. The complexity of role identification, the politics of sexuality, the inflections of professionalized discourse—all describe and impose boundary in my life, even as they confound one another in unfolding spirals of confrontation, deflection and dream. (256)

bell hooks, too, describes the "constricting notion of blackness":

> We have too long had imposed upon us *from both the outside and the inside* a narrow, *constricting* notion of blackness. Postmodern critiques of essentialism which challenge notions of universality and static over-determined identity within mass culture and mass consciousness can open up new possibilities for the *construction of self* and the assertion of agency. (28, italics added)

Given this confinement, along with the perverse corporeal semiotics of racism, it is not surprising that characters in these texts want to escape the confines of the body. While they cannot, like Joseph, change their bodies to confront and confound objectifying corporeal readings, they can and do escape them: characters in both texts are able to leave the confines of their bodies, leaving essentializing readings behind in the process.

In *Praisesong for the Widow,* Avey's mind leaves her body many times. As she packs to leave the ship at the beginning of the novel, "Her mind in a way wasn't even in her body, or for that matter, in the room." Her mind has "leaped ahead" to the time of her physical departure (10). Avey's grandmother, too, used this strategy: "Her body she always usta say might be in Tatem but her mind, her mind was long gone with the Ibos" (39). Avey's identity is so removed from her physical presence that she does not even recognize herself when that presence confronts her. When she is in the ship's mirror-walled dining room with Clarice and Thomasina, she "easily recognized them both in the distant mirror. But for a long confused moment Avey Johnson could not place the woman in beige crepe de Chine and pearls seated with them. This wasn't the first time it had happened" (48). Indeed, Avey is unable to recognize herself in department store mirrors, and once even in her own bathroom mirror. Her reflection is that of a "stranger" (48).

The choice to define oneself to oneself as that part which is not the body is not unusual in these texts. Tashi, in *Possessing the Secret of Joy*, repeatedly flies out of her body, becoming a bird in her mind.[12] When she leaves Africa, she tells us that only her "body had left. My soul had not" (116). Like Avey at the end of *Praisesong for the Widow*, Tashi has "the uncanny feeling that, just at the end of my life, I am beginning to reinhabit the body I long ago left" (110).

Another response to essentializing corporeal readings represented in *Possessing* is the reverse of escape: not leaving the body, but becoming the body. If leaving the body demonstrates pure subjectivity, becoming the body is pure objectivity. Mzee shows Tashi and Adam a film depicting a scene in which he believes he has "inadvertently interrupted a kind of ritual ceremony. . . . Everything . . . had *stopped,* the moment he and his entourage entered the ritual space. And what was also odd, he said, was how *no one spoke a word, or even moved,* as long as he and his people were there. *They literally froze* as the camera panned the area" (72, italics added). If Tashi's musing about herself and Adam as objects under the linden tree reflects an existential objectification, the ritual participants here literalize the process of what de Beauvoir calls being "fixed by the gaze of other persons." They "literally" freeze before the gaze of Mzee's entourage and the camera, *becoming* objects and, in so doing, making reading impossible. Indeed, Mzee is mistaken not only about the nature of the ritual, but even about the genders of its participants. The participants have turned what de Beauvoir calls the "petrified" and "fixed" body in the gaze of the other on itself, reflecting their object-ness back.

Both becoming a body and escaping it are strategies these fictional characters use to confront essentialist readings. But are all corporeal readings necessarily essentializing? Both Marshall and Walker also provide fictive models of alternative readings that provide open and complex (if not always accurate) understandings rather than a single closed and monolithic one, subjectivity rather than projected meaning. In order to do this, both authors create physicalized models of the psyche and spacial models of the body.

In *Praisesong*, Marshall's language, like the common metaphors of everyday discourse, relies upon and draws an interior and an exterior self. Because this interior, rather than the body, is the text that is often being read, characters try to peer "in" in order to read. When Avey remembers the man being beaten by policemen, she wonders, *"Where* had that night *surfaced* from?" (56, italics added). The night "surfaces" in her consciousness; the question "from where" suggests a geographical model of the psyche, one that comprises place ("where") and depth ("surfaced"). This depth model of the psyche is repeated when her husband Jay shaves his mustache: Marshall writes, "after a while it was as if he had always been clean-shaven. Nevertheless, *at a deeper level,* [Avey] remained unreconciled to the change, and as distressed and uneasy as she had been the first day" (130, italics added). Similarly, Jay's spirit is described physically. He carries "a weight on his spirit" (103). That his spirit is able to support a weight attests to its tangibility.

Paradoxically, it is the ability of these normally interiorized notions (will, mind, spirit) to *leave* the body that supports a reading of them as contained within it; the idea that they can escape means that the body normally holds them. The physicalization of these qualities, too, suggests a reading of the body as container or boundary. Avey's body is described as "flat, numb, emptied out . . . the same as her mind when she awoke yesterday morning . . . with the sense of a yawning hole where her life had once been" (214). Both her body and her mind—"emptied out . . . yawning hole[s]"—are empty containers. Likewise, the soothing (physicalized) presence of Lebert Joseph's spirit embodied in rum is able to fill the emptiness of Avey's body:

> In no more than seconds it had spread from her stomach out into the rest of her body, moving through her like the stream of cool dark air that had greeted her when she first entered the rum shop. Spilling into the dry river bed of her veins. Before she had finished half the glass, it had reached out to her dulled nerves, rousing and at the same time soothing them; and it was even causing the pall over her mind to lift again. (174)[13]

This idea of corporeal (and physicalized) mental containers is echoed in the image of Avey's sanity being held by a "china bowl" (91). After the bowl shatters, her mind is described as "a pile of angry shards" (92), an image which both supports the idea of a physicalized interiority and suggests a notion of a container (her mind, which has held her sanity) within a container (her body). This Russian-doll structure is a physicalized mirror of Avey's multiple selves.[14]

The notion of a physicalized interior contained within the body is a model for social interaction, too. However, these (black) characters, unlike Williams's "saleschild," are trying to peer inside the body, rather than reading that body itself as a text. Characters look at openings in the container (particularly eyes) and try to see in. The Grenadian taxi driver has a "smile that had the plan *behind* it" (73, italics added). Similarly, when Thomasina Moore wonders if she has "misread" Avey, she asks herself whether "there was more to her than she suspected: a force, a fire *beneath that reserved exterior* that was not to be trifled with? Her wondering *gaze* focused on the underlip which was still slightly pursed to *reveal* the no-nonsense edging of pink she had never seen before" (62, italics added). To keep herself from being "read," Avey has developed a "carefully *barred* gaze. She was clearly someone who kept her thoughts and feelings to herself" (48, italics added). Readings that allow for subjectivity also allow for interaction; Avey can at least attempt to *not* allow herself to be read. Lebert Joseph, the trickster, is able to read her anyway: "The feelings she sought to mask, the meanings that were beyond her—he saw and understood them all from the look he bent on her" (171).

Attempts to hide from the reading gaze of the other are as present in *Possessing the Secret of Joy* as they are in *Praisesong for the Widow*. Tashi is aware that "Nothing runs out of my eyes to greet [Adam]. It is as if my self is *hiding* behind an iron door" (45, italics added). Tashi's self is able to hide behind the door of her eyes; it seems as if the eyes here are not the windows, but the doors to the soul. Tashi's body is not only a text, but an intermediate barrier between the reader and her interior.

Another form of interaction in these texts is the way in which bodies that can be read can also speak. Jay, frustrated by looking for work, would "simply let his shoulders, collapsed under the jacket or coat, speak for him" (114). When making love to Avey, he speaks "with his body this time. A more powerful voice. Another kind of poetry" (127). Avey is able to understand the importance of their old rituals "in a way that went beyond words, that spoke from the blood" (137). The body is figured as "a more powerful voice," while blood can go "beyond words." Communication is figured here not as between a reading subject and an object, but as between two subjects.

In Walker's text, there is a similar model of (physicalized) interiority, and of the readability of that interior through and on the exterior, the body. Like Avey's, Tashi's interior has a geography, for her psychical recovery is imagined as a journey: "In my heart I thanked Mzee for [Raye], for I believed she would be plucky enough *to accompany me where he could not*" (134, italics added). When Tashi whispers to Raye that she has been circumcised, Raye doesn't understand. Tashi feels "as if I had handed her a small and precious pearl and she had promptly bitten into it and declared it a fake" (119). The "small and precious pearl" here simultaneously describes the shape of Tashi's excised clitoris and the physical rendering of her feelings, once externalized. A larger stone that is inside Tashi's body is the death of her sister:

> I took a deep breath and exhaled it against the *boulder* blocking my throat: I remembered my sister Dura's murder, I said, exploding the boulder. I felt a painful stitch throughout my body that I *knew stitched my tears to my soul*. (83, italics added)

Tashi's tears are "stitched" to her soul; the stitch is felt "throughout [her] body." That her soul can be "stitched" attests to its physicalization; that the stitch is felt "throughout [her] body" suggests its containment there. The idea of Tashi's body as container is emphasized by her memory of Dura's "bathing" being enabled by "a lid lifted off my brain." Being a container, her body can also be empty. Her mother used to "say, it is only hard work that fills the emptiness" (16).

In this text, the connection between the body and the psyche is central. As a novel about female circumcision, *Possessing the Secret of Joy* chronicles the discovery of the relationship between Tashi/Evelyn's physical scars (her circumcision) and her psychical one (her "deaths"). Conversely, Tashi's decision to be "bathed" (circumcised), connected to her patriotism, is figured as the result of her having in her "mind some outlandish outsized image of myself" (22). She wants to become physically Olinkan, finding courage in the "defiant" cheeks that "bore the mark of our withered tribe. These marks gave me courage. I wanted such a mark for myself" (24).[15]

An earlier psychical "death" occurs in Tashi after her sister's physical one. Not allowed to cry, mourn, or even speak of Dura (15), she becomes dead inside. Walker describes Tashi's psychical death by creating an opposition between her vital outside and her dead inside. This death is physically readable; other Olinkan children laugh at Tashi after her sister's death, crying, "Come see how Tashi has left our world. You can tell because her eyes have glazed over!" (20). This is not the only time that the irony of reading the unreadability of Tashi's eyes presents itself.[16] When Adam finds her in the Mbele camp, he reports, "The first thing I noticed was the flatness of her gaze. It frightened me" (40). Olivia, too, can tell that "her soul had been dealt a mortal blow. [It] was plain to anyone who dared look into her eyes" (66). Olivia believes that she can see the state of Tashi's soul by looking at—or into—her body.

If both books rely on physicalized models of an interior subjectivity, scenes of reading eyes, rather than bodies, represent corporeal readings that are not objectifying. When Tashi reads M'lissa's eyes, she says, "Her whole body is smiling her welcome; except for her eyes. They are wary and alert. What is that shadow, there in the depths? Is it apprehension? Is it fear?" (155). M'lissa, in turn, can see her "death in Tashi's eyes" (209). As Tashi observes, M'lissa's "is an x-ray gaze. But then, so is mine, now" (155). These women are communicating, although mutely; both are adept readers. Each sees the other as a subject.

Avey's self-discovery in Grenada is engendered through the Grenadians' refusal to participate in the types of corporeal reading strategies with which she is familiar. When she leaves the ship alone to go to Grenada, the people there refuse to believe the text she has written on her body:

> The problem was, she decided, none of them seemed aware of the fact that she was a stranger, a visitor, a tourist, although *this should have been obvious from the way she was dressed and the set of matching luggage at her side.* But from the way they were acting she could have been simply one of them there on the wharf. (69, italics added)

The out-islanders refuse to read Avey as a tourist; in fact, she can sense them rewriting the text:

> It was as if the moment they caught sight of her standing there, their eyes immediately stripped her of everything she had on and dressed her in one of the homemade cotton prints the women were wearing. Their eyes also banished the six suitcases at her side and placing a small overnight bag like the ones they were carrying in her hand, they were all set to take her along wherever it was they were going. (72)

The out-islanders do not see Avey as the "stranger" she sees in herself. Instead, they include her among themselves. Avey has finally come home, having never been at home in White Plains, where her flesh was "thick and inert" in her girdle, her body outside "its proper axis" in her high heels (223, 12). Finally, on Carriacou, after being massaged by Rosalie Parvay as if she were "clay that had yet to be shaped and fired," she orgasms back into her body (224). Avey, having arrived as a tourist, departs as a part of the whole. Her black skin, rather than objectifying her, invites the question "what's your nation?"; her skin color allows Lebert Joseph to assume a kinship with her.

51

Both Walker and Marshall demonstrate that bodily readings, to be communicative, rely on acceptance of the subjectivity associated with the text, a subjectivity that many have argued is associated in essentialist ideology with whiteness. Neither Marshall nor Walker take the assumption of their character's subjectivity for granted. By filling the bodies of their characters, by means of an interiority that is physically represented, Walker and Marshall are writing a semiotics of resistance. By writing strategies for repelling the psychical effects of an essentialist reading, and especially by providing models of alternative corporeal readings, they are insisting that, like Avey in her understanding of the old rituals of her marriage, we can go "beyond words," yet still communicate.

Possessing the Secret of Joy and *Praisesong for the Widow* demonstrate the frustrations and pleasures of body language, as well as resistance to it. They imagine ways in which the body, as the physical manifestation of the self in the world, can be regulated by that self in order to modify the image it imagines is projected. Because they are works of fiction, they are also able to demonstrate how corporeal semiotics works (and that it works).

The illustration of this structure is satisfying—it says what Williams's publisher did not allow her to say. It also illuminates some possible functions of the adjectives "black" and "white" in the two conversations with which I opened this essay. With the objectification of the other inherent in reading the body as a text (as only a body), the reader distances himself from the text. This is a Saussurean (and later, Derridean) concept as well: meaning is never present in a thing itself—it is always related to what the thing is defining itself against. By making "black" *mean* (in both senses of the word) in the first conversation, the speaker not only refers to a set of associations with blackness that he shares with his interlocutors, but distances himself from blackness itself: the final meaning is "not me." Which brings me back to my question: what does "white" mean in the second party conversation? It seems right to think that, as with the modifier "black" in the first one, at least part of its meaning is "not me": I cannot be read as a (white, middle-class, male) text.

This seems immediately related to contemporary references to the pre-1980s literary canon as "dead white men." Surprisingly, I have heard the term most often from white men. Though these men are not dead, the phrase clearly represents, like "five black guys" and "white middle-class male subject," more than the sum of the meanings of its words. The words "white" and "men" signify here as pejorative because the (white, usually male) group that uses the phrase has invested it with meaning. What I find particularly compelling about this phrase is that it reverses the logic of corporeal semiotics I have been describing up until this point: if the "old canon" has become "dead white men," then the texts that constitute it have become the bodies of the authors. I see a logic of corporeal substitution here; *Bleak House* becomes a "dead white man," and Dickens is substituted for his text.

Reading (literary) texts as bodies has become a habit of academic discourse. Paradoxically, in the current climate of the academy, with its claims of identity deconstruction and anti-essentialism, the urge to classify remains strong; to make sure that "difference" is included, it must be named. In "White Is a Color!" Leslie Roman points out that these terms of inclusion do not include at all, but separate "difference" from the hegemony. Summarizing arguments by Hazel Carby and C. T. Mohanty, she points out that

> efforts in the 1980s to integrate the curricula and the student bodies of universities under the aegis of "diversity" and "multiculturalism" (code words for racially subordinate groups) now serve as apologies for not living up to the promise of necessary affirmative action and widescale reform in higher education. (78)

bell hooks, too, notes that the inclusion of "diverse" texts in the canon serves as an excuse for not including "diverse" voices and epistemologies in the academy. Pointing to a "failure to recognize a critical black presence in . . . most scholarship and writing on postmodernism," she calls postmodernism itself

> a subject where those who discuss and write about it seem not to know black women exist or even to consider the possibility that we might be somewhere writing or saying something that should be listened to, or producing art that should be seen, heard, approached with intellectual seriousness. *This is especially the case with works that go on and on about the way in which postmodernist discourse has opened up a theoretical terrain where "difference and Otherness" can be considered legitimate issues in the academy.* (24, italics added)

Gesturing toward the need for "diversity" in the canon obviates, in the logic of textual/corporeal substitution, the need for the inclusion of "diversity" within the academy itself; texts are substituted for bodies.[17]

If texts can have racial identities usually attached to bodies, then decrying the textual "dead white men" makes room for other embodied texts. The logic of substitution makes sense, then, of white male aversion to "dead white men." I suggest that this is a fallout of anxieties about minority faculty hiring initiatives and related issues. I propose that these anxieties have produced two apparently opposite (yet strategically identical) reactions: (1) The cry that white men are being discriminated against, which is ubiquitous in the popular media; and (2) a misperception that various forms of oppression are associated somehow with "capital," which results in stated anti-white and anti-male positioning, even and especially among white males, in an attempt to gain this "capital."

This second strategy is what Roman calls "individual identities competing among hierarchies of oppression." In this climate, identity politics has replaced any notion of coalition politics, and authority is symbolically gained by claims to oppression. Now we can see that replacement of the literary text by the "dead white male" body, and the subsequent dismissal of that text, represent an attempt by the critic to distance his own live white male body from the dead one and gain this imagined "capital." It also becomes clear that the conversation at the first party was made possible by the essentialist practice of reading bodies as texts, while the second was related to a legacy of reading texts as bodies.

This logic of imagining texts as bodies results in what John Guillory, in *Cultural Capital,* points to as a

> certain confusion which both founds and vitiates the liberal pluralist critique of the canon, a confusion between representation in the political sense—the relation of a representative to a constituency—and representation in the rather different sense of the relation between an image and what the image represents.[18]

For bell hooks, it is "sadly ironic" that

> contemporary discourse . . . [, while] declaring breakthroughs that allow recognition of Otherness, still directs its critical voice primarily to a specialized audience that shares a common language rooted in the very master narratives it claims to challenge. (25)

Indeed, the "multicultural canon" discussed by students who reject "dead white men" in favor of colorful bodies (of work) is studied as an object, from the outside. The "objects" studied have changed, but the group that is "studying" them has not, nor has it become less self-authorizing, nor have the boundaries of the group become more mutable. The objectification of these works denies their multiplicity, in the same way that a racist reading substitutes a monolithic interior for a multifariously present one. hooks suggests a way to critique essentialism without reinscribing these colonialist paradigms:

> Employing a critique of essentialism allows African-Americans to acknowledge the way in which class mobility has altered collective black

experience so that racism does not necessarily have the same impact on our lives. Such a critique allows us to affirm multiple black identities, varied black experience. It also challenges colonial imperialist paradigms of black identity which represent blackness one-dimensionally in ways that reinforce and sustain white supremacy. (28)

Her prescription for changing the "exclusionary practice of postmodern discourse" is the enactment of "a postmodernism of resistance. Part of this intervention entails black intellectual participation in the discourse" (30). Of course, this prescription calls for more texts and *actual people* to be introduced into the system. It also calls for epistemologies that do not seek to replace one exclusionary system of authority with another.

[4]

WRITING IN RED INK DEBRA WALKER KING

Karla Holloway opens the first chapter of *Codes of Conduct* (1995) with a confession: "My grandmother warned me away from red."[1] I too was warned against red; and, during most of my adolescent years, I refused to wear it. For me, and others like me, red suggested an audaciousness, rebelliousness, and promiscuity condemned by the ethically and morally correct as vulgar and unclean. It suggested a face-to-face encounter with the reality of our bodies' interior spaces—sexual spaces with longings and desires, and the spaces where the rich, free, and sometimes dangerous flow of blood nudges budding flesh into maturity, awareness, and self-expression. Nice girls did not wear red, and I certainly wanted to be a "nice girl." Yet I wondered: why did the older girls—the ones with afros, dashikis, and bangles—wear it, especially the ones I considered "nice"? Why, I asked myself, would they chance their reputations on a color that informed against them?

What I did not realize was that I had little control over the interpretive gaze my body received regardless of how I dressed it. I did not realize that it was not the color of my clothes but the color of my body that informed against me. According to America's culturally constructed standards of morality and purity, not only did "nice girls" not wear red, their skin did not bear the racial indicator black, or brown, or yellow either. They were not called "Red Hot Mamas," "Brown Sugars," or "Exotics" simply because melanin colored their skin. Their bodies' public value was not predetermined and maintained by a system of name-calling that interpolated and disfigured its subject—labeling her whore, slut, or loose—even if that subject was costumed (as Anita Hill was during the Thomas confirmation hearings) in teal blue with "a modest row of military-like double buttons down the front" (Holloway, 15).

Today I look back with understanding at the older girls I once watched in wonder—the ones who wore afros, bangles, and that awesome color, red. Instead of accepting the value coding of a gendered and racialized fiction, they revised the code by appropriating it. As I see them now, they were young women living and writing the liberation of their "flesh"—that willfulness, courage, and subversive understanding of self that frees the mind and spirit from the assaults of conceptual violence that often accompany derogatory constructions of gender, race, and ethnicity.

This chapter is about that liberation as it appears in the fiction of black women writers. By reading a few images of captivity and liberation presented in selected works by Alice Walker, Toni Morrison, Gloria Naylor, and others, this essay traces the difficulties of writing the body in laughing rhythms and "white ink" (as French feminist critic and writer Hélène Cixous proposes) for those who discover that the public and private liberation of their flesh requires RED. [2]

The preponderance of stories about captivity, mutilation, and death in black women's literature is haunting. Who, for instance, having encountered Alice Walker's *The Third Life of Grange Copeland* (1970), Octavia Butler's *Kindred* (1979), or Gayl Jones's *Eva's Man* (1976), can forget the murdered Mem Copeland lying in "a pool of blood," Dana Franklin's violently severed left arm, or the imprisoned Eva Media Canada's oral castration of her lover? Images such as these sadden and even horrify us, but for black women writers and their readers, these events symbolize a struggle against socialized codes and values that denigrate subjective realities, hopes, and dreams. In each case, red emerges and spreads as blood flows freely from bodies experiencing physical and psychological wounding. This spilling of blood, a literal loosening of the flesh, intensifies moments of liberation and is often its prerequisite.

Images of bodily destruction occur so frequently in black women's literature that one begins to wonder what all this spilling of blood implies. Why is it necessary? The answer is simple: it brings into sharp focus that which our postmodern ideologies have taught us to disassociate from any possibility of sociocultural meaningfulness—our pain. We are taught to deny our suffering and feel so ashamed of our scars that we hide them beneath makeup or remove them with plastic surgery. In fact, we are told that we are stronger, better women if we endure our pain silently, ignore it, or medicate (and meditate) it away. We become likable and employable if we deny our need for deliverance from the wounds no one sees, or cares to see, but ourselves. The pain of black women in novels such as those mentioned above cannot be ignored; neither can its significance be diminished or its call for deliverance silenced.

Like a magnifying glass held up to the wounded spaces of our private lives, the physical and psychological injuries suffered by the characters of black women's fiction assist us in acknowledging and understanding our own pain. The blood we envision flowing from mutilated or injured fictional bodies offers us safe passage beyond our real-world suffering and fear. Our pain, no matter how different from that we read about, is somehow validated and justified as we witness the unveiling of its literary surrogate. The security found in witnessing yesterday's sorrow from a secure distance becomes our own and the failures of that past, fictionalized, provide the lessons that empower an audacious will to do more than survive. It provides us with the audacity to wear red: to be victorious in the face of oppositions and social divisions that threaten an inevitable and painful defeat.

Hélène Cixous denounces the instruments of such a defeat in "The Laugh of the Medusa" (1975) and suggests that our greatest weapon against them is writing the body. In an essay that makes incomparable use of her own body's rhythms, Cixous describes the black territory of Freud's "dark continent" as a place of "deadly brainwashing." According to Cixous, this male-constructed continent incarcerates and denigrates women's bodies while controlling and censoring their sexuality (336). Throughout the essay, Cixous demands a radical revision of how and by whom the female body should be written and interpreted. Her ideas are respected and taught in women's studies classes and feminist discussion groups today, and her primary arguments are examined at great length. Yet few of these discussions offer a thorough investigation of what writing in white ink, "that good mother's milk" (Cixous, 339), means for women of color. Before proceeding with my primary thesis, then, I want to focus on Cixous's use of metaphors and their implications for writing the black female body.

Using phrases such as "we are black and we are beautiful," Cixous encourages women to write themselves free from the discursive "apartheid" of masculine-prescribed body politics (336). Speaking of the self-degrading brainwashing women experience, Cixous writes:

> As soon as they begin to speak, at the same time as they're taught their name, they can be taught that their territory is black: Because you are Africa, you are black. Your continent is dark. Dark is dangerous. You can't see anything in the dark, and you're afraid. Don't move, you might fall. Most of all, don't go into the forest. And so we have internalized this horror of the dark. (336)

Cixous's version of feminine writing reclaims a darkness tainted with peril by offering a pen of illumination that writes the body in white ink. Unfortunately, the racialized fictions of black women's bodies remain unchallenged by her metaphors of discursive reconfiguration and subversion.

Writing in white ink allows women who are white to celebrate what Cixous identifies as their "cosmic" libido by inscribing their stories of decensored sexuality and "native strength" onto the pages of an already symbolically charged and racialized space of blackness (345). While effectively destroying the idea that women's bodies are unexplorable centers of lack, Cixous's choice of metaphor evades (if not supports) white masculine discourses that define blackness as an icon of extravagant eroticism and licentious desire. Through Cixous's use of metaphors, Medusa recovers her head and control of both the gaze and the interpolating call, while the "Red Hot Mama" remains an emasculating siren held captive within the dark continent of male-inscribed body politics.

As one of the "night crawlers," whom Cixous credits with "undermining the family and disintegrating the whole of American sociality," the "Red Hot Mama" haunts the fantasies and fictions of an illicit gaze (340). While some feminists try to redefine her by empowering her often pornographic display of body—especially if that body is white—she and the mythology of shame or empowerment surrounding her have been ignored by many black feminists. That is, ignored by some, but not by the red ink of black women's fiction.

We find her in Alice Walker's short story "Coming Apart" (1971), "twisted and contorted in such a way that her head is not even visible. Only her glistening body—her back and derriere [are displayed in the *Jivers* magazine]—so that she looks like a human turd at the man's feet" (43). In this short story a black female body, unlike its white counterpart, is nothing but a lump of human waste: something discarded and useless except for the pleasure her defeated (or defecated) body inspires. That the part of her anatomy from which thought, sensibility, and liberation emanate is excluded from the exotic picture is important. This decapitated figure has no power and no ability to break free of the illicit gaze that haunts her. She has no mind; therefore, she cannot think. She has no eyes with which to envision the other woman—the one who stands beyond the magazine's pages and struggles to break free of a body fiction that cripples and binds her public image.

The "human turd" that Walker presents has no advocate, no sister, to pull her from the darkness of the pornographic frame that misnames her. She also has no "brother" who understands that her degradation is more than a demonstration of his powerlessness in a white world. It is more than his disgrace. It is the cultural construction of his "self" that resides in the magazine's decapitated and denied black female body. If he looks closely enough, he will find that her complete body-ness and mindless presence offer a mirror through which he can locate a threat to his very existence. Captured and defined within the scope of a (supposedly white) pornographer's camera lens, her body—and, by extension, the womb that gestates a human "turd"—defines his lack while her degraded pose challenges his ability to see beyond the "Red Hot Mama."

An even more poignant picture of this abandoned siren and her relationship to the black man is drawn when a *Penthouse* centerfold makes her appearance in Gloria Naylor's *Linden Hills* (first published in 1985). Clothed in tantalizing "African" garb, she represents what the character Xavier Donnell calls black progress. Naylor draws the image of this vixen's captive body carefully. Being mindful of its historically informed fictions, she writes:

> There was an eight-page spread of lush, tropical forest and a very dark-skinned model with a short Afro. Her airbrushed body glistened between the thin leopard strips that crisscrossed under her high pointed breasts and fastened behind her back. She wore a pair of high, leopard-skin boots that stopped just below her knees, and she was posed to pull against an iron chain that was wrapped around her clenched fists. Each page offered the reader a different view of her perfectly formed pelvis, hips, and hints of her manicured pubic hair as she wrestled with the chain held by an invisible hand off camera. [On] the last page of the spread . . . [t]he model had snatched the chain and brought its mysterious holder to her feet. One leg was raised in victory on the shoulder of a scrawny white man in a safari outfit, and his thick bifocals had slipped below the bridge of his nose. (115)

There is nothing liberatory in the picture Naylor presents. Instead, she writes of a body held captive both figuratively and literally by the chains of white patriarchal iconography, a body that can only be called progress by those who assimilate and appreciate the illicit gaze of that brotherhood. Although black men like Xavier Donnell had no say in this fiction's historically racialized construction, they (but certainly not all black men) celebrate its commercial exploitation and fleshless vulnerability. I say *fleshless* because the image provides no sign of resistance against its racialized construction, no vehicle for breaking free from the implications of its own iconic force. There is no indication that the posed figure offers an awareness of self and ethnicity which precedes externally imposed and racialized body fictions.

There is a pleasure and violence in Naylor's representation of this "Red Hot Mama," but not one that "gives woman to the other woman" as Cixous demands. This is not a mama who "knocks the wind out of the codes" but one who maintains the codes by offering her body for its inscription (Cixous, 339). Naylor never revises this particular image of captivity, leaving the voiceless "Red Hot Mama" bound to the pages of her *Penthouse* spread to be shared by those to whom she belongs.

The free and subversive nature of writing as proposed by Cixous falls silent within these images. Although inspiring and liberatory for some women, Cixous's gendered metaphors are blind to the plight of those held captive by the racialized fictions Walker and Naylor portray. The symbolic agency of writing in "white ink," or good mother's milk, is clear when placed against the backdrop of an already erotic blackness, but how does this benefit the black daughters of Africa? What remedy do black women writers have when they reach for that pen of illumination and find the flow of mother's milk has dried up or has been stolen? "[T]hey took my milk," Sethe reminds us in Toni Morrison's *Beloved* (1987). "Held me down and took it" (17, 16). When we view blackness and mother's milk as more than metaphors for unknown territories and the unmasked *jouissance* of subversive writing, we cross the boundaries separating the unexplorable from the unspeakable.

On this path, the "goods" of mothering the self and others extend from a loss of body and body parts. They come from blood spilled and identifying that which was lost or injured as a sacrifice for life, for flesh. One of the clearest examples of this type of giving appears in Morrison's *Sula* (1973). Eva Peace, a woman who is accused of not loving her children, sacrifices her leg for their financial security and almost bleeds to death in an attempt to save her daughter, Hanna.

When this daughter asks Eva if she ever loved her children, "Eva's hand moved snail-like down her thigh toward her stump. . . . No. I don't reckon I did. Not the way you thinkin' . . . what you talkin' 'bout did I love you girl

I stayed alive for you" (67, 69). Hanna cannot grasp the concept of bodily mutilation as a gesture of love and a gift of life. She hungers for proof of affection, not love. The mother she thinks she needed as a child could "tickle [her] under the jaw and forget 'bout them sores in [her] mouth" (69). As a young black mother separated from her husband, Eva could not afford to pet her children. Like so many black mothers, she was too busy helping them survive. Perhaps Hanna's lack of understanding is why she dies a woman who only "dreamed of [wearing] a red bridal gown" (73). Perhaps her fleshless love is what taught her own daughter to watch her burn to death without even a moment of remorse. If we, as readers, can accept the goods and losses that result from Eva's kind of love, we, unlike Hanna, move closer to claiming as our own the power of flesh that writes its liberatory tales in red ink.

Morrison continues to draw upon this power as she tells the story of a woman whose "good" mother's milk is stolen. Morrison presents Sethe as "riveted . . . between the Medusa and the abyss"—to borrow from Cixous (341). Within this space she is the master of making ink. The man demanding her ink, called Schoolteacher in the text, likes the way she makes it. "It was [a white woman's] recipe," Sethe admits, "but he preferred how I mixed it and it was important to him because at night he sat down to write in his book . . . about us [the slaves]" (*Beloved*, 37). Just as Naylor's fleshless model provides the black body that her fictionalized version of *Penthouse* uses to inscribe its myth of sexuality, Sethe provides the ink that Schoolteacher uses to inscribe and define her degradation. Sethe, however, finds her ability to write her own story and nurture herself limited by something other than fleshlessness. She is limited by the thief of an essential ingredient in the recipe for feminine writing: "that good mother's milk."

As Mae Henderson proposes, "the image of Schoolteacher's ink conflates with the expropriation of Sethe's milk in a symbol that evokes" Cixous's metaphor for feminine writing.[3] While Henderson reads this symbolic exchange as one that facilitates Schoolteacher's inscription of paternity upon Sethe's body with a lash, I read it as the key to black feminine writing. To write in mother's milk, the author appropriates Cixous's recipe, but because her character's breasts have been violated—leaving behind a legacy of captive breasts through the sometimes haunting presence of rememory—Morrison, like Sethe, must mix the ingredients differently. In this case, Morrison adds a touch of red that revises Cixous's recipe for *écriture féminine* and allows Sethe to become the author of an unspeakable liberation story.

Having escaped the physical captivity of slavery, Sethe finds the impetus of that captivity chasing her and threatening to take her children to the place where breasts are raped and milk is stolen. To ensure their freedom from such violations, she decides to kill them, to "drag them through the veil . . . where no one could hurt them" (163). The death of the body through the spilling of blood liberates only one child from the physical and psychological consequences of captivity, however. Sethe and her daughter Denver become victims of limited mobility and psychological deterioration. The liberatory intent of Sethe's act of love collapses beneath the weight of social mandates defining "good" mothering until the residue of conceptual violation, in this case a physical manifestation of guilt and shame, haunts them. Sethe's psychological suffering assumes a material presence as the liberated flesh of the child, her "crawling already" baby girl whose throat she cut, returns in the form of a ghost.

Sethe's mother's milk, so necessary for the maintenance of self and others, is reconceptualized through this tragic story of liberation. Morrison describes both the breasts from which it flows and its acceptance by Sethe's surviving daughter, Denver:

> Sethe was aiming a bloody nipple into the baby's mouth. Baby Suggs [Sethe's mother-in law] slammed her fist on the table and shouted, "Clean up! Clean yourself up!"
>
> They fought then. Like rivals over the heart of the loved, they fought. Each struggling for the nursing child. Baby Suggs lost when she slipped in a red puddle and fell. So Denver took her mother's milk right along with the blood of her sister. (152–53)

In the eyes of Baby Suggs and others, Sethe's role as mother, as the source of goods, is tainted by the blood she spills. Baby Suggs cannot read beyond the body. She cannot see Sethe's "bloody nipple" as the ultimate gift of a supreme sacrifice, the chalice of a Passover meal that pays homage to a "passing" that promises the liberation of Denver's flesh—a commemorative "last supper" offered in a mixture of milk and blood, nurture and life. Instead, Baby Suggs reads an infant's dead body, falls in that which death spilled, and misinterprets a ritual of the spirit that nurtures and frees the flesh. If we read the death of the body in *Beloved* as infanticide we too are horrified; but if we read the flesh, we understand Sethe's decision to kill—for she only kills that which holds the spirit of black subjectivity captive. She only kills the body.

By highlighting moments in fiction such as this, moments that mutilate or kill the body, I am not suggesting that a denial of the black body is preferable to celebrating its beauty and stunning grace; and neither are black women writers. Hortense Spillers's 1987 essay "Mama's Baby, Papa's

Maybe" is helpful in opening up and explaining the dichotomy of body and flesh which Morrison and other black women writers explore. In that essay, Spillers revises and inverts Cixous's body metaphor so that the body speaks of captivity, bleeding breasts, scarred backs, and branded limbs while the flesh is representative of a liberty that pre-existed the captivity of those for whom blackness is both a physical reality and a lived experience. Spillers comments that "before the 'body' there is the 'flesh,' that zero degree of social conceptualization that does not escape concealment under the brush of discourse, or the reflexes of iconography."[4]

The body is where the assaults of slavery, social oppression, and repressive value coding bombard African Americans, registering their dismembering and disfiguring influence. It is also the physical site of a mental wounding engendered by interpretive discourses that misname and unname, in mythic proportions, the agency and spirit of liberated black subject positions—the "flesh." For those of us existing outside texts like *Beloved*, it is only by metaphorically turning the body inside out that the conceptual violence of racism is diminished and that a zero degree of self-actualization reveals its power. In black women's fiction, however, the metaphor is transformed into action. This literal manifestation of body wounding is often misread by characters (and readers) standing outside or beyond the actual event (or text). In many cases, these misreadings usurp the positive effects of turning the body inside out—especially if it is the subject of body wounding who does the misreading.

Beloved's bloody death is a publicly displayed and tangible indicator of her position as the subject of body wounding. As Sethe leaves the site of liberty's battle, her wounds are not so easily accessed. Only the blood that covers her dress speaks of them. The narrator tells us that "The hot sun dried Sethe's dress, stiff, like rigor mortis" (152–53). This image of life held captive in the grip of death repeats and revises Sethe's earlier experiences of spiritual and physical wounding, when her milk is stolen and her back is inscribed by Schoolteacher's whip[pen]. It also attests to the psychological wounding she suffers while producing, or rather drawing forth, the red ink that writes her daughters' liberation. It is this symbol of her pain that she must read against codes that would bind her to a self-imposed captivity. Sethe fails at this task. Although she can write the story of her children's liberation publicly, she has not learned the secret of privately breaking free of her own bondage.

Like the community that comes to gaze upon her pain, Sethe cannot embrace, for herself, the liberatory implication of her actions. The community reads her clothes through codes that deny the flesh and dismisses

Sethe as a bad mother. For Sethe, the red that envelops her body colors not only her clothes but also her ability to reap the rewards of knowing and celebrating her own flesh. Secure in the knowledge that at least one of her daughters is free of slavery's chains, Sethe experiences a moment of intro-spective reflection and painful sublimation that others misinterpret. The text tells us, "She climbed into the cart, her profile knife-clean against a cheery blue sky. . . . Was her head a bit too high? Her back a little too straight? Probably. Otherwise . . . [the] sound [of singing] would have quickly been wrapped around her, like arms to hold and steady her on the way" (152). Sethe's submission to this silence and communal alienation acts as a barrier to her ability to move beyond the socially constructed story her blood-soaked garment tells.

It is only by acknowledging the separation of her flesh from the icons of captivity her body wears that Sethe is able to begin self-recovery. She must embrace the flesh. Only when she discovers the "Sethe" within—that self who turns the body inside out and reveals her private stash of red ink—can she arise and walk unfettered by yesterday's pain and today's concern for a community's scorn. Only then is she able to release the ghosts who hold her mind prisoner along with the ruling episteme of her body's captivity. Sethe achieves this moment of freedom with the help of the man she loves. Unlike Xavier Donnell, who celebrates the "Red Hot Mama" bound to the pages of Naylor's *Penthouse* magazine, the man, Paul D., who gazes upon Sethe's pain understands her need for flesh and encourages her toward it: "You your best thing, Sethe. You are" (273).

"Woman for Woman," Cixous claims when writing of the mother func-tion (woman as nurturer and giver of goods) and women in relationships with each other. But Paul D.'s presence and his function as Sethe's nurturer ask of the black woman and man something different. They ask us to mix the recipe differently. "Woman gives woman to the other woman," Cixous claims (339), but, in the case of black bodies, the woman given is too often bruised, mutilated, abused, or publicly scorned and denied. She must face the often hidden lash of racism—the same lash that black men struggle against—daily. In some cases, these struggles exhaust even the goods of female nurture, woman's gift to woman, leaving little in its wake.

Many women are like Sethe—they have not yet discovered how to sepa-rate their flesh from the instruments of racial captivity our culture uses to bind them. These are the women who wear a dress of relentless fear and suspicion. We have all seen them. They are the women who cannot find their way to the other woman, even if that woman shares their race and especially if she is racially or ethnically different. Some share the sentiments of Sherley Anne Williams's Dessa Rose, for whom white women are the progeny of pain and betrayal: "White woman was everything I feared and hated."[5] Or maybe they, like Williams's Rufel, cannot "buy" the story of black women's wounding without first seeing the scars we have been taught to hide (169). Then there are those who mistake fear for disgust and turn away from the other woman, afraid that the wounds which remain in the whites of her eyes mirror too closely their own suffering and rejected selves. In such cases, bonds of gender collapse, allowing the stains from racism's wounds to tighten around the self-alienated "like rigor mortis" (*Beloved*, 253). For the black woman who wears this dress, only the hands of black men who understand and share her need for flesh can reach her, redefine or remove the stains that cover her garment, or, at the very least, help her find the clarity and confidence to see the other woman within and heal herself.

There is no separation between bodies, male and female, when the stains of racism's wounds besmirch us. Before African American women can give fully and with wholeness to the other woman, black bodies must give flesh to black bodies. This does not mean that cross-cultural and interracial unity is impossible. My intent here is to suggest that, in the process of developing this unity, African Americans must move through the imposed darkness of racism with a clear and secure understanding of our private stashes of red ink. That ink is pure, void of jealousy and pride, reinforced by respect, strengthened by love, and purchased by a history of bloodstained and broken black bodies. It is the "me" inside: the one that stands above the plane of racist assaults, gendered fragmentation, and petty grievances to share itself with "you." Whenever black men treat black women as "fleshless" flesh, as bodies designed for their pleasure and subsequent dismissal, they fall on the slippery floor of their own manhood. There lies the blood that liberation spilled, a liberation that was somehow forgotten or overlooked in a lustful rush for sexual gratification or masculine validation.

The bonds and abuses of which I speak present themselves boldly in black women's literature in texts as vastly different as Terry McMillan's *Waiting to Exhale* (1992) and Naylor's *Linden Hills*. For McMillan's characters, woman gives back to woman that which the novel's male characters have corrupted or denounced: a respect and love for black womanhood. Her characters achieve wholeness through female bonding, but, for Naylor's characters, situations in which women find themselves alienated and alone result in ominous and lethal forms of body wounding. It is precisely the absence of black male/female bonding, acceptance, and aid that strikes the blows of private and public wounding experienced by the captive female bodies of *Linden Hills*.

Red ink drips from the pages of this novel, creating a tale of bonds broken by a constructed body politics that pushes each of its primary players (male and female) into the hollow arms of absolute negation. From Evelyn Creton's private experience of bulimic emaciation to the bloody site of Laurel Dumont's public suicide, the devaluation and rejection of black women by black men exacerbates experiences of pain and alienation. Yet, even in this novel, the metatext of extreme body wounding functions as a salve that frees the flesh and releases the captive, especially the captive who reads beyond the horrors of its bloody and fire-engulfed ending.

Novels like *Linden Hills* force those living outside the text to see the blood spilled by liberty and to acknowledge their own connection to it. Like the viewer of a boxing match, we are forced to see the body as body: limited, vulnerable, and dying. In this way, Naylor's *Linden Hills* forces its reader to not only see but feel the weight of that which holds us all captive: historical silencing and absence, myths of mothering and mandatory sacrifice, dreams deferred (or rather, dreams subordinated to masculine desire), colorism, and excessive materialism. Each of these are represented as modes of captivity for black women in *Linden Hills*. Unfortunately, we are often so overpowered by the hopelessness of the body's bondage and ultimate demise that we miss the freedom captivity's death provides. We read the body and are dismayed by its message when we should read the flesh and live the hope of its liberatory offering.

Naylor leaves the silent "Red Hot Mama" bound to the pages of her *Penthouse* spread to be shared by those to whom she belongs, but, for those who dare to read beyond the iconography of the body, she offers a vehicle for freedom from such fictionalized and fleshless images of black womanhood. By wounding the posed and photographed body of Priscilla McGuire, for instance, Naylor sends a message of liberatory empowerment. We meet the deceased Priscilla through Willa Prescott Nedeed, whose husband has locked her in a basement with their dead son. As Willa turns the pages of Priscilla's private photograph album, she reads body wounding. Within each family photograph Priscilla disappears beneath the figures of her husband and her son until she is lost in the bonding of masculinity that surrounds and overshadows her. Willa pages through the photo album until she notices that something is missing:

> [Priscilla's] face was gone. The photo album trembled in [Willa's] cold hands as she realized there was no mistaking what she now saw: Priscilla McGuire ended at the neck—and without her features, she was only a

flattened outline pressed beneath cellophane. The narrow chin, up-turned nose, and deep fiery eyes were a beige blur between the two grown men on each side of her. The entire face, the size of a large thumbprint, had been removed. This had been done on purpose. There was no way this wasn't done on purpose. Cleaning fluid. Bleach. A drop of hot grease. Over and over, page after page, the smeared hole gaped out into the dim light. . . . [Until s]he came to the last photograph. And scrawled across the empty hole in lilac-colored ink was the word *me*. (249, Naylor's italics)

The pictures Willa contemplates are of a woman erased first by the domination of one man, her husband, who uses her body to duplicate himself in the form of a dark-skinned son and discards it thereafter. This son, who sees her as merely the vessel through which his body passed before finding life with his father, provides the second source of her domination and erasure from the photograph. The third vehicle of erasure she provides herself, by writing over both men's fleshless codes and discourses about her and reinscribing her own. Through the destructive mechanism of her own hand, she enacts symbolically a body wounding which resists their discursive shadows and frees her flesh.

Although Priscilla writes over male-defined stories of absence and lack in lilac-colored ink, red fills this scene. It is framed by the image of blood spilled during Laurel Dumont's public suicide and it is viewed through the eyes of a character who sees everything beneath a veil of blood. Willa's gaze is colored by a rage the narrator describes as "scratch[ing] at the scars in her mind." We are told that "she trembled as fresh blood seeped through the opening wounds. . . . Blood from the open scars dripped down behind her eyes" (204). Priscilla McGuire discovers the "me" inside and finds that her stash of ink is lilac, indicating a knowledge of self that is weak and not fully formed—but for Naylor the ink is red. She fills the scene and our vision of it with blood that frees both our minds and her character, Willa, from captivity.

Willa allows the bloody evidence of her psychological wounding and physical captivity to write over the fictions her husband inscribes until his definition of her as a flawed reproductive machine is silenced. For Willa, the body becomes "a mere shelter for the mating of unfathomable will to unfathomable possibility. And," we are told, "in that amber germ of truth she . . . conceived and reconceived" herself (288). This recognition and acceptance of the "me" inside creates within the text a space of stability and security where those (the reader included) who find themselves subject only to their own will and imagination can congregate.

As Willa escapes the basement of her captivity, her body is subordinate to an experience of liberation that renders its death by fire ineffective. The fire kills nothing of eternal value, self-realization, or ethnic truth—these we, the readers of this bloody story, carry from the text. Naylor's red ink conjures a mode of transference that not only calls Willa into recognition of her internal will and strength, but also calls the reader into a realization of life and renewal. If we read the flesh and not the corpse that housed it, we, like Willa, find the ability to free ourselves from gendered and racial-ized forms of captivity. We discover a way not only to survive but to live.

Cixous advances the idea that our strength as women derives, in part, from "the gestation drive—just like the desire to write: a desire to live self from within, a desire for the swollen belly, for language, for blood" (346). This is a powerful statement undermined only by its association with an illuminating pen of whiteness, a pen that marks out the primary vehicle of rememory and transference in black women's texts. Writers, like Walker, Naylor, and Morrison, take their "mother's milk right along with [their] sister's blood" and so should we. With this revised recipe for writing and living, black women inscribe their flesh and renew their strength. The blood black women writers draw from the vein of history's silence and rememory's labor is the blood for which we thirst. The desire for blood, then, is not a desire for gestation, for that which is to come, but rather a desire for the right to acknowledge today's pain while clearing a space of recognition that gives voice to the voiceless and flesh to the fleshless. Using red ink we fill the belly of our personal, creative, and professional desires with life—a life that strikes against the malicious whims and misrepresen-tations of body fictions. We live our defiance proudly in recognition of who we are, what we have become, and what we shall be; lest we forget that below our feet lies the blood of our mothers' and sisters' struggles against the wounds of slavery, disfranchisement, Jim Crow, sexism, exclusion, deg-radation, invisibility, poverty, and distortion.

We have all heard of the glass ceiling, but have we all heard of the slippery floor, a floor covered with the blood that liberty spilled? Through Morrison's depiction of Baby Suggs, we understand that if we do not ac-cept the sacred chalice provided by the wounded bodies of our sisters we fall in the blood that liberty spilled and captivity challenged. This chalice filled with blood and mother's milk is the trope through which we reclaim ourselves, our history, and our pain—without feeling ashamed or embar-rassed. It secures our feet as we stand upon the slippery floor and pound against the glass ceiling, knowing we, like our ancestors before us, can break the codes of body fictions that attempt daily to hold us captive or bind us to debilitating labels that cloak our intelligence, mark us as expendable bodies, or sacrifice our sexuality to images of baby machines, sex toys, and emasculating vixens.

The injuries and deaths of characters in black women's texts call forth the healing powers of the flesh we need to survive today's struggles. We must read the flesh in these stories. Without it we too die or become disfigured by the codes and myths that wound their protagonists. To use Morrison's play on words, these are not stories to "pass on"; they are stories to claim, pass through, and survive. Within them lies a message of hope, defying body fictions that inform against us and hold us captive. It is a message of spirit and of flesh with the power to liberate us all, black and white, male and female, if only we take the time to look beyond "the" body.

[5]

MYTHS AND MONSTERS:
THE FEMALE BODY AS THE SITE FOR
POLITICAL AGENDAS **S. YUMIKO
HULVEY**

Recently I began noticing images of the *yamauba* (mountain Furies) lurking in the narratives of several Japanese women writers. In texts by Enchi Fumiko (1905–86), Ōba Minako (1930–), Kurahashi Yumiko (1935–), and Tsushima Yūko (1947–),[1] the yamauba topos is appropriated to deal with problematic issues such as identity, sexuality, and the traditional role of women in modern society. Enchi's "Haru no Uta" ("Spring Song," 1971) and *Saimu* (*Colored Mist,* 1975), among others, reflect images of women who "drain" the life force from the men with whom they have had sex and suggest men as victims of supernatural, empowered women in the yamauba tradition. Ōba's "The Smile of the Mountain Witch" ("Yamauba no Bishō," 1976) and "Candlefish" ("Rōsuku Uo," 1986) offer updated versions of the yamauba topos from an insider's point of view, rendering a sympathetic feminist revision of the female demon of the past. Kurahashi's "The Long Passage of Dreams" ("Nagai Yumeji," 1968) and "Spring Night Dreams" ("Haru no Yo no Yume," 1989) suggest that women are capable of becoming demons, merging dream and reality, as women seeking sexual satisfaction talk of devouring and ravaging men as if they were modern reincarnations of yamauba. Tsushima's "Maboroshi" ("Illusions") and "Yume no Michi" ("Path of Dreams") offer images of women running through the mountains, mountain paths leading to seemingly uninhabited mountain huts, mothers who inadvertently hurt their children, and aging women who transform into yamauba simply by growing old.

A number of questions come to mind: Why would these women writers choose to incorporate such a negative image of a man-eating female monster into their texts, and after having done so, what do these writers hope to achieve by placing the yamauba in their narratives? In the course of trying to refine the image of the yamauba, I began to sense that the yamauba may have some mysterious relationship to powerful female archetypes from ancient stories or myths. Perhaps the yamauba of traditional Japanese folk tales harkens back to female prototypes in ancient creation myths that impart a sense of empowerment to women. Maybe by choosing to write about the challenge of living as women in patriarchal society, women writers are able to exorcise or alleviate their feelings of frustration. Why would most of these writers choose to promote negative images of women, if not to express their ambivalence or anger at having to cope with living in patriarchal society?

In this chapter, I do not seek the modern version of the yamauba found in the texts of modern female authors. Here, I present two creation myths, the Japanese and the great mother, as prototypes from which a cycle of folk tales about the yamauba evolved and developed. I argue that the creation myths provide inspiration for the yamauba topos by introducing female prototypes that give birth later to a variety of female demons. I propose that the Japanese creation myth, which posits the female body as the site of defilement and pollution, was a ploy adopted by patriarchy to associate females with negative attributes in order to gain control of property and inheritance rights that were originally under the jurisdiction of females.[2] I refer to studies of the great mother creation myth to suggest the privileged position, based on their procreative ability, that was occupied by females in prehistoric times and that was usurped later by patriarchy. Finally, I extrapolate reasons why some modern women writers choose this topos as a vehicle for literary expression.

Studies of the yamauba traditionally begin with medieval short stories, then proceed to medieval Nō dramas with a more literary flair, and conclude with folk tales collected from all over Japan at the turn of the twentieth century. The folklore studies I have read thus far do not refer to myths as the source or inspiration of the yamauba topos nor identify her nature as the two-faced "terrible mother," sometimes a nurturer and other times a destroyer. Only when I delved into the study of myth did I discover the work of Yoshida Atsuhiko, who locates the true origin of the yamauba topos in the creation myths of the Japanese and the great mother. To my knowledge, no study in English focuses exclusively on the connection between the yamauba topos and these creation myths.

What or who is a yamauba? *Yamauba* is most commonly translated as "mountain witch" or "crone." Classical Japanese dictionary definitions make a distinction between *yamauba* and *yamanba*, but modern dictionaries treat the two words identically. A yamauba is usually defined as a woman with superhuman strength (*kairyoku*) who lives deep in the mountains, or a female demon (*kijo*) who lives in remote mountains. The medieval pronunciation with the medial nasalization, *yamanba*, is most often defined in classical dictionaries in terms of its relationship to the Nō play titled *Yamanba*, sometimes referring to the Nō mask (*men*), the Nō dance (*kusemai*), or the main characters in the play, Yamanba and Hyakuma Yamanba.[3] Classical Japanese dictionaries do not specify the age of yamauba, but modern dictionaries define both yamauba and yamanba as old female monsters (*rōjo no kaibutsu*) who live deep in the mountains. The recent trend toward treating the two terms identically leads to some misunderstanding of the character of the yamauba.

Meera Viswanathan, in "In Pursuit of Yamamba: The Question of Female Resistance," defines the yamauba as a

> terrifying old woman with long gray hair, possessing superhuman strength and prescience, dwelling in the mountains, preying on stray male travelers who intrude on her as she occupies herself with the task of spinning; she is capable of extraordinary transformations, ranging from animal to beautiful maiden. Should her prey attempt to escape, she chases it down in the mountains and devours it with uncanny delight. Yet, interestingly, this figure of dread also appears in alternative disguise in folk tales: as a comical dupe, a fool, a greedy and selfish creature, who is ultimately punished for her unnatural ways. Here the threat posed by the figure of the *yamauba* becomes doubly contained in these narratives, first, by her failure to realize her desires, and second, by the denaturing of her character through her representation as an object of ridicule.[4]

While Viswanathan provides a much-needed introduction to the yamauba topos, her work is not without problems. Viswanathan falls under the spell of Ōba Minako's modern metamorphosis of the yamauba in the short narrative "The Smile of the Mountain Witch," and confuses Ōba's modern version with the traditional yamauba. Viswanathan assumes that Ōba's creative transformation of the yamauba reflects characteristics of traditional yamauba. First, she mistakenly endows traditional yamauba with the ability to read people's minds, when telepathy is never mentioned in medieval stories or folk tales about the yamauba. Second, she accepts Ōba's invention of the yamauba's "uncanny delight" in devouring their victims, when traditional folk tales never describe the monster's actions with emotional detail. Third, she adopts Ōba's description of yamauba as old women with long gray hair, when in some folk tales yamauba are beautiful young women who have not yet revealed their supernatural quality or they are not described in any detail, making it difficult to gauge their age. Finally, although Viswanathan mentions a connection to the Japanese creation myth in a note referring to an article by Ōba Minako and Mizuta Noriko, her study makes no further mention of the relationship between the prototype and the yamauba figure.[5] From my perspective, striking similarities between the yamauba and the female deities indicate that the inspiration for the yamauba topos originated in the creation myth recorded in the *Kojiki* (*Record of Ancient Matters,* ca. 712) and the *Nihongi* (*Chronicles of Japan,* also *Nihon Shoki,* ca. 720).

Myths are powerful tools that shape the values of society and legitimize the political ideals of the ruling hegemony. Merlin Stone offers a perceptive reading of myth:

> Myths present ideas that guide perception, conditioning us to think and even perceive in a particular way, especially when we are young and impressionable. Often they portray the actions of people who are rewarded or punished for their behavior, and we are encouraged to view these as examples to emulate or avoid. So many of the stories told to us from the time we are just old enough to understand deeply affect our attitudes and comprehension of the world about us and ourselves. Our ethics, morals, conduct, values, sense of duty and even sense of humor are often developed from simple childhood parables and fables. From them we learn what is socially acceptable in the society from which they come. They define good and bad, right and wrong, what is natural and what is unnatural among the people who hold the myths as meaningful. It was quite apparent that the myths and legends that grew from, and were propagated by, a religion in which the deity was female, and revered as wise, valiant, powerful and just, provided very different images of womanhood from those which we are offered by the male-oriented religions of today.[6]

Keeping the persuasive power of myth in mind, I will present some of the most important elements of the Japanese creation myth from the *Kojiki:*

Izanami (Female *Kami* Who Invites) and Izanagi (Male *Kami* Who Invites) stand on the Heavenly Floating Bridge and use the Heavenly Jeweled Spear to create Onogoro Island. They descend to this island and erect a heavenly pillar and a spacious palace. They walk around the pillar in opposite directions before having intercourse, and she speaks first. A leech child (Hiruko) is born. They make a reed boat and cast the child adrift. Izanagi says that it is not proper for a woman to speak first. They consult other deities and a divination is performed, revealing that because she spoke first the child was malformed. They perform the ritual around the pillar again, and this time the male speaks first, producing good deities and land. But Izanami suffers a fatal injury while giving birth to the fire god. She suffers greatly, sickens, and dies. Sadly Izanagi buries her body near the border of the lands of Izumo and Hahaki. In anger, he beheads the fire god with his sword, engendering still more deities from the fire god's splattering blood. But Izanagi misses Izanami so much that he ventures into the land of the dead to retrieve her. Izanagi finds a palace in the dark land, knocks at the door, and is surprised when Izanami answers the door. He reveals his longing for her and asks that she return with him so they can finish the act of creating land. She answers that it is too late, for she has already eaten food in the land of the dead. She feels sorry for him and is touched that he came to visit her, so she goes to consult the kami who rules the land of the dead. She tells Izanagi not to look at her body and goes back inside the palace. He gets tired of waiting for her and tries to enter the palace, but it is so dark that he breaks a male pillar (otokobashira) from his wooden comb and lights it to find his way into the palace. Then he sees her body decomposing, teeming with maggots, and spawning eight thunder gods from her head, chest, stomach, genitals, arms, and legs.

Izanami tells him that he shames her by violating the prohibition and that he must be punished. First, she summons the eight ugly females of Yomi (Yomotsu Shikome) and sends them to vanquish Izanagi. But he runs away and throws down his headdress, which transforms into grapes. The Shikome stop to eat the grapes, giving him a little lead. As the Shikome draw close again, he throws his comb, which transforms into bamboo shoots that the Shikome devour, allowing him to gain more ground. Next Izanami sends the eight thunder gods at the head of the Yomi army (Yomi no Kuni no Gunzei) against Izanagi. But Izanagi draws his sword and waves it behind him until he reaches the sloping pass that separates the land of the living from that of the dead (Yomotsu Hirasaka). There he takes three peaches and hurls them at the thunder gods, causing them to turn back. Izanagi thanks the peach tree and asks that peaches may grow in the land of the living to help people in need. He climbs the hill to the land of the living and places the boulder (Chibiki no Iwa) that can be moved only by the strength of one thousand people over the entrance. Finally Izanami herself chases Izanagi to the pass. There Izanami and Izanagi face each other

75

through the boulder that blocks the passage between two worlds. She vows to strangle to death a thousand people a day and Izanagi counters with a pledge to build one thousand five hundred parturition huts each day (that is, to give birth to fifteen hundred new lives a day). Thus they break their troth.[7]

Izanagi goes to the river to purify and exorcise himself of defilements collected by going to an unclean land and gives birth to numerous deities, the most important of which are Amaterasu Ōmikami, the sun goddess, who springs from washing his left eye; Tsukuyomi no Mikoto, the moon god, from his right eye; and Susanoo no Mikoto, the storm god, from his nose. Izanagi gives Amaterasu his necklace and charges her with governing *Takama no Hara* (the Heavens), and entrusts the rule of the night to the moon god and of the ocean to Susanoo.

But Susanoo wails and rages, causing destruction, and is expelled by Izanagi. Before Susanoo leaves he ascends to the heavens to say farewell to his sister, Amaterasu. Distrusting him, she dons male war attire to battle him for her territory. However, Susanoo asks that she test whether his intentions are good or evil by bearing children. Standing on the opposite side of the riverbank from him, she breaks a sword into three pieces, rinses the pieces, then chews them and spits them out, while making jingling sounds with her jewels. Three deities are born. Then Susanoo asks for Amaterasu's long strand of myriad beads wrapped around various parts of her body: her left hair-bunch, her right hair-bunch, the vine securing her hair, her left arm, and her right arm. All told he gives birth to five male deities as compared to the three female deities borne by Amaterasu. His intentions are judged to be good because he bore male offspring, but he goes to Amaterasu's fields and breaks down the ridges between rows of rice and fills in the ditches. Then he defecates and throws feces around the hall where the first fruits are tasted. Amaterasu does not reprove him but speaks with good intentions. However, Susanoo's actions become more flagrant. While Amaterasu and her attendant are in the sacred weaving hall, he opens a hole in the roof and drops down a flayed dappled pony from heaven. The heavenly maiden is alarmed at this, strikes her genitals against the shuttle, and dies. Amaterasu, seeing this, is afraid, and opening a door to a cave in the rock, shuts herself inside. When all is in darkness, the deities devise a plan to return light to the darkened world. They have a smith forge a large mirror, have a long string of myriad *magatama* (comma-shaped) beads made, and perform divinations and rituals. Then Ame no Uzume no Mikoto becomes divinely possessed, exposes her breasts, and pushes her skirt down to her genitals, producing laughter among the myriad deities. Amaterasu, thinking it strange that they are enjoying themselves when all should be shrouded in darkness, opens a crack in the heavenly rock cave, and is tricked by the mirror into believing there is a deity more brilliant than she herself. Then another deity takes Amaterasu by the hand and pulls her out of the cave, returning light to the Central Land of the Reed Plains. Susanoo is exorcised and expelled again.[8]

With the plot of the Japanese creation myth providing guide posts, I will now turn to the yamauba in all her various guises spawned from myth.

Yamauba are known by various names. Combining *yama* (mountain) with a variety of words referring to women creates compounds such as *yamahaha* (mountain mother), *yamahime* (mountain princess), *yamaonna* (mountain woman), and *yamababa* (mountain crone), words that describe females living in the mountains with connections to divinity through the mountain kami with whom the yamauba is often linked.

The connection between yamauba and the mountain kami is probably inspired by the story of Iwanagahime (Long Rock Princess) and Konohana no Sakuyabime (Flowers Blooming on the Trees Princess), daughters of the mountain deity Ōyamatsumi no Kami from another part of the Japanese creation myth. Ōyamatsumi sends both his daughters as brides to Ninigi no Mikoto, the son of Amaterasu no Ōmikami (or Susanoo, according to some sources). Ninigi no Mikoto accepts the beautiful Sakuyabime and deigns to sleep with her for just one night, but he sends the ugly Iwanagahime back to her father without touching her. After Iwanagahime is sent home, Ōyamatsumi no Kami explains that he sent his daughters together for a purpose: to insure that the lives of humans would be long-enduring like rocks and beautiful like blossoming flowers. Because Ninigi no Mikoto rejects Iwanagahime for her ugliness, human life spans are shortened, resembling the ephemeral flowers rather than enduring like rocks (Philippi, 144–47). Some variants of this myth have Iwanagahime herself proclaim that humankind will be doomed to ephemerality as a result of Ninigi no Mikoto's rejection of her.[9] Like Izanami, who is made to proclaim that she will kill a thousand people each day, Iwanagahime is blamed for shortening the lives of human beings (Yoshida, 61–73). Both are depicted as dangerous women.

Other variant names by which yamauba are known emphasize the malevolent, supernatural aspect of aged females: *onibaba* (demon crone), *oni* (demon), and *oni no haha* (demon's mother), perhaps a reflection of patriarchal views of females who have outlived their traditional roles in patriarchal society. The medieval stories and folk tales related below employ the entire gamut of variant names to refer to women who fit the yamauba mold.

Yamauba who appear in one of the earliest collections, such as *The Tales of Times Now Past* (*Konjaku Monogatari,* ca. 1120), are simply called oni (demons), but they display attributes of yamauba recorded in more recent folk tales. For instance, in "How a Woman Who Was Bearing a Child Went to South Yamashina, Encountered an Oni, and Escaped," from *The Tales of Times Now Past,* a pregnant woman leaves the capital to find a place in the mountains to bear her child. She and her maid come upon an abandoned estate, go inside, and discover an old woman living there. The old woman kindly invites the young woman to have her baby there and stay until the period of defilement is over. A few days later, the mother overhears the old woman saying that the baby boy looks incredibly edible. So the mother, maid, and baby leave the house immediately and return to the capital.[10] The old woman is referred to as an oni, never as a yamauba, but her circumstances fit the image of a yamauba living on the fringes of society. It is worth noting that the old woman in this story does not possess supernatural powers, such as telepathy or the ability to transform; she is just an old woman who says the baby boy is cute enough to eat. The old woman shows the benevolent side of her personality in providing shelter for the unwed mother, but equally important is her hidden aspect: a potentially dangerous yamauba looking for male prey. The mother and maid may feel threatened by the old woman, but clearly the only object of her sinister gaze is the male baby. One wonders if she would have been equally menacing if the baby had been female rather than male.

In "How the Hunters' Mother Became an Oni and Tried to Devour Her Children," also from *The Tales of Times Now Past,* two brothers hunt at night to support themselves and their frail, aged mother. One night, while perched in a tree waiting to shoot deer, the elder brother finds himself being hauled higher up the tree by a supernatural being. He asks his younger brother to save him by shooting an arrow above the place from which his voice emanates. The younger brother shoots an arrow and when the elder brother reaches up, he finds a hand dangling from his topknot. When they return home, they discover their mother moaning in her cottage. After examining the hand closely, they conclude it is their mother's hand. They decide that she must have become an oni and followed them into the mountains to devour them. She dies of her wound soon afterward.[11] Here a sickly old woman displays superhuman strength by climbing a tree higher than her sons and hauling up one of her sons by the hair until her hand is shot off. The narrator's concluding remark, that women turn into oni when they age, reflects a patriarchal stance that sees women past the age of childbearing and sexuality as vile and threatening. There are other stories that depict mothers trying to devour or actually devouring their male children.

In the two medieval stories of female oni, both women are old, beyond the age of childbearing, and at least one of them demonstrates superhuman strength. The two women also match the description of yamauba in that they live in remote mountainous areas, yet their behavior differs quite markedly from this point on. The old woman who gives the unwed mother shelter cannot be unequivocally called an oni, since she never acts upon her verbal appreciation of the baby's culinary appeal, but the mother of the two hunters is quite malevolent, displaying superhuman strength as she acts upon the urge to devour her own children. Threatening female monsters continue to appear in the yamauba cycle of folk tales of more recent times, collected and catalogued by the pioneer folklore scholar Yanagita Kunio.

Yamauba appear under all sorts of names in folk tales such as "The Three Charms" (Sanmai no Gofuda), "O Sun The Chain" (Tentō-san Kane no Kusari), "The Ox-Leader and the Yamauba" (Ushikata Yamauba), and "The Woman Who Eats Nothing" (Kuwazu Nyōbō).[12] Although there are many versions of each of these folk tales, major elements that recur in story after story are worth examining.

In "The Three Charms," a novice asks a priest to send him into the mountains to gather flowers and is given three charms to throw at demons, should any accost him. While the boy is gathering branches, an old woman says she will give him something good if he comes to her house, so he goes along. He decides to spend the night there, but the rain wakes him and tells him to go look at granny's face. He sees that she has turned into an oni and knows he must escape. So he pretends that he has to go to the bathroom and she allows him to leave the house with a rope tied around his waist to a grindstone. The yamauba keeps asking, "are you through yet?" and he keeps answering, "not yet." He has the first charm answer while he escapes. When she discovers that he has escaped, she begins chasing him. He throws the second charm and shouts, "Big river." Then a big river blocks the yamauba's path. When she almost catches up to him, he throws his last charm and shouts, "Big mountain." While she is crossing the mountain, the novice reaches the temple. The priest hides him in a cupboard. When the yamauba leaps into the temple and threatens to eat the priest, the priest challenges her to a transformation duel. He tells her to turn into a bean and when she does, he sticks it into a *mochi* (rice cake) and eats it (Mayer, 102–105). This story resounds with echoes from the creation myth: a woman chases a man with intent to kill; a man "sees" the hidden side of a woman that causes fear; and a man throws things at a woman to cause delays that enable him to escape. The story also connects yamauba with mochi, a thread we can trace to other tales in which the yamauba makes an appearance, most likely sown from ancient agricultural beliefs in the great mother as the provider of food and sustenance.

The second oldest record of the Japanese creation myth preserved in the *Nihongi* (*Chronicles of Japan,* ca. 720) reveals an interesting variation on Izanagi's flight from the Shikome, the ugly females of Yomi. While Izanagi is running away from the Shikome, he urinates against a large tree. The urine immediately turns into a great river. While the Shikome are trying to cross the river, Izanagi is able to reach the pass to the land of the living, and to place the boulder across the pass.[13] This version provides an archetypal image of a river as an obstacle to slow down women in pursuit of a fleeing male, linking this folk tale to a variant version of the creation myth from the *Nihongi*.

In "O Sun The Chain," three brothers are told to be good while their mother is away. She warns them that a man-eater may come, so they should be very careful. That night someone knocks at the door and the oldest boy answers. He thinks the visitor looks like his mother but he notices that she has hair all over her hands, so he shuts the door. Then the man-eater scrapes the hair off with a potato grater and knocks again. This time the boy lets her in, but wakes up in the night when he hears his mother eating. He asks her what she is eating and she answers by throwing a bloody finger at him. He wakes up his remaining younger brother and together they run out of the house. They climb a peach tree but she climbs up after them. So the boys cry out, "O Sun, please save us," and a chain comes down from the sky. They climb it to safety. She also calls on the sun for help, but the chain breaks when she climbs it. She falls, hitting her head on a stone, and dies. Her blood stains the roots of the corn red and the corn continues to grow with red roots from then on (Mayer, 105–107).

There are whispers from the creation myth: the peach tree which Izanagi told to help humankind gives temporary refuge to the boys; the image of a woman chasing young boys is similar to Izanami's chase; and the stone, reminiscent of the boulder that blocked the pass between the world of the living and that of the dead, is often associated with yamauba for the rock caves in which they give birth to offspring or the rocks on which they leave marks etched during the pain of childbirth. Prototypes of child-devouring mothers are found in the figure of Lilith and in Jungian interpretations of the myth of the great mother, which posits the development of individual personality as a path away from the mother's engulfing effects on the child. Variants of this story contain celestial images of the stars and moon, not surprising when one recalls the title, "O Sun The Chain," another link to cosmology and divinity.

In "The Ox-Leader and Yamauba," a man leading an ox (or a horse) loaded with salt mackerel meets a yamauba at a mountain pass. She follows him, begging him for the mackerel, until he gives her the entire load. She then begs for the ox. When she has finished off the ox, she comes after the ox-leader. He runs off frantically and finds a lonely house at the foot of the mountains. It is the yamauba's house. He hides in the rafters of the house. When she comes home, she builds a fire and begins toasting mochi. When she dozes off, he takes a piece of thatch from the roof and picks up a piece of mochi to eat. She wakes up and screams, "Who took my mochi?" He answers, "Fire god." She says that if it is the fire god there is nothing she can do. She gets a kettle to heat some sweet wine (or makes *miso* soup) and nods off again. The man again takes a piece of thatch and sucks up all the wine (or soup). She wakes up and shouts, "Who drank my wine (or soup)?" Again he answers, "Fire god." So she decides it might be better to go to sleep on a night like this. She gets inside a wooden chest and goes to sleep. He comes down quietly, puts a lid on the chest, and puts a heavy rock on the lid to trap her. He stokes the fire, boils a lot of water, and drills holes into the chest. He then pours scalding water through the holes and avenges himself on the yamauba. In some versions, he sells the remains of her body as medicine and becomes wealthy.[14]

This story, linking food to the yamauba through the images of mochi and wine (or soup), is related to the idea of the great mother as the provider of sustenance. The yamauba's death by boiling is equally related to cooking, as is illustrated by Jōmon clay pots with human heads and breasts that signify feeding off the body of the mother goddess.[15] Yoshida contends that the sale of the yamauba's scalded body as medicine, which makes the man wealthy, is related to the principle that beneficial things are produced from the body of the yamauba. The most interesting elements are the inclusion of the "fire god" and that the yamauba's death is ultimately due to fire. In the creation myth, Izanami is fatally injured while giving birth to the fire god and descends into the darkness of the land of the dead; similarly, the yamauba secludes herself in a dark chamber and dies. The fire god binds the creation myth to folk tales through the image of a female who dies by fire. But in some variants, the yamauba turns into a spider after being boiled to death, a filament we will trace in the following tale.

In "The Woman Who Eats Nothing," a miserly, middle-aged man finally gets married when he finds a beautiful woman who supposedly eats nothing. He is happily married for a while until he has a friend go to his house disguised as a healer, since his wife is ill, or an old woman warns him that his wife is more than just an ordinary wife.[16] In either case, he peeps and discovers a hidden side of his wife: she secretly eats vast quantities of food through a hole in the top of her head. When the husband discovers the true nature of his wife, he is horrified. He runs but she chases him and quickly catches him. She puts him in a tub and hauls him into the mountains; he holds onto a tree branch and escapes. He hides in the bushes where irises and mugworts grow and the vegetation acts as a yamauba repellent. In some versions the yamauba is just held at bay by irises and mugworts; in others, she is killed.[17] In other extant versions, the yamauba turns into a spider when her secret is discovered and sometimes tries to eat him. In both of these versions, after the yamauba transforms into a spider, the spider is killed.

Here the woman displays supernatural attributes such as a hole on the top of her head, the ability to eat massive quantities of food, and the power to transform into spiders in some versions. Like Izanami and Izanagi in the creation myth, this couple is happily married until one day he "sees" a side of his wife of which he had not previously been aware. Furthermore, the husband has to run for his life when he shames his wife by looking, as did Izanagi when he violated Izanami's prohibition. This story also shows the dual nature of the yamauba: depending on who is doing the "looking," she is viewed either as a beautiful woman or as a demon. When the yamauba transforms into spiders, she is posited as a negative female figure, a hunter who weaves a web of deceit to lure victims into her trap. In some variants, the image of a spider is introduced into the story by the yamauba's occupation as a weaver.[18]

The image of weaving also occurs in a variant version of the creation myth recorded in the *Nihongi*. Amaterasu is in the sacred weaving hall making garments for the gods when Susanoo breaks a hole in the roof tiles and throws down a flayed piebald colt of Heaven (Aston, 40–48). She is so shocked that she wounds her genitals on the shuttle and locks herself up in the Rock Cave of Heaven, bringing darkness to the Central Land of the Reed Plains. The rest follows the story recorded in the *Kojiki*, but some scholars believe this may be the earlier version since it is the sun goddess herself who is wounded by the shuttle, whereas the *Kojiki* takes the insult away from the sun goddess and places it upon a lesser female attendant. In either case, the images of yamauba and weaving are linked to the creation myth.

In a variant version of "The Woman Who Eats Nothing," after the woman is killed by being exposed to irises and mugworts, she turns into a spider. Her life as the wife of a miserly man, contributing to his prosperity by denying herself sustenance, is thus shown to have been still more "fantastic," and more of a lie, than it appeared. Spiders are connected to women through the image of weaving webs, something yamauba are known to do as they lay traps for male victims or wait to attack men who chance upon them in remote mountainous regions. Food as sustenance and mountains are encountered again in other stories of the female demon.

Yoshida introduces several other folk tales in which yamauba assume interesting guises. He cites tales that highlight the yamauba's dual nature as nurturer and destroyer. Yamauba can help people by providing bountiful crops or wealth if they are treated with respect. There is a folk tale with several variants in which an old woman shows up in a village asking to help in the year-end work of pounding cooked rice into mochi cakes in preparation for the New Year's celebration. In one version, everyone refuses the old woman until a young couple, the poorest in the village, invite the old woman to add her contribution of two or three cups of rice to their meager supply. The couple is surprised to find that for every cup of rice they pound, five are produced. The next day when the old woman returns they give her her share of the increase and she goes away satisfied. Every year thereafter, the old woman returns and is given a generous portion of the increased rice. The young couple grow ever more prosperous, until they are the wealthiest family in the village. But when the couple grow old and hand their house over to their son, the son discontinues the practice his parents had begun, and turns the old woman away. Thereafter, the yield of his crops decreases and his family reverts to being the poorest in the village (Yoshida, 18–19).

Again echoes of the mother goddess as the provider of food and life reverberate in this story. When Izanami's decaying body produces the gods of gold, clay, water, and bountiful crops in the creation myth, this genesis is directly related to the belief that the mother goddess's body provides sustenance for the people. Jōmon cooking pots decorated with human heads and breasts illustrate the concept that food comes from the pregnant, fecund body of the mother goddess. And this brings to mind the variant story in the *Nihongi* in which Ukemochi no Kami, the food goddess, produced food from her mouth. The story also seems to suggest that yamauba must be honored and respected or the yield of the crops will decrease.

Another story that emphasizes the yamauba's need for honor and respect is tied to her reproductive cycle and the mountain deity. There are tales of yamauba giving birth to multiple offspring in dark caves and dying by fire. In one, a yamauba retreats to a cave when she feels that she is about to give birth. While she is in the cave, some villagers make plans to burn fields to prepare the land for future plantings. The villagers do not know the yamauba is in the cave, so they inadvertently burn her to death as she gives birth. Thereafter many inauspicious things occur in the village, such as illnesses and natural disasters. Someone suspects a yamauba may be involved in the pestilence, so the villagers go to the cave and bring out her skull. They enshrine her remains and make the yamauba a mountain kami. Soon afterward, the illnesses and disasters cease (Yoshida, 58–59). Some variants have the villagers intentionally planning the yamauba's death rather than accidentally burning her, but nonetheless, this tale focuses on the deification of a yamauba, when she is enshrined as a mountain kami. As mentioned earlier, the inspiration for the connection between the yamauba and the mountain kami comes from the Japanese creation myth through Iwanagahime and Konohana no Sakuyabime, the daughters of the mountain deity Ōyamatsumi no Kami. Both yamauba, the one who increases the yield of mochi and the one who gives birth to many children at once, demand respect and exact retribution in its absence in the form of decreased production or pestilence and illness; the stories thus allude to the two-faced character of the yamauba.

Both yamauba and Izanami possess dual natures: they may be frightening demons intent on killing men or nurturing women bestowing wealth and bountiful crops. There are a number of parallels between them. First, the archetypal image of a woman chasing a man with intent to kill is embodied by Izanami chasing Izanagi; similarly, the prototypical image of the yamauba is the chase to capture male prey. Second, Izanami gives birth first to islands and then to many deities; this is echoed in the yamauba tradition when she gives birth painfully to many offspring in rock caves—and sometimes dies by fire as did Izanami. Third, Izanami and Izanagi are happily married at first and she does not show her demonic nature until Izanagi violates her prohibition of looking at her body; likewise, yamauba sometimes marry men who are quite content until they see the demonic side of their wives' personality. Fourth, various parts of Izanami's decomposing body produce thunder gods and her feces, urine, and vomit give birth to gods of gold, clay, water, and bountiful crops; in the same vein, there are some folk tales in which a yamauba imparts wealth or beneficial products to those who treat her with honor and respect. Finally, Izanami no Mikoto ironically becomes associated with death in the divorce decree as patriarchal society seeks to counteract the powerful procreative powers women possess in reality; furthermore, the daughters of the mountain kami, Iwanagahime and Konohana no Sakuyabime, shorten the lives of humankind; and the yamauba also becomes the agent of death by chasing male prey to kill and eat.

Tracing patriarchal elements in the Japanese creation myth reveals an attempt to displace belief in the great mother with male-dominated belief systems. For instance, when Izanagi and Izanami first descend to Onogoro Island and have intercourse, Izanami speaks before Izanagi and a leech child is born. After consulting other kami, they enact the ritual again, this time with Izanagi speaking first. In this way, legitimate offspring are produced and recognized until Izanami is mortally injured bearing the fire deity. The message of the courtship ritual is clear: when the female kami Izanami speaks first, a leech child is born, something deformed or lacking, not fit to be recognized as the offspring of kami. But when the male Izanagi speaks first, worthy offspring are produced. The story dictates that females should assume a passive role in sexual relations; that is, women should wait to be chosen, while males should play an active role in choosing females as mates. This is evidence of the attempt by patriarchal society to counteract the universal practice of mother goddess worship, in which females actively chose males to mate with because paternity was not important in ancient matriarchal societies. Patriarchy used myth and morality to promote monogamy and control female sexuality, putting an end to the active role females played in sexual relations. This was the beginning of the double standard males have enjoyed up to the present.

The phallic symbols in the Japanese creation myth may actually refer to rituals honoring the great mother. The ritual of circling around the Heavenly Pillar in opposite directions is interpreted as "foreplay" by one feminist historian.[19] Although the form of the pillar resembles the shape of a phallus, another feminist historian maintains that pillars made from trees carved into statues were an integral part of rituals honoring the mother goddess (Stone, 175, 214–18). Philippi cites supportive evidence from pillars and ancient Japanese customs: rites of walking around a pillar were designed to increase human fecundity; a procession of men and women singing around a pillar was an ancient form of a Japanese marriage ceremony; and rituals to summon a deity from the heavens were also enacted around pillars (Philippi, 398). Since, as I have argued, myth is a potent repository for literary motifs and plots, it would not be surprising to find Izanagi and Izanami's rite of walking around a pillar before engaging in intercourse as a model for ancient marriage rites. The three rites listed by Philippi have in common fecundity, intercourse, and the summoning of deities, suggesting some intimate connections to ancient mother goddess worship.

In the Japanese creation myth, the female body becomes the site of ritual defilement. At first, Izanagi notices Izanami's genitals and suggests that he insert that part of his body that is formed to excess into the place in her body that is not whole, so that she may give birth to land. But the vagina that originally invited his attention later becomes the sight/site of his revulsion when her vagina is burned while she gives birth to the fire god. Izanagi is even more repulsed when he lights a tooth from his comb and sees her decomposing, with maggots crawling over her body.

The patriarchal ideology at play in the creation myth upholds the integrity of the male body at the expense of the female body: Izanagi produces various kami from his body without being physically harmed, but Izanami's body is vulnerable to physical decay. She suffers a great illness after giving birth to the fire god and descends into the land of the dead. A national scholar (*kokugakusha*) of the Edo period, Hirata Atsutane, proposes a link between fire and blood due to the color red. He states that Izanami's giving birth to the fire deity may actually refer to either the afterbirth or menstrual blood, since in his time menstruation was euphemistically referred to as "fire," and the practice of remaining in seclusion during the monthly defilement is perhaps associated with Izanami's illness and withdrawal (Philippi, 399–400). Menstrual blood is thought to be the worst kind of defilement because it emanates from the vagina. Other scholars suggest that the association between fire and blood may have been derived from the ancient custom of burning parturition huts after birth. Another link between fire and blood is formed when Izanagi beheads the fire god and the fire god's blood gives birth to other deities. Thus the association of fire, blood, and birth is clearly established in the creation myth. Fire, like water, is one of the elements used to purify the defilement of birth, connected to both blood and the vagina.[20]

In the *Kojiki* account, after Izanagi returns from the unclean land of the dead, he bathes in water and produces the most important deities of the Japanese pantheon, Amaterasu Ōmikami, the sun goddess, and her brother, Susanoo no Ōmikami, the storm god. In the land of the dead, Izanagi sees Izanami's rotting corpse and flees in fear and horror at the sight. Therefore, putrefaction is associated with the female body while purity is

associated with the male body, and the kami born of the male body symbolize the politico-religious, agricultural, and military aspects of ancient Japanese society.[21]

The most damaging blow dealt to females by the compilers of the creation myth was the association of females with death rather than birth.
Although in actuality females are the ones capable of creating life, the
compilers of the creation myth denied biological fact by making females
the reviled gender that threatened humanity with death. In the service of
their political agenda, they launched a double-pronged attack on females:
they made females the counterpart of the Grim Reaper and made the
female body the site of ritual defilement in a thought system that values
purity above all else. As harbingers of death and defilement in the Japanese creation myth, females are handicapped by negative associations that
are hard to overcome even when facts to the contrary have been revealed.
The female body thus becomes the site for political agendas: patriarchy
sought to displace matrilineal lines of descent and gain access to property
and inheritance by denigrating females, who were originally worshipped
and honored for their procreative ability.

As if Izanami's connection to death were not enough, the Japanese creation myth also uses Iwanagahime to reinforce the idea that women are
responsible for shortening the lives of humankind. The stories of Iwanagahime, Konohana no Sakuyabime, and Izanami involve enclosures, fire,
and the birth of multiple offspring. Like Izanami giving birth to the fire
god, Konohana no Sakuyabime is made to prove the paternity of her children to Ninigi no Mikoto by building a parturition hut, sealing herself
up inside it (creating a cave-like enclosure), and setting it on fire before
bearing three offspring. This story is linked to both Izanami and the yamauba in several ways: females retreat to an enclosed space, bear more
than one child at one time, and die by fire. Some scholars speculate that
the custom of proving the legitimacy of the child by ordeal may have been
derived from shamanistic practices involving deities who come to wed a
female shaman for just one night or from the custom of burning parturition huts after birth to ward off evil spirits. Women were required to
prove the legitimacy of their children and attest their faithfulness through
ordeal by fire; this brings to mind ordeals in which women have been
drowned to prove their innocence of witchcraft. Thus the creation myth
provides the archetypal stories from which tales of the yamauba grew.

The association of the female deities Izanami, Iwanagahime, and Konohana no Sakuyabime with death and defilement spoiled any chance for
mortal females to escape negative associations in life. Similarly, the yama-

uba, spawned from archetypes found in the Japanese and great mother creation myths, is reviled in traditional Japanese folk tales as a female monster who threatens to devour and kill men. In the Shintō belief system, which values purity, the female body cannot ever be ritually cleansed because it is the site of defilement through its association with blood, illness, and putrefaction. By extension, the bloody image of the yamauba, a man-eating female monster, can be nothing but negative.

The power of myth is so strong and pervasive that to this day women writers instinctively feel a primordial connection to the image of the yamauba. Women writers may even realize that the yamauba owes her inspiration to the vilified female deities of the Japanese and great mother creation myths, but even if they do not, they seem to sense some mysterious kinship between the female monster and archetypes of threatening, empowered females. Perhaps the female psyche intuitively recognizes the maligned image of the yamauba as a figure worth reviving in the world in which we live. What is astonishing is that some women writers, like Enchi Fumiko, actually revel in the negative associations of dangerous women, employing images of vampires and femmes fatales who lure men to their doom, perhaps for the same reason that some religions believe that contact with defilement can sometimes empower those who dare it. Using images of blood and bald assertions of female sexuality and desire, women writers today challenge patriarchal norms by appropriating formerly negative associations as active, positive means of expressing discontent.

Because the power of myth makes it difficult to dissociate females from death, conscious effort must be made to understand the political agendas that drove the compilers of the myth to distort facts and create negative associations with the gender they sought to subjugate. Like Eve's guilt for humankind's expulsion from the Garden of Eden, Izanami's association with death and defilement excludes women from the Shintō ideal of purity. If, however, negative associations cannot be dispelled, contemporary Japanese women writers seem to brandish the yamauba topos as a sword to mow down misconceptions of the female condition. Like the yamauba herself, if women today cannot be revered or worshipped as the creators of life, they prefer to be feared as agents of death, as decreed by myth, rather than bow down meekly as the oppressed Other.

[6]

AGENCY AND AMBIVALENCE: A READING OF WORKS BY COCO FUSCO **CAROLINE VERCOE**

"We've been working on our conversational abilities with our fantastic HOT INTERNATIONAL guide, which comes with translations for love and sex in seven different languages. . . . Ready? Or should I say *listo?*"[1]

Two rows in front of me a middle-aged woman shuffles nervously as "Rosa," dressed in floral hot pants, large hair, and a boob-tube, invites audience members up on stage to join in an Afro-Frenetic Dance Extravaganza. Beside me, an excited young man waves his blue ticket in the air and is duly led on stage. Behind him, three friends crack up laughing as the volunteers are led through their steps. To the side, I notice a man in a suit and spectacles march out of the auditorium—he is offended. Exploring the ambivalence and complexity of cross-cultural engagement, Coco Fusco uses her own body to highlight the ways in which identity, as perceived through stereotype, constructs cultural myths and contributes to collective memories. While her writing deals with a range of cultural concerns, her solo and collaborative performance works characteristically explore the function and agency of cultural representation, social inscription, and the Other's body. [2]

In perhaps her most well known performance collaboration, *Two Undiscovered Amerindians Visit . . .* (1992), Fusco and Guillermo Gómez-Peña were displayed in a cage in various public spaces around the world. The performance was envisaged as a reflexive, playful satire on the display strategies of turn-of-the-century cultural expositions where many members of non-Western cultural groups were exhibited in conditions not unlike today's zoos.[3] The two artists presented themselves as indigenous Amerindians from an island in the gulf of Mexico that had somehow not been discovered by European voyagers. Exploring the politics of colonial containment, they drew on the vernacular of nineteenth-century cultural expositions and were presented as ethnographic specimens in museums, public squares, and universities, with cultural experts available to answer questions from a curious public.

Fusco's performance contexts blend fiction and apparent reality in a manner designed to entice viewer interaction. Presenting her body as a site of colonial desire and fantasy, she highlights the ways in which fascination with the Other can remain firmly entrenched in contemporary society, regardless of present-day multi-cultural initiatives or the onslaught of global philosophies. Like Freud's magic slate, which leaves traces of its original inscription after it has been wiped "clean," the West's fascination with its exotic Other is indelibly streaked with a legacy of colonial nostalgia and fetishistic yearnings. By constructing performances which interrogate the complexities of sites such as the museum and tourism, she works to expose the mechanisms by which non-Western cultures are maintained as marginal within colonial hegemonies. "The object of colonial discourse," writes Homi Bhabha, "is to construe the colonized as a population of degenerate types on the basis of racial origin, in order to justify conquest and to establish systems of administration and instruction."[4] bell hooks telescopes these concerns into a contemporary context, using metaphors of eating and encounter to describe strategies in which colored voices and bodies are maintained in colonial servitude. "When race and ethnicity become commodified as resources for pleasure, the culture of the specific groups, as well as the bodies of individuals, can be seen as constituting an alternative playground where members of dominating races, genders, sexual practices affirm their power-over intimate encounters with the Other."[5] Within this fraught space Fusco creates performance-fictions which challenge conventional readings of cross-cultural encounter and work to unearth personal responses, confronting viewers with the "horror" of their own colonial, racist fantasies.

Fusco presents the colonial Other in the continuum—in a postcolonial and global world. With Gómez-Peña, she followed up *Two Undiscovered Amerindians Visit . . .* with *Mexarcane International* (1994), which took place in shopping malls in Britain and Canada. In this piece, the artists set up a fictitious market research center, which aimed to custom-design exotic experiences for shoppers. Posing as representatives of a corporation specializing in global encounters, Fusco interviewed shoppers about their ideal exotic experience and Gómez-Peña performed an interpretation of it, based on the results of the interview. The performance environment was situated between conventional mall shops and was located near a food hall for maximum exposure. Gómez-Peña sat in a bamboo cage set on an artificial patch of grass, posing as the ubiquitous noble savage. Communication with him was mediated by Fusco, who approached potential clients employing market research strategies of engagement.

These encounter-performances situated the Other's body within sites of contemporary cultural consumption—the museum, the public square, the shopping mall, the gallery. Each of the works reflects histories or contexts in which native cultures and bodies have been contained and displayed for the colonial gaze. These metaphors recur throughout Fusco's oeuvre, in her exploration of the implications of cultural consumption and its role in the creation of images of identity. Her encounter-performances seek to interrupt audience complacency in relation to the viewing and reading of cultural difference, and to elicit unfiltered reactions. These goals can be seen in the obvious structure of the cage and more obliquely in the containment of native bodies within the prescriptive fixity of stereotypes. Highlighting the role of stereotypes in the process of cultural consumption, Fusco reworks key sites of encounter to stage performances which bring to light the mechanisms that are employed to fix the Other as curio, as partial, and as lacking.

In all of Fusco's projects, elaborate props and contextualizing paraphernalia are employed to set the scene. In *Two Undiscovered Amerindians Visit . . .* , Fusco and Gómez-Peña presented themselves in a range of adornments signifying Otherness. Blending myth, apparent realism, and fiction, they framed themselves against a background of paraphernalia associated with nineteenth-century cultural expositions, providing "authentic" artifacts from their make-believe homeland accompanied by dances and legends and "proof" in the form of docents to answer questions from the public. They also blended elements of kitsch into this collage—tourist badges and plastic sunglasses. Fusco wore a leopardskin-printed print bikini top and a grass skirt, Gómez-Peña a studded collar and a Mexican wrestling mask. A range of props surrounded them in their cage, enhancing their living cargo-culture diorama—a plastic snake, brightly colored fabrics, and a gaudy souvenir tablecloth. The artists used their props as fetish objects, constituting a discourse of colonial nostalgia and primitivist fantasies.

The performance of encounter was made even more elastic by literally drawing the audience into its frame of reference—the camera's frame. A side-show dynamic was enhanced by the sale of Polaroid images of audience members and the "savages," allowing moments of this experience to be captured and taken away by each purchaser. Implicating viewers in the theater of encounter by fixing their images alongside those of the Other becomes a way of interrogating the pleasures and ambivalences of cultural consumption. The camera has been firmly sited within colonial discourse as a mechanism enabling the capture of native bodies and landscapes and the inscription of ownership and difference onto them.[6] This photographic service, along with "traditional" stories told in a fictitious language by Gómez-Peña and dances performed by Fusco for a nominal fee, helped to create a carnival atmosphere in which the bizarre spectacle seemed unproblematic.

Fusco states that their aim was not to represent an actual existing indigenous culture, but rather to re-enact the idea of Otherness. Linking this notion firmly to the culture of nineteenth-century cultural expositions, she suggests that visitors wished to see their idea of the Other—"cultural stereotypes in the flesh to be looked at, rather than . . . individuals from cultures different from their own" ("History," 37–63). It is not the colonized body that is the site of fascination and consumption, but its excess. When highly theatrical props are added to the already familiar stereotype-charged environment focusing on the Other's body, theater and the real became blurred, inviting spectators to suspend their disbelief and engage in the encounter in purely scopic terms. The success of this endeavor is perhaps best illustrated in the cynical but revealing response of *Art Forum*'s Jan Avgikos, who smugly states, "I had thought about what I was probably supposed to be thinking, and what in fact I was thinking, as I stood gazing at the installation/performance. . . . What I did think about was how beautiful Fusco's scantily clad body was—which is probably what just about everyone else was thinking too."[7] The ambivalent gaze is nurtured by parallel ambivalences relating to the stereotype and notions of primitivism, nostalgia, and revilement. The Other can be simultaneously abject and beloved. While the essential ethos of the Other has for centuries provided base ingredients for Western artists and capitalists alike (tourism being a crucial case in point), the body of the Other remains fixed in an objectifying discourse in which it is framed concurrently as sexualized and exotic, as a menial worker, curio, muse, nurturer, and degenerate.

By presenting the performance as realist—complete with docents giving detailed and informed explanations to the public and providing evidence in the form of maps and texts which specifically showed the location—the site—of Guatinaui, Fusco and Gómez-Peña constructed, for some, a mythical reality. Since the performance had a minimum of prearrival publicity, the public was often caught off guard, and many viewers engaged with the performance in a nonfictional capacity—actually believing that the staged scenario was real and the couple in the cage were legitimate. Fusco expresses her surprise that their satire was mistaken for truth: "We did not anticipate that our self-conscious commentary on this practice could be believable. We underestimated public faith in museums as bastions of truth, and institutional investment in that role. Furthermore, we did not anticipate that literalism would dominate the interpretation of our world" (*English Broken*, 50).

Fusco co-produced a video, *The Couple in the Cage: A Guatinaui Odyssey* (1993),[8] which juxtaposes encounters filmed during their performance and actual footage from cultural expositions and circuses in which indigenous people were exhibited as curio and spectacle. Movies featuring Hollywood exotics and primitive savages were also contrasted with contemporary reactions, highlighting the blend of truth and fiction which often informs an individual's awareness and readings of cultural difference. The majority of present-day responses judged the authenticity of the performance by the physical appearance of the couple. While the documentary reflected a range of reactions, each seemed marked by a deep ambivalence. This ambivalence appeared to go hand in hand with an anxiety on the part of many viewers, who often seemed unsure how they were supposed to act under the circumstances. Fusco discusses a number of reactions she encountered whilst ensconced in the cage-performance:

> Artists and cultural bureaucrats, the self-proclaimed elite, exhibited skeptical reactions that were often the most anxiety-ridden. They sometimes have expressed a desire to rupture the fiction publicly by naming us. . . . Several feminist artists and intellectuals at performances in the U.S. have approached me in the cage to complain that my role is "too passive," to berate me for not speaking and only dancing, as if my activities should support their political agenda. . . . A group of skinheads attacked Gómez-Peña in London and had to be pulled away by audience members. . . . No American ever asked about the legitimacy of the map (though two Mexicans have to date), or the taxonomic information on the signs, Gómez-Peña's made-up language. . . . In Spain there were many complaints that our skin was not dark enough for us to be "real" primitives. ("History," 158–62)

Ambivalence functions as a pivotal strategy in both the construction and the maintenance of cultural stereotypes and the dynamics of the colonial gaze. It also plays a key role within the framework and reception of Fusco's performances. Bhabha's treatise on ambivalence and its shaping role within colonial discourse has cast an indelible shadow over the landscape of postcolonial thought. His essays "Of Mimicry and Man: The Ambivalence of Colonial Discourse" and "The Other Question: Stereotypes, Discrimination and the Discourse of Colonialism" situate the native body firmly within the discourse of colonialism as a crucial signifier of difference and inferiority. [9] The construction and consumption of the Other's body is necessary in order to legitimize the supremacy of the colonizer; its containment and display are imperative to the maintenance of "his" control.

Bhabha maintains that two key strategies are used to create, disseminate, and maintain imperialist hegemonies—mimicry and the stereotype. His notion of mimicry refers to the partial assimilation of colonial dictums; as he puts it, "colonial mimicry is the desire for a reformed, recognizable Other, *as a subject of a difference that is almost the same, but not quite.*"[10] By introducing codes of behavior and articulation which cannot fully be attained by the colonized, the strategy of mimicry works to highlight both their difference and their innate inferiority. It also instills a sense of lack in the Other, caused by the constant reminder of this difference. Bhabha's mimicry comprises pure repetition; its partial nature affords it no identity "behind its mask" ("Mimicry," 88). However, it is the very nature of this partial or anomalous presence which highlights the instability and split nature of its construction. "Under cover of camouflage," he writes, "mimicry, like the fetish, is a part-object that radically revalues the normative knowledges of the priority of race, writing and history. For the fetish mimes the forms of authority at the point at which it deauthorizes them" ("Mimicry," 91).

A number of writers have criticized Bhabha for his essentializing reading of the subaltern and his insistence that the colonized have agency and pose a real threat to colonial discourse.[11] The lack of empirical treatment afforded his work by the writer himself has also led some to suggest that his grand treatise of the ambivalent and anomalous Other is somewhat "lacking" in practice. It is within the body of Fusco's work, however, that the ambivalent, anomalous, and threatening Other materializes. She embodies what Bhabha calls "the hidden threat of the partial gaze," for while she appears to be the object of pure scopophilic gratification, the gaze is returned ("Mimicry," 89). The complexity of reception that ensues encompasses an ambivalence that even Bhabha may wonder at, for it is the intersection of the viewer's gaze and the performer's gaze which is highlighted and explored. In the same way that Bhabha's colonial discourse relies on a conflictual and ambivalent encounter of colonizer and colonized, Fusco's performances pivot on the presence of a returned ambivalent gaze. In an ironic reversal of Bhabha's partial Other, who can *almost but not quite* emulate the Master's culture, Fusco's performances present the Other who can *almost but not quite* convince its audiences of its legitimacy as Other.

While *Two Undiscovered Amerindians Visit . . .* initiated a voyeuristic relationship between viewer and performer, *Mexarcane International,* by siting itself within shopping malls, offered up the Other's body as a product to be appraised, customized, and purchased. This intensified scopic spectacle pivoted on the interface between shoppers' desire to consume products and their fascination with exoticized cultures as commodities to be consumed. The shopping mall is a kind of modern-day marketplace, providing for a range of needs and enjoyments. Positioned within the interstices of larger shopping spaces lie a number of smaller sites—information stations, demonstration carts, and market researchers—aiming to question passersby about their shopping experience. These sites employ a more hands-on strategy, one of direct approach as opposed to allurement. These spectacles function within the carnivalesque to provide unusual and comical forms of entertainment. Like carnival sideshows, the smaller sites of product promotion and consumption—featuring magic pens, glass blowers, and caricature artists—provide sites for amusement and wonder for the cultural consumer. These smaller, more peripheral spaces within the context of the "marketplace" operate as carnivalesque moments within the overall shopping experience. They provide sites for Bakhtinian "ritual spectacle" within the overall marketplace/carnival paradigm, a spectacle existing on the border between art and life, shaped "according to a certain pattern of play."[12]

Mexarcane International also featured an elaborately constructed performance environment, designed to lure viewers into the encounter. As with *Two Undiscovered Amerindians Visit . . . ,* the mutual alienation of the public and the figure on display was heightened by the fact that Gómez-Peña did not speak in English, but conveyed his messages in a fictitious language. In the mall performance, clients of *Mexarcane International* were interviewed by Fusco, who asked questions about their preferred exotic experiences. Having completed the interview, the clients were encouraged to approach the cage and request Live Action A, B, D, or O, according to the results of the questionnaire—which in fact had no real correlation with Gómez-Peña's response. At this point, Gómez-Peña would perform an arbitrary activity—e.g., eating a human heart made of rubber, performing a "native" dance, or addressing his viewer in a fractured, fictitious language. Fusco and Gómez-Peña, aware of the power that evidence and trophies play in creating the authentic Otherness, surrounded themselves with a range of signifiers which served to suggest that their activities were legitimate, part of the overall shopping experience. Legal documents clarified the natives' authenticity, along with work permits from governmental agencies that reinforced their presence as legal.[13] Large glossy photographs were also displayed to illustrate the range of exotic types which could be hired out for corporate occasions. A range of cultural artifacts and props set the scene for this exotic encounter with Otherness. By situating their product within the context of the shopping mall and by employing conventional strategies of market research promotions, the performers were able to suspend their shopping audiences' disbelief and engage them in the poetics and politics of scopophilia, fetishism, and the Other's body as commodity.

bell hooks describes this curiosity about and fascination with exoticized cultures as a phenomenon in Western mass culture (hooks, 21). This form of cultural consumption, however, does not embrace the complexities of the cultures or bodies fetishized; rather, it fixates on particular images and impressions which provide stylized and palatable stereotypes of race and ethnicity. "Whereas mournful imperialist nostalgia constitutes the betrayed and abandoned world of the Other as an accumulation of lack and loss, contemporary longing for the "primitive" is expressed by the projection onto the Other of a sense of plenty, bounty, a field of dreams" (hooks, 25). The Other remains fixed in an ambivalent state, the object of desire and also of pity, a signifier of pleasure and of danger.

The politics and poetics of cultural consumption and the Other's body were again the focus of Fusco's solo performance *Better Yet When Dead* (1996–97). Fusco re-enacted the wakes of prominent Latinas, including Frida Kahlo, Selena, and Ana Mendieta, who have become iconic cultural figures and symbols of Latin femininity, and whose fame in the West has largely come posthumously. Fusco explains, "In 1995 I was trying to figure out how to develop the containment theme more to deal with issues of gender when the Tex-Mex singer Selena was killed. What really struck me was that she became a household name all over the U.S. as a result of her death, not her creative pursuits in life. . . . I started to take notes as I compared the Selena story to those of other Latinas who have occupied a special place in the American imagination and who have all died in particularly tragic or violent circumstances, making their deaths into a kind of performance of female sacrifice, which relates to Marianism in Latin Catholicism, the counterpoint to machismo, which dictates that good women should be martyrs, or that through sacrifice one achieves transcendence."[14]

Fusco lay in a coffin, dressed to resemble each woman, in a room adorned to reflect mourning rituals in Latin Catholic churches. Once more the environment was constructed to create an overall ambience enhancing the scenario—the lighting was dim, the walls were covered in black velvet, and a soundtrack featuring the chanting of the rosary was continuously played. Viewers were invited into the gallery to mourn and contemplate the "dead" female icons. Once more the Other's body becomes the site of fetishistic encounter.

Better Yet When Dead continues Fusco's exploration of notions of containment, display, and the Other's body. Extending Gayatri Spivak's suggestion that the only sites prescribed for subaltern voices to speak from are positions of self-sacrifice, sati, and suicide, Fusco creates a contemplative space in which viewers are invited to interact with and quietly consume the dead body of the Other.[15] The coffin acts as a poignant metaphor for the containment and display of non-Western voices and bodies, and for the construction of popular cultural myths relating to women and martyrdom. Spivak suggests that the subaltern is prescribed no positions of enunciation, but rather she is either spoken for—inscribed in the politics and pleasures of the Master's voice—or allocated alternate positions of articulation which do not correspond to her own subject position. As a result, Spivak despairs of efforts to establish counter-histories as means of breaking down or balancing imperial narratives, because the colonizing process has established the hegemonies of subject positions within colonial discourse, which are often deemed historical or legitimate in the continuum. "One never encounters the testimony of the women's voice-conscious," writes Spivak:

> Such a testimony would not be ideology-transcendent or "fully" subjective, of course, but it would have constituted the ingredients for producing a countersentence. As one goes down the grotesquely mistranscribed names of these women, the sacrificed widows, in the police reports . . . one cannot put together a "voice." The most one can sense is the immense heterogeneity breaking through even such a skeletal and ignorant account. (Spivak, 93)

Sites of silence and self-sacrifice emerge for Spivak as prescribed sites for subaltern voices, and Fusco's performance would seem to re-enact these spaces.

In the three performances discussed so far, the Other's body has been presented as a disempowered, scopic object. The cage and coffin provide explicit visual referents to colonial acts of seizure and containment. Because Fusco infused her performances with parody, exaggerated staging, and bizarre spectacle, viewers' reactions often seemed to pivot between a willingness to engage and an anxiety not to appear stupid or ignorant. The theater of encounter was staged from a distance, so to speak. Fixed within the confines of cage or coffin, viewers were able to mediate their experience, whether knowingly or otherwise. They could choose to engage or remain anonymous within the comfort zone of the crowd. In her next performance, *STUFF* (1996), a collaboration with artist Nao Bustamante, the performers took on a more active role. They physically interacted with their audience and addressed them directly. Staged in theater spaces, *STUFF* explored tourist strategies relating to the creation of cultural stereotypes and myths. The artists re-enacted a range of interactive experiences dealing with gendered stereotypes, Latin women, and food in an exploration and interrogation of touristic modes of cross-cultural encounter. Documentary techniques, game show dynamics, and promotional hype were combined to construct a performance revolving around a number of vignettes, telling stories about food, sex, exchange, consent, and the politics of cross-cultural negotiation in a "world" where touristic imperialism has replaced colonial hegemonies.

Aspects of spiritual and sexual tourism were re-enacted, blending strategies of mimicry and parody to highlight both the complexity and transparency of touristic desires and their implications. The audience was exposed to a range of cultural stereotypes referencing different aspects of touristic encounters: go-go girls, sex workers, waitresses, cultural center performers, street vendors, and travel guides. Brecht's notion of theater as providing entertainment as well as being a site for potentially transformative experiences is embraced in this performance. Humor and parody function as crucial vehicles for audience engagement. Fusco's and Bustamante's roles within the piece mimicked highly engaging and sexualized stereotypes of Latinas who engage with the audience but are intrinsically passive and nonthreatening.

Unlike previous works, *STUFF* is heavily scripted, with audience participation occurring throughout the performance. While it references many of the issues seen in previous works, the combination of cabaret techniques (of audience response, role playing, and sing-alongs) and its duration of over an hour make the performance a more complex and densely packed piece. On entering the theater each member of the audience is given one of four different-colored tickets. Individuals are selected from among those who volunteer their tickets when asked (plus those who attract the attention of Rosa's "magic elbow"). The prospect or threat of interaction creates a certain air of tension throughout the performance.

This highlights the fact that there is a preordained routine being played out. While seeming impromptu, *STUFF* is well planned and choreographed, mimicking similar performances staged by tourist industries.

STUFF opens with Fusco and Bustamante seated at dressing tables on opposite ends of the stage writing postcards which they read to the audience. The contents of the postcards are based on experiences the artists have had while traveling, documenting their encounters with various occidental "Others" who project their preconceived desires onto the pair. There are elements of self-reflexivity, as the performers look directly at the audience while reading. Bustamante's first postcard recounts an experience she had of being propositioned by a young local as she walked home in the early hours of the morning in Copenhagen. Intrigued by her looks, he offered her salsa and corn chips to lure her into his bed. In another reading Fusco, writing to "Kim from Toronto," tells of an experience she had at a film festival when she was criticized for articulating a personal view which did not wholeheartedly support "third-world film." The postcard readings highlight a range of perspectives and views relating to cross-cultural experiences which sharply contrast with the binary tourist clichés usually seen adorning the backs of postcards. By "sending" the various cards from different (predominantly European) parts of the world, they site themselves as international voices, who ironically remain fixed as exotic and sexualized.

According to Bhabha, stereotypes are located within the realms of the fetishistic, the scopic, and the Imaginary. He suggests that fantasy plays a formative role in colonial exercises of power. Bhabha describes the mechanisms of cultural stereotypes as embodying elements of fixity, repetition, fantasy, and ambivalence and suggests that if certain types of images are constantly presented in a range of different contexts, they will become imprinted on the collective memory of viewers and inscribed within a collective vernacular ("Question," 66–84). Fusco's performances rely heavily on the power of stereotyped signifiers to trigger reactions. She mimics stereotypes relating to sexist and racist behavior and dress, in order to create circumstances which arouse exoticizing and fetishistic memories or reactions in her viewers. Rosa and Blanca (alias Bustamante and Fusco) are the first character-stereotypes to feature in the performance. They are introduced by Elizardo Eduardo Encarnacion Jones (also known as Triple E), the Director of the Institute for Southern Hemispheric Wholeness, as representatives of an agency specializing in providing exotic services to tourists, or Travel Tasters. His Institute offers authentic global encounters, in the realms of sexual and spiritual tourism. Triple E interacts with the audience and performers via a video projection, offering trouble-free tourist packages, guaranteeing the very best of holiday experiences, and monitoring the actions of Rosa and Blanca as they go about realizing his requests: "heat without sweat, ritual without revolution and delicacies without dysentery." His promise of "post-spatial travel" offers no-strings-attached, guilt-free travel experiences—which include generic user-friendly landscapes, climate, and people. Triple E gives an assurance that the glossy tourist brochure simulacra can be real. The notions of consumption, eating, and anthropophagy work within each piece as multi-layered metaphors, reflecting the ways in which native bodies are packaged into stereotypes and consumed by a range of audiences. The gaze is returned in Fusco's performances and the process and experience of cultural consumption become somewhat disturbing for the viewer.

By constructing the performance around the voices of touristic subalterns, Fusco and Bustamante problematize the snug binary of victim/exploiter. Agency exists not only on the part of the tourist but also on that of the tourist worker, and the ambivalence felt by many tourists in relation to their cultural encounters is mirrored in the experiences of their providers. Considering that for many non-Western countries the tourist dollar constitutes a significant contribution to economies, it is not surprising that industries quickly emerge to cater to touristic needs. Host countries have an investment in the fixed imaging of "only positive" and authentic culture. One sequence illustrating this notion features Fusco "as a child selling Zapatista dolls." A voice-over in Spanish is translated into English text and projected onto the theater wall:

> I've never seen the real Marcos, but I have dolls of Marcos, Ramona, Trini, Moises and David. . . . Sometimes there are people who will even buy me a meal, and then I always ask for chicken. I always try to see if my friends and my mother can come too. Then we can sit in the restaurants where we usually get thrown out and the waiters can't say anything.

As with many of the stories told and re-enacted in *STUFF*, this sequence was based on an encounter that the artists experienced—this time with a young girl in Chiapas. The girl explained that she dresses "traditionally" in order to gain more income. Ironically, the Zapatista dolls were the invention of a Spanish journalist who asked a local woman to sew a mask on one of her dolls for him to take home as an authentic and personalized memento of his stay.[16]

The ability to frame and construct one's body in a number of cultural stereotypes works to reflect the body's intrinsic malleability as a form of representation. It also subverts the notion of fixity in which the stereotype is inscribed. Fusco's work differs from politically explicit performance art, which tends to project a fixed set of meanings onto viewers. Serving viewers an array of stereotypes enacting different experiences of Otherness, she invites them to interact with them within a relatively unmediated environment. Delayed reactions, however, highlight the layers of ambivalence, transgression, and subverted roles in play within the works. Viewers may for instance have engaged enthusiastically with aspects of the performance, only to feel on reflection that the dynamic was humiliating or disrespectful.

Not only the performers but also the audience are subjected to the inscription of cultural stereotypes. The artists stage a re-enactment of a ritual honoring Cuxtamali, "keeper of the earth, the mother of all things," which is the first of several audience-based pieces.[17] Triple E names each audience participant: François, the economist searching for authentic pre-Columbian food; Wanda Desert Flower, a New-Ager wanting to train as a medicine woman; Bert, who wants to give up smoking; and Tippy O'Toole, a Body Shop consultant. All of these labels reference Western archetypes of a search for some perceived authentic or spiritual truths in non-Western cultures. Props are again a feature of the performance, echoing previous works. Each participant is provided with a spiritual guidebook from which to recite mantras (reciting foreign terms being a common strategy of touristic interactions) and with the necessary accessories to perform a meal ritual. During the re-enactment, Blanca acts the role of scribe and interpreter, a modern-day oracle, who reads from an oversized tome which is ceremoniously lowered from the ceiling. She describes the blissful environment of "pre-contact" life, focusing on native rituals surrounding food gathering, consumption, and the honoring of the deity Cuxtamali, their most revered goddess.

As she recounts information relating to the goddess (in particular her insatiable sexual appetite requiring the attentions of three lovers, "water, wind and fire") and her benevolent provision of food for the people, the Travel Tasters recite incantations to the goddess. At one stage they merrily demand "Self sacrifice!" on Blanca's insistence, calling for Cuxtamali to perform a ritual bloodletting act. Cuxtamali (alias Rosa) is incarnated, however, "as Chicana canteen worker" complete with white cafeteria smock, cigarette, and food trolley. She seems tired, even bored in her role as mother and provider. The text of the native myth contrasts parodically with the visual representation of Cuxtamali. This juxtapositioning of trivial objects and authentic ritual highlights the facile and commodified nature of similar touristic endeavors and the fact that some rituals have been exhausted of any real value through their excessive use and abuse within tourist contexts. Although each participant is encouraged to blow "sanctified melodies with horns of giant shells" in order to "commemorate the rise and fall of the great goddess's love affairs with wind, water and fire," the Travel Tasters in reality blow party whistles, highlighting humorous ways in which "authentic" rituals are made accessible and available for touristic consumption.

The performance reaches its crescendo as Cuxtamali goes into a trance and spins around out of control, brandishing a sacred knife, as the participants smile nervously. Once they are led back to their seats, Blanca tells Cuxtamali off and threatens, "I can find somebody else to do this with, you know." By blending impressive mythic rhetoric with the banal, the disappointing, and the everyday, the performers uncover and play with emic and etic perspectives of cultural encounters, performance, and display. While the girls are fighting it out, our host, Triple E, re-emerges to ask the audience, "Isn't it simply marvelous to move in and out of a distant time and place at the flick of a switch?" This lack of overt didactic content may be disconcerting for viewers expecting a cathartic or transformative experience. What Fusco serves up is an array of stereotypes enacting different experiences of Otherness, which she invites her viewer to consume. By presenting open-ended narratives the artists invite a range of responses, though they cannot control the ways in which they are read nor can they mediate the gazing dynamics generated.

A criticism leveled at the performance emerges as one of its greatest strengths—that *STUFF* is too entertaining, too much fun, that the audience doesn't leave feeling sufficiently guilt-ridden, and that its political content is not obvious enough. This dynamic, however, can be a very effective means of presenting an audience with its own deep-seated desires and fantasies by recreating them without overt or obvious critique. Both Fusco and Bustamante have employed this strategy in previous performances. In Bustamante's *Indig/urrito* (1992) she presented herself complete with G-string and strap-on burrito dildo, offering male "penitents" absolution from colonial guilt through partaking—on bended knee—of the burrito. *Two Undiscovered Amerindians Visit . . .* also parodies cultural-exposition displays of Othered cultures. The dynamics of these performances rely on audiences' response in order for individuals to draw parallels, based on their own experiences, with aspects of the performance. They also depend on humor and laughter as a strategy to carry the audience through potentially difficult and disturbing issues. Bakhtin describes laughter as crucial to the destabilizing of audience preconceptions:

> It is precisely laughter that destroys the epic, and in general destroys any hierarchical (distancing and valorized) distance. As a distanced image a subject cannot be comical; to be made comical, it must be brought close. . . . As it draws an object to itself and makes it familiar, laughter delivers the object into the fearless hands of investigative experiment—both scientific and artistic—and into the hands of free experimental fantasy.[18]

In a reflexive moment, Fusco reads a postcard addressed "to the audience": "Dear Audience, I think it's time to explain why we are so interested in Latin women and food." She states specifically the precepts on which the performance is based: consumption, "our" bodies, "our" myths, and food. Using metaphors of cannibalism and consumption, she suggests that the act of cultural encounter is mediated by both the eater and the consumed: "So when you come charging in our direction, running from whatever it is you're running from—you may not think that we who serve you could be eating as well."

Fusco's performances work on a number of levels. Characteristically they are not overtly political but rely heavily on the power of the stereotypical signifiers presented to trigger reactions. Fusco actively and knowingly mimics sexist and racist dress and behavior, in order to create a certain set of circumstances that may arouse racist and fetishistic memories and reactions in her audiences. However, in these works the gaze is returned and the process and experience of cultural consumption on the part of the viewer become problematized and disturbing upon reflection.

Foucault suggests that historical discourse is composed of sedimentary strata rather than a continuous chronology of events creating a singular "history proper." He suggests that total or linear history is disrupted when discontinuous elements break its chronology into "an ever-increasing number of strata."[19] Artists and writers exploring the entangled relationships of colonial and colonized fields of knowledge often point to the presence of a layering of perspectives which construct master narratives. The acknowledgement that histories are not linear and that historical texts are not fixed or closed allows for the presence of alternative perspectives within the discourse's overall structure.[20] Increasingly, feminism, postcolonialism, and poststructuralism have sought to highlight the complexity of colonizing narratives by positioning alternative voices, perspectives, and points of departure within and around them. As this process becomes more and more elastic, sites of counter-practice emerge within the narrative's infrastructure. Within these liminal spaces, representations of Othered cultures are reinvented and re-enacted, accentuating the complexity of cross-cultural encounter. Coco Fusco's performances embody the potential for stratified readings. This act of stratified reading becomes both arbitrary and prescribed within her performance contexts, creating an ambivalent and dialogic space in which various meanings can be encountered in the act of gazing at and consuming the Other's body.

[7]

PERFORMING BODIES, PERFORMING CULTURE:
AN INTERVIEW WITH COCO FUSCO AND
NAO BUSTAMANTE **ROSEMARY**
WEATHERSTON

Nao Bustamante is a performance artist pioneer who has been based in San Francisco's Mission District for over a decade. Notorious for her edgy improvisational pieces in which both she and her audiences are on display, she describes her artistic method as one of disarming audience members "with a sense of vulnerability and sensuality, only to confront them with a startling wake-up call." Using her own body "as a source of image, narrative, and emotion," Bustamante generates performances that "communicate on the level of subconscious language, taking the spectator on a bizarre journey, cracking stereotypes by embodying them."[1] Among her numerous solo works—*The Soul Sentence of MisDemeanor* (1990), *Ice Queen on a Soapbox* (1991), *The Frigid Bride* (1991), *Rosa Does Joan* (1992), *Playball!* (1993), *The Patriarchy Blues* (1993), *La Musica Del Corazón* (1993), *Dangerous Curves* (1995), and *A Tribute to Those Who Have Eaten Food Before Us* (1998)—perhaps her best known pieces are *Indig/urrito* (1992), in which she offered absolution from the sin of colonial oppression to any white male audience member willing to take a bite of her strap-on vegetarian burrito/dildo; and *America, the Beautiful* (1995, 1998), in which she used packing tape to transform herself into an hour-glass-shaped sex kitten, who unsteadily attempted to balance American patriotic and feminine ideals while traversing a ladder in four-inch heels.

In addition to her work as a solo performer, Bustamante has collaborated with artists from a wide range of disciplines, such as the experimental dance group Osseus Labyrint in *Umphallos Epos* (1994), which toured in Taiwan and Hong Kong; on-line artist David Baal in *In the Ring with Rosa;* and Miguel Calderón in the video project *The Chain South* (1994–95). She has also been a guest curator at a number of prestigious art institutions, had her writings published in *Revista Paralax Journal* (1993) and *On Our Backs* (1995), and begun producing visual art exhibitions, including the site-specific installation *Postcolonial Día de la Raza* (1997) and the mixed-media group show *When Borders Migrate* (1998).

Coco Fusco is a New York–based interdisciplinary artist and writer whose work, like Bustamante's, has met with international success. Taking what she calls an "obsession with culture" and her belief in cultural representation as a key site of political struggle, Fusco creates "media-based art, performance, and other experimental forms that dramatize, in their production and reception, the process of cultures meeting, clashing, and mixing."[2] Between 1989 and 1995 many of her projects were created in collaboration with Mexican artist and writer Guillermo Gómez-Peña and interrogated historic, economic, and cultural relations between North and South Americas. Among their joint works were *Norte:Sur* (1990), *La Chavela Realty Company* (1991), *1992: The Year of the White Bear* (1992), and *Mexarcane International* (1994). *Two Undiscovered Amerindians Visit . . .* , the performance component of *1992: The Year of the White Bear,* in which Fusco and Gómez-Peña toured as a caged indigenous couple from the undiscovered (imaginary) island of Guatinaui in the Gulf of Mexico, was selected for the 1992 Sydney Biennial and the 1993 Whitney Biennial. The award-winning video documentary of their experiences performing as imaginary Amerindians, *The Couple in the Cage: A Guatinaui Odyssey,* was directed and produced by Fusco with Paula Heredia in 1994. Fusco's most recent solo works include *Better Yet When Dead* (1996–97) a performance installation examining the fetishization of Latin American women artists after their deaths, and *Rights of Passage* (1997), a site-specific performance installation in Johannesburg, South Africa, about race, space, and power in the postapartheid era.

As successful a facilitator and writer as she is an artist, Fusco has curated a number of international exhibitions on subjects ranging from black American short films and videos to Latin American performance art. Her articles have appeared in such publications as the *Village Voice*, the *Los Angeles Times*, the *Washington Post*, the *Nation*, *Art in America*, *Frieze*, *Nka: The Journal of African Art*, *Afterimage*, *Screen and Third Text* (Britain), and *La Jornada and Poliester* (Mexico), as well as in several anthologies. Her collection of essays on art, media, and cultural politics titled *English Is Broken Here: Notes on Cultural Fusion in the Americas* (New Press, 1995) won the 1995 Critics' Choice Award from the American Educational Studies Association.

In this interview, conducted on the campus of UC San Diego in June 1998, Nao, Coco, and I use their collaborative work, *STUFF*, as a springboard from which to discuss some of the larger issues of community, consumption, performance, and resistance that surround it. During the course of our conversation we cover subjects ranging from their research into the sexual and indigenous tourism industries to their personal struggles as Latina artists with the sexist and nationalistic views of both Latin and Anglo communities, to their rejection of the view of "art as social work" which dominates today's cultural funding agendas. Refusing a narrow definition of serious cultural critique, we look at the value of humor, irony, and confrontation in challenging oppressive stereotypes, and attempt to dismantle the assumptions of authenticity and representation that result in the limitation of women performers of color to the roles of cultural informants and art therapists. The result is a no-holds-barred look at the relations among gender, commerce, race, and art, and a richer understanding of the potential for performance to both reveal and subvert oppressive body politics and their material.

RW: The last time I saw *STUFF* was in December of 1996 at Highway's performance space in Santa Monica, California; today you just completed a studio taping of the show in front of a live audience at UC San Diego— how did you two originally come to collaborate on *STUFF*, and how has the piece evolved over the last year and a half?

CF: Well, the first time I heard about Nao's work was several years ago, while she was performing *Indig/urrito* [1992], a piece in which she strapped a burrito to herself like a dildo and invited white guys on stage to take bites and thereby absolve themselves of five hundred years of colonization. I really liked the irreverence of the piece, and I really liked the fact that she was brave enough to be iconoclastic and avoid the protectionism and excessive sentimentality of a lot of Latino performance. At the time, I was writing an article about postcolonial performance and I called and asked her to send me a picture of the performance to illustrate it. Then I saw her perform *America, the Beautiful* [1995] in Los Angeles and really liked the piece, so I asked her if she wanted to work on something together.

RW: Because you are both such powerful artists in your own right, I would have thought news of your collaboration would have been met with a lot of professional interest, but, Coco, you mentioned to me that when you two embarked on this project, you were just beginning to raise your head professionally after terminating your collaboration with Guillermo Gó-mez-Peña and, as a result, found yourself to be considered far less fund-able. Why do you think that was so?

CF: It was a real lesson to me to experience how people who consider themselves fairly enlightened nonetheless perceive male-female collabo-ration in a sexist manner, according the male the primary role as creator. There are many reasons for this, and some are even more acutely evident in a Latino or a multicultural context. Straight men of color benefit from patriarchal privilege *and* from a very powerful alliance with white women who use their support for these men as a form of symbolic revenge against white men *and* as a way of masking their fear of women of color. Within Latino cultural contexts, where very often institutions are dominated by social conservatives and cultural nationalists, there is little support for the development of an autonomous feminist discourse. To be "good girls" we're supposed to help the "community," "*la familia*"; and our men, who are supposedly more threatened than we are.

RW: So, some people saw you as having "helped" Gómez-Peña, rather than as having been an equal contributor to the partnership?

CF: When I think about how things actually functioned in our collabora-tion, that assessment is fairly absurd. But this is the reality women perform-ers live with. Compare today's market value of women performance artists from the seventies, versus male performance artists from the seventies. In the seventies they were probably getting the same amount of attention; now the men are millionaires and women are barely scraping by. I think that that is just a reflection of gender dynamics in the art world. Male-male collaborations are not dealt with in the same way. It isn't assumed when two men are collaborating that one of them is the real artist and that the other one isn't. But I can't force people not to look at things that way. The situations in which Nao and I working together have done best is either in entirely new relationships with presenters that we've formed on our own, or with gay presenters or strongly female-identified presenters.

RW: Besides being a new collaboration, *STUFF* is a formal departure for both of you, isn't it? It seems much more scripted and theater-oriented than a lot of your previous works.

CF: Well, we knew we wanted to develop a piece that could be presented in a proscenium context, and we knew that that was going to be kind of dangerous because neither of us comes out of "theater" theater background. And whenever you move your work into a proscenium context you end up being dealt with by theater critics who just yell at you because it's not "theater" enough. But the possibilities of presenting performance work in nontheatrical contexts were shrinking, and I knew I, personally, was either going to have to make a transition for the time being into this space, or get out of performance altogether because, basically, I wouldn't be able to afford to do it. There were a lot of goals with *STUFF* that were not necessarily format, that had to do with us saying, "OK, let's take the limitations of this particular kind of production and try to make them work for us. Let's do something that doesn't have a lot of props and is fairly easy to do as text so we can travel, so we don't have to carry a stage manager along with us, etc., etc."

RW: And how did you come to focus on stereotypes about Latin women, food, and sexuality?

NB: In the beginning we started with really basic, stripped-away ideas. We knew we wanted to work together, we knew we had the energy to put together a project, and we were both in the place of wanting to begin anew. So we asked, "What do we have in common?" "Well," we said, "we're both women, we're both Latina, we both have these trips around being mama-type characters which have to do with food and sensuality." Then we started comparing our shared experiences of growing up in, living in, and moving through the world as Latina women. At a certain point that conversation started intersecting with Coco's investigations of prostitution in Cuba.

CF: I was also looking for dynamics that articulated power relationships between cultures. I had recently come from doing a piece in a shopping mall with Guillermo called *Mexarcane International* [1994], in which we posed as representatives from a corporation that distributed and marketed exotic talent for special events. During the performance, we went around giving people in the mall little "samples" of what kind of exotic activity they might enjoy being a part of, and I was really interested in finding other dynamics that were already in the larger culture that I could drag onto stage and represent in an exaggerated manner in order to show

how the cultures of North and South Americas are constantly bouncing off of and influencing one another. Food and sex seemed to be two other arenas in which these sort of interactions happened. And, actually, they seemed to represent the primary relationships that North Americans have with Latin cultures. With food, those relationships range from the majority of Mexican immigrants coming to the U.S. to be part of the food industry—either in agricultural labor or working in restaurants—to the fact that everybody in the Southwest eats Mexican food.

NB: I remember Coco saying that a lot of times people's first encounter, their *primary* encounter with a culture is through that culture's food. That point immediately struck me as something simple, but really true. When I was growing up, the only contact with Chinese people I had was going with my family to eat at a Chinese restaurant, or going to a family-owned Chinese supermarket. I clearly remember thinking: this is Chinese food, these are Chinese people, and this is Chinese culture. Now, as an adult, and after having performed in Taiwan and Hong Kong and having been peripherally exposed to Chinese culture, I know how removed those childhood experiences were. But the fact remains that people do often connect culturally with other people through their food, and that's something to both be celebrated and looked at.

RW: And how did you move from looking at cultural connections made by means of food to those made by means of Latin women's bodies?

CF: We wanted to look at the commodification of Latina sexuality because, since the 1920s really, Americans have gone to the Caribbean and to Mexico in search of an experience that supposedly puts them in touch with sexuality that they don't have access to in their own culture.

RW: I thought one of the real strengths of *STUFF* was your undermining of any benign notion of those types of searches, and of the idea of "cultural consumerism" in general. I especially appreciated the way you embodied the points of view of women and children whose economic survival depends on their daily contact with foreigners, and their ability to manipulate the stereotypes those foreigners projected upon them. Could you talk a little bit about your experience researching culture tourism in Chiapas, Mexico, and sex tourism in Cuba?

NB: We were both aware of the political situation in Chiapas, but we really went there on a residency to write. While we were in Chiapas, however, the environment started making its way into the script. We realized that a whole other type of tourism was happening there, a kind of spiritual/ intellectual tourism.

RW: Which you refer to as "indigenous culture" tourism?

NB: Right, in the same way that Europeans and North Americans are going to the Caribbean to have sexual experiences, people are going to Chiapas to have a spiritual experience. We would sit in outdoor cafés and see European tourists follow a stoned Mexican out to the *zócolo,* the square, and play Bob Marley tunes on a guitar and think that they were becoming somehow more enlightened.

CF: And the "culture tours" in Chiapas are so specialized. You can go on tours to see shamans, tours to see revolutionaries, tours to see Indians who speak a particular language and who are hyper-traditionalists, tours to see barrios where Fundamentalist evangelicals dominate, all of which, in one way or another, romanticize abject poverty and push the idea that the "Indian" is a conduit of the spiritual. The people who are taking these tours buy into the notion that by getting close to "authentic" Indians, they will somehow purify themselves.

NB: There is a rush to take advantage of the last purity in that area of the world. People realize that they are destroying it, but they also think they are experiencing some sort of authenticity. At the same time, when Coco and I made friends with the kids who were vendors and selling little bracelets that they made, they would tell us the stories like the one told by [a] little girl in *STUFF* about the German who bought her her outfit so that she would look more "authentic" when she sold things. She would only wear that dress when she was trying to sell to the tourists. The whole idea of bumping up against a culture, and of how a culture represents itself, and who has the power isn't as simple as "authentic" versus "unauthentic." *STUFF*'s script takes a lot of complicated turns because we are not trying to say, "Because the tourists are coming to look at this person, they are somehow being taken advantage of." We're more saying, "Look at the relationship: this is one side of the story and here is the other side of the story and how do they interact?" If you really look at it, the idea of consuming culture becomes pretty complicated.

CF: Chiapas is the state in Mexico that has the largest indigenous population, and even though the majority of Mexico's people have indigenous backgrounds, very few of the people in Mexico actually speak native languages as their primary language or live according to what is identified as

111

indigenous traditions. That's why Chiapas is the place where tourists go to see the "real thing," the "real Indian culture," not the ones that are totally . . .

RW: "Ruined"?

CF: Right, "ruined," so to speak, by European and American influences.

RW: A lot of tourists, and even a lot of people in the United States who want to purchase cultural goods or view ethnic or multicultural events, do seem to have this bizarre expectation that the cultures with which they are interacting maintain a certain level of "purity." It's like the idea of cultural reciprocity or hybridity seems somehow unauthentic, even distasteful. In *STUFF*, though, you very intentionally show that exchange and contact never move in just one direction, that so-called third-world or indigenous populations are actually very savvy about the types of stereotypes tourists bring with them.

CF: But also, Mexico—like many other Latin countries—is *extremely* adept at inventing fictions of identity for foreigners to consume. It is a *business* that the government is involved with and that Mexicans themselves are involved with *constantly,* and any sophisticated anthropologist would recognize that. Most Mexicans who are involved in negotiating with tourists understand at an intuitive level that they *must* produce a fiction in order to survive. And I really think that fact is a particularly difficult thing for American leftists and multiculturalists to swallow, because everybody wants to believe that they will find the "real thing" that nobody else found. As far as I am concerned, the "real thing" doesn't exist; all that exists are fictions of the real and audiences who want them.

RW: Do you think that with the increase in international consumerism and the rise of the global market there are now *global* body fictions and stories? Does the world now occur as a single, giant banquet in which people are expecting to partake?

NB: It definitely breaks down into relationships of the consumer and the producer, whether the producer is weaving the fabric or working in the factory or picking the fruit—the idea of cultures and people being presented as commodities is still a really basic model. And it's a model that is especially rampant on the Internet. You can find these "world marketplace" sites that have every kind of handcrafted item from all over the world. Just like Triple E says in our script, you can have delicacies without dysentery and ritual without revolution and poverty. You can just point and click your mouse and have these handcraft goods hand-delivered to your postbox.

CF: As a matter of fact, most people don't want to go and have to deal with the dirt; the simulation is much more attractive. Let's go back to our research for a minute, though, because we didn't really deal with the Cuban sexual tourism side of this. I have been going back and forth to Cuba for fourteen years and I witnessed the return of massive-scale prostitution beginning in 1989 to 1994, when it really hit full force.

RW: What caused the explosion?

CF: A number of factors. One was the fall of the Berlin wall and the end of Soviet subsidy to the island, which sent the economy into a total shambles. By 1993, Cuba entered something called the "Special Period," with the most horrifically drastic reduction in supplies. People were getting scurvy, they were getting optic neuritis for lack of vitamin B in their diet, basically every type of bodily dysfunction one can get from not having enough to eat and from drinking contaminated water. At the same time, dollar possession was legalized, which made it easier for prostitution to be more out in the open and to grow. And, from the eighties onward, tourism became a more and more significant part of the hard-currency economy, supplanting sugar and everything else. So the demand for women to service the tourists grew until it became a kind of self-fulfilling prophecy. Cuba already had a history of being an international brothel and that stereotype was revived in order to draw tourists to the island. So tourists were going there thinking they were going to find what existed in the fifties.

RW: Are the types of cultural and sexual body fictions that you address in *STUFF* those that have had the strongest impact on you personally?

CF: I can only speak for myself, but yes, insofar as that they are the primary stereotypes with which Latin women are associated. I don't think that there's absolutely no reality that corresponds to the stereotypes, but I think that [there] are ways in which the stereotypes can be much too rigid. I also think that, whether I like it or not, there are certain things that my body signifies to people that are associated with those stereotypes, and so my experience has been marked by their negative impact. But I also think that global culture is all about the recycling of these kinds of stereotypes. There is nothing new in global culture; it's just the facility with which we, as consumers, have access that is new; not the product, the product is the same. And, whether you are a consumer getting access by logging on through your Internet shopping or a tourist taking a trip to Acapulco, you are still in search of these very old types. I know that there are some relationships that end up becoming more profound than that, but the stereotypical dominates the dynamic.

RW: How strongly do you think increased access has exacerbated that dynamic?

CF: Well, think about it, tourism is the second largest source of global employment. Only five percent of the world population have enough money to travel for leisure, but the international tourist industry is the second or third largest employer in the world. In the Caribbean and in Mexico it is among the top sources of hard currency and employment. And the reality is that the majority of tourism is about spirituality, food, and sex. As developed-world societies become more and more associated with virtual disembodiment and electronic culture, it's the cultures of the South that are associated more and more with physicality and sexuality. To a certain extent there are cultural stereotypes at work in the choice that people make to find sexual partners in Latin America, but I also think it is an economic relationship that gets racialized. It's about men looking for a country where they can take advantage of women who have much less power than them and have no legal recourse. It's also about people wanting to be able to live in a level of splendor and comfort during their holiday times that being in an impoverished country provides, you know? Because you can feel like a king with twenty-five dollars.

NB: I've had that experience.

CF: I have too. But it's important to realize that while these are economic relationships that are racialized as a result [of] the geographic displacement, at the same time these older, firmly entrenched stereotypes about hypersexual Latinas get activated in order to catalyze that fundamentally economic relationship. And it's usually stereotypes about the spitfire, sexpot Latina or the submissive Asian, because these are the two main groups of women who are involved in the international sex trade.

RW: Do you think that the relationship between the consumer and the consumable is an inherently gendered relationship? Are all countries and people put in that position of a commodity—even those who, as you suggest, take advantage of those fictions for survival—are inherently feminized?

NB: Well, in this day and age when you are talking about gender you're not necessarily even talking about the sexes. But if you wanted to say, "Are the relationships gendered?" Yeah, I would say they are gendered.

RW: Are the "commodities" inherently feminized?

NB: It depends how you are modeling it, you know? If you are modeling it on a feminist paradigm or if you are modeling it on qualities that are considered feminine, or qualities that are considered masculine . . .

CF: I don't think you can make those kinds of generalizations. I have a theory about this exact type of overgeneralization that has to do specifically with Latino culture.

NB: Lay it on them, sister.

CF: Because Latin masculinity is very flamboyant and very theatrical . . .

NB: It's like a rooster.

CF: Because it's the opposite of the expression of Anglo masculinity, it is very often confused with being feminine. Anglo masculinity is all about the gray suit, neutrality, and rationality; but what is the stereotype of the macho? It's somebody who is out of control, who wears his masculinity on his sleeve, who's always overdoing it, always overstating himself, and always being extremely theatrical. Plus, Latin Catholicism theatricalizes male masochism. Male masochism *is* the primary ritual of Catholicism: the Passion is Jesus Christ carrying the cross, Jesus Christ being beaten; it's *San Sebastián* who is having arrows being flung into him. It's all these *men* who are allowing all these things to be done to their bodies which, in a non-Latin context, may be looked upon as feminine. But it is *not* feminine and it is not the domain of female expression in Latin culture. And, in that sense, I think that Americans completely misunderstand how men have the advantage in the domain of the theatrical. Because the tropes that we would, in an American context, call "feminine" are, in a Latin context, the macho's terrain. In Latin culture it is the macho's terrain to be public, to flail, to flagellate yourself to draw attention to your body, to keep the focus on you the way that Greta Garbo keeps the focus on her. That's what men get to do. And when women do it, they are marginalized or represented as extremely threatening to the culture, or out of their minds.

RW: You just brought up a really, really good point. Another thing many American "leftists and multiculturalists" tend to forget, myself obviously included, is that the cultural stereotypes that we try to critique—multi or not—are often nation-specific. You have another piece, don't you, *Better Yet When Dead* [1996–97], that deals specifically with the threat that the visible Latina artist holds for Latin cultures?

CF: Yes, I did that piece three times. I think that the public presence of Latin women occurs mostly after their death and through the fetishization of the dead body as an object. I mean, who are the women, the Latin women, that are known and have iconic status? The ones who die and then have their cadavers fetishized: Evita Peron, Aria Mendieta, Sor Juana Ines de la Cruz, Frida Kahlo, Selena. They perform death as female sacrifice and cults crop up to their memory.

RW: I find it really interesting to hear you describe visibility and physicality as the province of the male in Latin culture, or those characteristics are culturally threatening when engaged in by Latin women, because both of you seem to me to be very physical performers, and to use transformations of your own bodies as the driving engine of your works. How would each of you characterize your own relationship to your body, both within a performance context and within some of these cultural contexts that you were just describing?

CF: Well, I would just step back for a moment and point out that most of the support that we get is not from Latinos. We actually have much more support from the gay community and from people who are interested in performance. But, then again, within a Latino culturalist/nationalist context, Latinas have never done well as performers. The most prominent Latina performers, women like Marga Gomez or Carmelita Tropicana, made their careers through the women's theater circuit, and through the gay and lesbian theater circuit. Most Latino/a performance artists in general make it through the gay circuit more than they do through the Latino circuit, with the exception of groups, like Culture Clash, who are really closer to theater. And, if you notice, Culture Clash never touches anything that is a dangerous subject for Latinos. I am not saying they aren't interesting performers. But they don't deal with homophobia, they don't deal with feminist issues, they don't even have women in the group. They take a very safe approach in dealing with what Latino culture is. And that's what I mean about Latina women being kept on the edge and at the fringe: unless we want to play the suffering mother role, where we are obviously desexualized by being menopausal, we are not even considered. And therefore, we have a much more problematic status to being an informant, to being able to speak for the culture in a kind of nationalistic sense.

RW: Nao, have you come up against the same type of problems in your career?

NB: I would say that most of my support also comes from artistic cultures, rather than from the Latino culture, although I have had opportunities presented to me though Latino arts centers like the Mission Cultural Center or *Galleria de la Raza*. Right now, a Chicago Mexican museum is interested in bringing my work there. I think it's a good sign when Latino cultural communities are bringing me in, but I don't necessarily want to be a Latino representative.

RW: Why not? Do you feel as an individual that you aren't "representative," or do you reject the entire notion of being a cultural informant or cultural representative?

NB: Well, I do feel representative of a certain sector of the population of California-born Mexicans who have experienced a schism with tradition and who have one foot in Mexican traditional culture and one foot in California and global pop culture. So I do have a voice for a certain sector, so I do think it's a good sign when the Latin community brings me in. But I haven't depended on the Latin community. Primarily, I've just been really focused on the work, and taking opportunities when they come to me.

RW: No matter where they come from.

NB: No matter where they come from. My audience is usually pretty mixed. I have support from the queer community, from women's communities, from the Latin community, the visual arts communities also support my work, so I have a pretty big crossover in terms of who my audience is, who I am speaking to, or who will come and actually check out the work. And the issues have covered artistic issues as well as political issues and personal issues. Thinking specifically in terms of visibility and physicality, some of my work has dealt intensely with women's body issues.

RW: Such as?

NB: The last solo piece I was touring, *America, the Beautiful* [1995, 1998], dealt mostly with the idea of transforming the body on stage and the relationship between the performer and the audience: forcing people to look at the body, forcing their love. I mean, I was naked and binding my body with tape, actually sculpting the fat on my body into tiers. And that's really hard for a lot of people to see; even just to show fat on stage is really a big no-no right now.

RW: I read a great line of yours: "If you don't like this," or "if you're not comfortable with this, leave your body."

NB: That was from *Indig/urrito* [1992], where I was saying to the audience, "If you're not comfortable, just leave your body." That was also a reference to work I was doing at the time with incest survivors. A lot of women who have been abused have had the experience of leaving their bodies. Coco was talking before about my irreverent approach to the work, and that line is a really prime example of how I interact with audiences, of my desire to get people to take more responsibility in general for what they're feeling and what they are experiencing, of just telling people, "If you're not into it, leave your body." Some people have left the room when I'm performing and that's okay, too. I like a lot of different kinds of audience interaction, I like when people get rowdy and heckle me. I like performing in clubs. There are all kinds of situations under which I'm available to work. Getting back to the question of how we see our bodies: it's a struggle. I think it's a very complicated issue because we have our own self-imposed and socially imposed impressions about our bodies as women, and how we move in the world, and how people look at our bodies. At the same time though, we're *bodies,* we're human beings, we're on stage, we're there to be seen. We want to present ourselves with strength and clarity and—and vulnerability when the character calls for it. So, I don't know, Coco, do you want to add more to that?

CF: I'm glad you see me as a very physical performer, because I usually have to face the perception that I am much too intellectual. But the reason that I am interested in performance is because I think it's an artistic medium in which I can explore the problem of the body on a metaphorical level. And I feel directly implicated by that process, because, even though I am not dissatisfied with my body as a person, I feel like my body has caused me to experience a lot of unpleasant things in my life.

RW: In what ways?

CF: Well, I am the product of an interracial couple. I'm much lighter-skinned than my mother's family, but I was identified by some members of my father's family as belonging to the "black" tribe. And those contrasts produced a lot of tension. My adolescent and college memories are of generating a lot of confusion with my presence. We're talking about the sixties, seventies, here; nobody understood, or knew the term "bi-racial," there wasn't really a category in the Northeast for people who were "light-skinned but of African descent," so people just didn't know what to *do* with me. I was constantly asked, "What *are* you?"

RW: "What are you *really*?"

CF: "What *are* you?" Right? Later it became not just a question related to my body, but also a question of how could I be so intellectual, and so well educated, and trained, and tri-lingual and dance the rhumba? Then it became a question of "Well, with the way you look, and your background and everything, maybe you are not really American." And then it became a matter of my ideology: How could I travel to Cuba and not be fanatically anti-Castro? I never have been, I'm still not, even though I am somewhat critical of the revolution. Yet, when I would go to Cuba, even though I am American-born, I was identified by my body-type as a Cuban, and mistaken for a Cuban many times, and even mistaken for a prostitute there many times. So I've been through all these experiences where my body is the big issue, where there's a disjuncture between the voice that comes out of me and the body that's there. That's what I've been working on in a lot of performances, and not just so I can narrate my life experiences, but because I think that that disjuncture is a product of larger social situations and experienced by a lot of people.

RW: One of the questions this anthology is asking is how do you start to take apart the oppressive power dynamics and body fictions that result in those type of "disjunctures"; or, at least, how can you aggressively challenge them? Why is it that both of you chose performance as the arena in which to engage these issues? What is it about performance that so attracts you, and, perhaps a more difficult question, do you think that performance can have material impacts on the audience, or the communities, or the fictions with which it engages?

NB: I know that there are impacts and real changes because people tell me and because of my own personal experiences from viewing performances. I came to performance as an artist through seeing other performers. I felt things physically change in my body when I would watch performance. I would feel my understandings open up for different issues, I would feel actual, almost neurological pathways being expanded. And I know that people are having mental or physical encounters when they see our performances because people come and tell us so after they see us perform. They tell us that they appreciated the treatment of the subject, or, with *STUFF*, that they enjoyed making fun of the Travel Taster's rhumba lesson, or they felt really sad for a particular character. So I think that performance still affects people and I think it affects them in a way that other mediums, such as cinema, can't. It really seems to be based on the live interaction of performance, particularly the way that we work with the audience, because we bring the audience onto the stage, which causes other audience members to have a deeper empathy for the people on stage and for themselves as audience members. There is even a little bit of fear involved.

RW: The "Don't pick me!" fear.

NB: (Laughter) Yeah, "Don't pick me!" People can get a little afraid, so there's sort of a tension that happens in the audience, and I think that they feel more included, more a part of the picture within the context of the performance. They don't just feel like we're talking and they're listening: *they're* the Travel Tasters, they're there to experience; we're doing it for them. In today's performance, for instance, I really had fun doing the section where I'm asking people to visualize their favorite vegetable to use as a dildo. When we were writing *STUFF*, Coco had to drag that story out of me because I really do work as a sales associate, mail-order sex educator in a woman-owned sex store, and I usually don't make direct crossovers between my personal information and my performance work. But Coco kept saying, "You *have* to use that, you have to use that story." And today, it was really interesting, because at this point in the show, the lights are turned up on the audience and all of the sudden I am questioning *their* sexuality, and asking them very specific questions.

RW: "Would you prefer the long cucumber . . .

NB: . . . or short, or the hooked-nose squash?" People really went for the g-spot prostate stimulation squash today (laughter). But you know, although we do the whole vegetable-visualization as a joke, it really works because it gives people an opportunity to participate at a very personal level. In some ways it really works because people feel like little kids; they think that if they can hide by closing their eyes and if no one else is going to see what they choose, then they can really participate. That's really the main thing that keeps me going—that people have experiences and that they tell me about them. The other rewards are less compelling.

CF: I started out in theater in high school. Actually, before that. When I was younger I use to create plays with my brothers and my neighbors, I was really into the idea of dramatizing everything. Every time we would go on a trip as a family, my brothers and I would come back and make a play about what we just saw, so the bullfight in Spain became a play, the Christmas procession became a play. In high school I was still really interested in drama, but when I got to college, to Brown, I was a semiotics major and became immersed in film. All of the cultural theory and critical theory I was reading at the time was telling me the real way to change people's consciousness was through media. Media was, is, the dominant language of popular culture and so you have to use media to change the way that people see themselves and the way that they see the world. I got very wrapped up in that for a while. But in the early stages of theorizing media spectatorship I don't think that there was really an understanding of just how *passive* it is and just how editing techniques can be elaborated in order to encourage more passivity. And like many, many people, I came to understand that the optimism of people like Walter Benjamin about the possibility of film has been attenuated by the realization that mass culture outstrips by far the possibilities of individual, independent filmmakers to make central statements using the media. It was growing dissatisfied with the critical power of film and media that took me back to performance. One of the things I liked specifically about performance art was the amount of artistic control you have over the material: you write it, you produce it, you direct it, it's *your* material. You're not there to have your head twisted by some wacky director.

RW: You *are* the wacky director.

CF: So I went back to performance, thinking that in a world that's media-saturated, direct encounters may actually have a value that I hadn't originally appreciated. One of the significant things that happened with performance during this time, during the eighties, was that it became a space for the articulation of alternative identity formations and alternative communities. Primarily because you don't have to sell ten thousand tickets to make your money back in performance. If you have two hundred people that's good. This was particularly true for the gay community and in the feminist community—in those communities performance art took on an incredibly important role. It was a place where people met to be together and to find one another as a community.

NB: It is a platform, even, to express ideas or create a dialogue.

CF: If you go back prior to that time, to the Cabaret Voltaire or to Judson Memorial Church, performance was a reaction against the *salons* controlling the arts and a move towards artists controlling art for themselves. Performance was the vehicle through which artists could begin to control art for themselves. They made performance for themselves, not for the bourgeoisie. It wasn't a bunch of dealers from Fifth Avenue going to see them, it was *other artists*. So I think performance carries with it that history of distanciation from the market and provides a space for engaging a smaller audience.

NB: Performance has always been distant from the market.

CF: Yeah. And those were the things that drew me back to it. Also, people lie through their teeth about who they really feel they are, what they really believe, and about their racism quotient and their sexuality. But there are certain things about the immediate, direct encounter of performance that prevent you from lying as effectively. And you can't fool yourself as much because if you really are surprised, it will show; if you really are shocked, it will show; if you really get caught off guard, it will show. And every time we perform this piece, somebody's shocked, somebody's caught off guard, somebody gets embarrassed, and it all shows.

RW: In general, audience reaction to *STUFF* has been really positive, and I know you've been selling out your venues. At the same time, however, some critics, from both Latino and Anglo artistic communities, have accused you and Nao of not being avant-garde enough, or have suggested that your use of parody and comedy, and of popular cultural images, somehow "pollutes" your critical intent. Why do you think the response to *STUFF* has been mixed? Do you think the critics' response is indicative of a sexist or Eurocentric understanding of cultural critique?

CF: I think that there are a lot of different reasons why there have been reactions of that kind. I think, to be somewhat humble, that we started our tour a bit too early and that the show was really raw. But financial limitations and scheduling commitments from the commissioning body didn't leave us with much choice; we just had to go on. At the same time, however, I had early experiences when I was touring with Guillermo where we slapped things together and went on and didn't get the same negative response. The first time I did *New World Border* with him in 1992, we literally took the script on stage, sat down, and read it to the audience. We didn't have *anything:* we didn't have light changes, we didn't have any costume changes, there was no staging. Once upon a time it was acceptable to do that.

NB: You could develop work on stage.

CF: But that's no longer acceptable. Presenters want a polished piece from the get-go. But who's paying for it? Right? And who's giving you the time and space to do it? So in that sense I think that some of people's negative reactions at the beginning may have been negative reactions to a show that was still raw, that needed more work. Which we gave it. We added material that helped the rhythm of the show and that revealed more about ourselves, so that we are not just there at the beginning, that we come back in the middle. My encounter at the end with the cop is another way of coming back to the piece to remind the audience always that this is us and not-us. You know? We worked with a director, Ellen Sebastian-Chang, to make our staging a little bit tighter, we turned the song into a karaoke tune. There are ways in which I think the show became more coherent over time and it's generated a lot more positive responses from the audiences . . .

NB: And the press.

CF: And the press subsequent to that. In terms of people not being able to deal with parody, that is something I have encountered over and over again, with everything I have ever done. People and critics like that are always serious, and say, "Parody isn't serious." They're usually either hard-core lefties who just don't believe that anybody who suffers ever have a laugh, and to them I say, "I think you have spent too much time in a library and have never been to a war." And I have been to more than one. I've danced at parties with soldiers with rifles on their back. And I say to them that people who live in much more horrible conditions than any of us can imagine laugh, and make jokes, and make fun of their suffering—that's how they survive. I admire the character of a person who's able to find humor in the most horrible situations. Maybe people who can't understand that are too—I don't know, maybe they don't know how to have fun, or they don't know how to enjoy, or they don't see the radical potential of comedy to be able to show that side of life. I think that there's also going to be high modernists who are never going to go for any parodic script or strategy because it's not original, right? The standard modernist critique of parody is that it is parasitical, that it is derivative. I also think that there are people who are tired of this type of content. We produced this piece, in a way, too late.

RW: Too late for what?

CF: If we had done it five years ago we would have probably gotten a much more positive reaction, but by doing it after the backlash we put ourselves in a situation where a lot of people would say, "Let's not talk about sloppy, unpleasant aspects of intercultural dynamics because we don't want to be embarrassed by it," or "That's been done, this has already been talked about," or "Adrian Piper already danced for people in a museum." I respect Adrian Piper and like her work, but I don't feel like she covered *everything* with one performance. I'm not going to completely change myself into a cyber girl who only works with plastic or bacteria just because that's what's in fashion. Then there's the fact that we are dealing with the areas that implicate most people who consider themselves not to be racist, and to be really hip and together. But I could tell you stories about very high-minded intellectuals who have begged me for merengue lessons when nobody is looking, or had asked me what to do with the Puerto Rican hairdresser they picked up the night before and they want to get rid of. The bottom line is that all of us still, in some way, fall into these paradigms all the time. I mean, Nao and I have both been tourists. We've both been caught in a lot [of] situations that we examine in the piece, both on the side of the more powerful and the side of the less powerful, so why not explore it? There are also some people who are involved with the arts and multiculturalism who want art to act like a Band-Aid: they want us to produce work that solves the problems of the world, and I don't think that art does that very well. I think that what we can do is to offer people a space in which to reflect upon the problems of the world, but we can't solve the problems of the world by what we do.

NB: I think critics are very important in terms of the food chain of the art world, but they are also a small part of the audience. I think of critics as audience members, and we've had both positive and not-so-positive experiences of critics, and we've had both positive and not-so-positive experiences of audience members. Getting back to the audience experience and the comparison of performance and other mediums, like cinema. Last night we went and saw a movie, and my experience was almost like leaving my body. I move into the screen, and I enter into that world, and in its own way it's fantastic, right? But in performance I think audience members become *more* in themselves, become more a part of their *own* bodies, and maybe that's part of what we offer people. And maybe that's partly why live performance still exists, because people go there and they have an experience that reflects the fact that *they're* sitting in the chair, *they're* in their body, they can't really escape that. It's not a space for them to move into like a fantasy; it's a space for them to view from and be critical from. I don't know how else to put it except that when you view something like cinema, you move out of yourself and into the screen, and when you view performance you stay in your own body. It's a different kind of viewing.

RW: Since so much of your work involves the audience members being willing to reflect back on themselves and to be critical, to be implicated, do you think it is possible for a parody to fail if people don't "get it"? Or is a failed parody a misnomer? I'm thinking, for example, of the Highway's performance of *STUFF* when a male audience member really slapped Blanca for "misbehaving"; or, Coco, in your collaboration with Guillermo Gómez-Peña called *Two Undiscovered Amerindians Visit.* . . . A lot of people didn't seem to realize you two were engaged in performance art and thought you were a caged anthropological exhibit.

NB: Well, you are always going to have people at different levels of understanding, but that's part of it, part of it is the person who gets mad at the person next to them who's just laughed, and the person who's *sorry* they just laughed, and the other person who is just laughing because they think it's funny. People are going to see different layers, and some people are going to get some of the jokes and other people won't. It's kind of great, actually, the thing that happens in the audience, the way that audience members really feed off of each other, the person who thinks, "Hey, how come that person laughed? I don't get it." That happens a lot in *STUFF,* especially in the "Sex Tours" dialogue where we are translating between English and Spanish. We do translate most of the Spanish, but there's this really great moment of tension when some people have laughed, and other people don't know what's been said until we translate it into English, and then there's a delayed laugh, a delayed recognition that happens.

CF: I agree with Nao, you cannot control how people respond to your work. With regards to the cage piece, the general understanding of people who didn't see the piece was that *all* these people didn't get it. Well, a lot of people may not have gotten it for some period of time, but I think it's important to clarify that because I think that there's a way in which that's been mystified. Most people don't understand what the hell they're looking at when they look at artwork for a long time *anyway,* you know? Where would you have the opportunity to go into a museum of art and have Jasper Johns, or Robert Rauschenberg, or Frank Stella stand next to their paintings and tell you what it is, right? So it doesn't surprise me that some people were confused, particularly because we put the piece in a non-art context. I think that what happens with performances like the cage piece and *STUFF* is that we are dealing in a very ironic way with issues that most people who like multiculturalism think have to be dealt with in a very serious way.

NB: In a "delicate" way.

CF: In a delicate way. I've been told by people, "How could you possibly make fun of that poor guy you bring on stage during the sex tourist dialogue because he can't pronounce words properly?" Or "How could you laugh about prostitution?" No one, *no one* in Latin America would ever, ever say that to me! They would probably say this is tasteless, they would probably say this is not art, but they wouldn't say there is something wrong about laughing about human frailty, or that there is something wrong with being parodic about social problems.

NB: We've also had a real gamut of people who come on stage with us. We've had everything from the person who lays on the ground with me during the trance dance and goes crazy, to the person that Coco has to coach because he's about ready to faint.

CF: But it's also about a function of a type of cultural protectionism that still exists, particularly among minority intellectuals. There's this sense of "The mainstream culture fucks us over, so we have to take care of our icons. We have to take care of our cultural symbols, we have to take care of our culture, we can only show the good." That doesn't convince *anybody!* It doesn't begin to address just how complex the cultural dynamics that we're dealing with are! And it's *boring* for one as an artist to be limited to only telling happy stories. Happy stories are not interesting. I really cannot insist on that enough because it comes up every single time I perform or do a presentation. I did a videotape a few years ago, *Pochonovela* [1995], that makes fun of *telenovelas,* and I got responses like "Oh my god, you are making fun of our culture, we shouldn't make fun"—I say, "Why *not?*" you know? If we don't, who will? Isn't it better to understand your foibles? Isn't it better to understand your weaknesses than to pretend that everything is fantastic?

RW: It sounds like you are describing a set of rules about what is and isn't seen as allowable in multicultural theater performances. What [do] you think most American audiences are looking for when they go to see so-called ethnic/multicultural performances? Do they expect happy stories?

Do they expect to be given authentic accounts by cultural informants? Or do they view the work as some sort of transparent political activism, as—to paraphrase you, Coco—a predictable form of Otherness to view from a safe distance?[3]

NB: Actually the more critical comments we've received have been from people who don't feel like we've beaten them up enough. They don't feel like they've been hit over the head enough and want to be made to feel more guilty.

CF: That always comes from people who are either really rich, or who manage a lot of cultural funding, which tells me a lot about the comment. It's never from some Joe Shmoe in the audience, it's always from people who think that culture should guilt-trip people, and that showing audiences how much everyone suffers is going to change the world. We *all know* how much suffering there is in the world! I'm not sure people's lives will be transformed by experiencing one workshop with a visiting performer, which is the other thing that funders want. They want you to move into a town for two weeks, and change the life of someone who is about to die or who is an at-risk youth. If you say your work can do that, then you can get money thrown at you.

RW: Which is another version of someone telling you, "Give me a spiritual transformation."

CF: Of course!

RW: The difference is that you, the Latina performer, are now in the position of indigenous informant, or . . .

CF: . . . of social provider.

RW: Exactly.

CF: Or of social worker. All of this is about turning art into social work, and about being able to measure how much of an impact an individual artwork has on a particular public with some kind of wacky utilitarian ruler. It's a product of the bureaucratization of multiculturalism that took place in the eighties and nineties, and it hasn't really done very much good for anyone. It certainly hasn't produced a lot of great work.

NB: There is even sort of, well, I don't even know if I should say this, but to even say "multicultural" work—there's some sort of taintedness about the term. I feel like the term is very uncritical and unaesthetic.

RW: What terms do you prefer?

NB: I think what we do is more akin to experimental theater, but, in truth, it's pretty mixed up. There are definitely performance art aspects about it, definitely theatrical aspects, but we don't work in a traditional theatrical structure. *STUFF* is "multicultural" in the sense that it represents a lot of different cultures: we have a "German" character, a "French" character, but we also have "deadbeat" characters.

CF: To tell you the truth, everybody who's involved with any kind of administration of cultures knows how much "difference quotient" you need in a grant proposal, or in the calendar of a performing arts center, to get by. They know how much "difference" they have to do. And the type of institution you're talking about determines whether they're either going to book Anna Deavere Smith or whether they are going to bring somebody in from *Ballet Folklorico.*

RW: Have either of you been brought in by an institution to fulfill a difference quotient or been put in the position of cultural informant?

NB: If I ask the question "Am I a cultural informant?" no organization is going to tell me that I'm invited because of quotients. So I couldn't honestly tell you. But I do know that people who have a more layered and complex view of cultural identity and aesthetics are more interesting to work with.

CF: I know I'm often hired, contracted, invited to fulfill difference quotients. Nobody likes to admit that, but it's true. Things get really crazy around Black History Month and Women's History Month. There are really very few funding bodies that support multicultural performance-oriented work, and unfortunately this type of work is driven today by a very specific funding agenda: to save at-risk groups and revive a sense of community among social sectors that are considered to be on the fringe. I think that younger people are becoming less and less interested in the kind of social-work agenda that is connected with those funding sources. I see it among my students, they don't want to know *anything* about that kind of work whatsoever. So they go into another circuit. They might be in the gay circuit, they might be in the alternative scene, they might be Christian rockers, but they're not going to go for those social-work agendas.

RW: While I certainly wouldn't describe your work as having a social-work agenda, it does engage in social and political critique, and both of you have described the cultural sphere as a political space where political activism can take place. How does the cultural sphere show up as the political for you? Is it a *personally* effective space for you, or is the cultural an arena that many people can make politically effective?

NB: Well, there's a basic level of activism in the very nature of the work that we're doing. We are doing work that is important to us, that we believe in enough to continue forward on it even though we're not getting a lot of financial compensation. There is a certain amount of resistance to traditional culture in what we're doing, and then there's the different issues that we bring into the work. Fortunately or unfortunately, because of who we are, and because of the time that we're in, we can't really escape the political or the social comment. If I make a statement about culture or politics then I'm a Latina making these statements in my work. If I don't make these comments, I'm a Latina not commenting.

RW: Which is making a different type of statement.

NB: Right, making a different kind of statement by not commenting on these situations. I don't really look at it like a "Damned if you do, or damned if you don't" situation.

CF: But you are.

NB: But I think that it's more about how others are viewing me in the context of the art world than what I'm actually producing. My work touches on a pretty wide range of issues, everything from basic movement and aesthetic issues, personal issues, a range of women's issues, and then moving into broader political and cultural issues.

CF: In terms of culture and performance being political—everything's political. I'm drawn to topics that have some kind of overt sociopolitical critique in them because those are the things that interest me, those are the things [that] get my mind going in ways that are not utterly self-involved and therefore, to me, somewhat trivial. I've never been an artist, or student or critic for that matter, that's interested in pure formalism; I've always been interested in how do you take the social and shape it a way that draws out its formal dimension in an interesting way? How do I make people think about the environment that they're in in a way that will shed a different light on it? My decision to concentrate specifically on gender issues in Latin culture and in intercultural dynamics with non-Latin cultures is part of a political decision. My decision to work with other women is a political decision, my decision to manage my own art business is a political decision, because I don't want to give up my work to a management structure or bureaucracy that's going to try and *force* me into a position of submission in relationship to a community. And I think that Latino cultural discourse in this country up to this point has been dominated by the attitude that "You give everything to *la Raza*. You give everything to the *familia*. You give everything to the *Causa*." You erase yourself, you submit, and—and then the group advances. But what in actuality has happened is that Latin women submit and Latin men advance themselves. I don't want to be part of that dynamic anymore, I don't want to encourage it, and so my political orientation is as much directed towards developing a critique of cultural nationalism *among* Latinos as it is directed out towards the larger culture. It's a terrible shame, but the type of powerful African American women's movement, particularly in the arts, that came out in full force in the late seventies and the eighties and that really changed the way that Americans understood what black culture in this country was about, and who black intellectuals were, hasn't happened yet for Latinas, and I very much want to be part of that sort of a Latin discourse.

NB: As do I.

RW: Well, if each of your artistic and political commitments is any indication, I'd say you were both at the forefront of that sort of discourse. Thank you, thank you both very much.

[8]

WOMEN SINGING, WOMEN GESTURING:
MUSIC VIDEOS **MAUREEN TURIM**

From the suggestive, masturbatory images of a singer stroking herself in a video clip to the subtle directional movement of an actor's eyes in a close-up image in which nothing else moves, filmic and televisual gesture cover a wide range of coded, and yet elusive, movements of the body. I will look at how such gestures are understood and will specifically explore the meaning of the sexualized gesture as used differently by white and black women, straight women and lesbians in videos from the years 1993–94, when the emphatic sexual gesture hit its stride.

Displays of sexuality by vocalists and lead instrumental performers have long been an element of musical stage and club performance. In fact, flirtation is central to many operas, from *La Noce di Figaro* to *Carmen* to *Lulu;* flirtation, whether by tenors or sopranos, but especially by sopranos, depends in modern stagings on the corporeal as well as the vocal gesture. So it should be no surprise that in the even more adventurous and youthful theaters of blues, rock, and hip-hop, popular musicians have long been testing how suggestive or direct the evocation of sexual desire, availability, prowess can be.

Music video performance grows out of these traditions, performative and narrative, but with a different history constraining its mass dissemination, a history that has been fraught with a struggle with internal censorship. This struggle has been heightened by music video's obvious appeal to a very young and very large audience. Issues of racial and gender inclusion and parity have haunted the music video industry, and have been the subject of much of the critical and theoretical writing on it.

My purpose here is to focus on the specificities of visual gestures in music videos and address issues that are the concerns of this entire volume, concerns about how bodies are presented as implying or creating meanings that affect the psyches and beings of women. Representations of women's gestures are inherently available to regimes of invigoration or betrayal, substantive expression or equally substantive deception, and the manipulation of identities.

Music video offers us one example of an extremely commercial and mass-cultural formatting of bodily representations, and one in which many talents construct a performer's body, voice, narratives, and myths. Here I focus on analyzing the videos as representations of women's bodies, and use the question of gesture as my means of entry. Preliminary to that entry, I find I must start by indicating how the study of gesture in general is at a certain impasse, and what directions I propose as I move into this look at women's gesture in music video.

A telling entry in Griemas's 1986 dictionary of semiotics under "gesture" indicates this impasse, while still mapping in detail the advances made to date and the promise of future research, not the least of which is his *Semiotiques des Passions,* recently translated as *Semiotics of Emotions.* Griemas offers a concise delineation of the problems of a semiotics of gesture, which can be summarized as the difficulty of moving beyond taxonomies of the most clearly coded gestures of direct communication. The semiotic dream of a comprehensive classification often moved the study of gesture into scientific observation, measurement, and categorization. While advances in zoosemiotics and semiotic anthropology (including books on French and Central African gesture, as well as a cultural history of gesture ranging from the medieval period to the twentieth century) are in many ways impressive, the impasse is most evident in the textual inscription of gesture, where far more fluid and contextual methods are needed. Analysis here must be open to idiosyncrasy and inventiveness, as well as irony and poetics.

A poetics of gesture, a theory of gesture, promises a move beyond the image, a life beyond the signs of a dead end. In the writings of Julia Kristeva both the genotext (in opposition to the phenotext) and the semiotic (in opposition to the symbolic) bear traces of the gestural that is brought to the fore by her work on Bellini. Barthes's "third meaning," as well, could be reinterpreted as a contemplation of the gestural traced in the image as an excess. Damisch, in addressing the history and limits of iconography and its debt to the uncovering of forgery, focuses on the specificity of the rendered gesture. And yet gesture remains elusive in semiotics even as it points to a horizon on which deconstruction will dance. Jacques Derrida's interview, "Choreography," observes the theoretical implications of the dance as a trance almost granted an alterity to language, to writing.

This paradoxical dance, though, is already choreo*graphy,* already written. Derrida's dominant metaphor of writing writes the chora as a feminine limit that is not outside writing, but constitutes a border, *almost* elsewhere. The dancing feet come down to another space of writing, but one now ironically marked by a sort of gendered difference and assigned a distinct role as an emblem of the less-than-written in writing.

The danger in this strategy is that women dance here as "primitives," giving us a vision of primary and primal gesture. Ironically, the theoretical incorporation of gesture into deconstruction ultimately finds gesture as auxiliary to more familiar textualities. Gesture has been inscribed within the text as limit, a move made possible by the theoretical refusal of the specificity of the visual, musical, and gestural signifier. This refusal to analyze the specificity marking kinds of writing and kinds of signifiers leaves us bereft of a means of considering a complex medium such as music video in which visual, musical, and, above all, gestural signifiers are on display. Gesture escapes analysis, its elusiveness confirmed.

Alternative to this have been loose notions of gesture as sign in cultural studies, where the object of study itself is so thoroughly gestural that one is hard pressed not to focus there. Performance art, photography, advertising, music video: all induce writers to speak of gestures as signifiers. Ironically though, this is a cultural studies still grasping for, or perhaps after, methodology, characterized by a looseness of terminology in fact borrowed from the semiotic approach. John Fiske's look at music video as a Bakhtinian carnival style in *Television Culture* bears within it an implicit theory of gesture in a series of crude oppositions between other sorts of texts (literature, film) and music video. Fiske gives us the following chart:

ideology: pop pleasures
sd: sr [signified: signifier]
meanings: physical sensations
depth: surface
subjectivity: body

responsibility: fun
sense: nonsense
unity: fragmentation
homogeneity: heterogeneity
the terrain of control: the terrain of resistance[1]

Laced in these oppositions is a theory of gesture in music video as physical sensation without meaning or signifieds, a sensation that speaks the body in fragmentation and heterogeneity. "Fun" is very nearly equated with resistance, surely providing the mass consumer the easiest entry imaginable into a political opposition.

Any closer and more semiotically precise analysis of music video hardly shows gesture to be as systematically "nonsensical" as Fiske would have it. On the contrary, while gesture is indeed at the heart of music video, it signifies there in ways clearly decipherable and constantly deciphered with acuity by an audience clearly capable of interpreting these signs.

E. Ann Kaplin recognizes this in her more ideologically informed study of music video, which nonetheless concentrates, as Fiske's did, on the carnivalesque, the rapidity of montage, the flurry of reiteration as postmodern incomprehensibility.[2] Yet this conclusion is overdetermined by the refusal to consider precedents, particularly in the avant-garde. It refuses to see how video, as a cutting on gesture, makes the gestural emphatic. While Kaplin's work offers one of the best attempts to date to look at gendering in music video, it cannot really bring this gender analysis together with an examination of music video's celebration of physical sensation associated with a variety of meanings.

Gesture is gendered in music video. A critical look at this gendering is one way of exploring the poetics of these clips.

The comparison of music video to early cinema deserves note. Performance and what has been called the "cinema of attractions" dominated early cinema, providing such spectacles of flesh, exposed and undulating, as *Lola's Turkish Dance* and *The Serpentine Dance*. The fascination with movement itself becomes coupled with another fascination, that of women's sexuality, which is in turn laden with exotic connotations of otherness, the primitive, the "oriental," and the bestial. As the American term "exotic dancer" comes to signify the performer of a sexually arousing dance, it gives us an encapsulation of the process by which authentic Middle Eastern dances which serve as the remote source are transformed by popular cultural performance into both distillation and legitimization of the "sexual." The "Turkish" in *Lola's Turkish Dance* merely signals a loose agglomeration of "orientalisms," but covers its display with an ersatz "ethnography." In the title "The Serpentine Dance" we get both the metaphoric comparison of woman and snake, dancing to the charmed notes or movements of a man's offscreen instrument, and the description of her sinuous movement both as resembling a serpent and as "subtly sly and tempting" (the cultural connotation of "serpentine"). In both films the woman moves to music that in early kinetoscope presentations was unheard, but that could be provided in the mass context of nickelodeons. These short films from the earliest exploitation of cinema as mass spectacle clearly prefigure music video not only in structure and function, but in the process of blending connotations into the transformed appeal of a new hybrid and modern culture.

It is not just the gesture of parallel performance in early film that is of comparative interest with that of music video, but gesture in fiction film from its historical beginnings as well. It has been well established that early films borrow heavily from theatrical, melodramatic gesture, but that a more subtle approach to gesture ensues from the adoption of framing and amplification devices of analytic editing, especially the close-up. In her recent book *Eloquent Gestures* (1992), Pearson systematically traces the interaction between what she calls the "histrionic" and "verisimilar" codes of gesture. While Pearson's study elucidates something quite specific concerning the years of transition 1908–15, her oppositional comparison between more demonstrative and exaggerated codification of gesture and those performative gestures that seek to suggest through litotes and juxtaposition the "natural" and "everyday experience" is useful as a means of assessing the range of gesture and gestural styles in fiction film. From the histrionic, clearly, other specifically coded gestural systems evolve, such as expressionist and surrealist gesture. The ironic hyper-gesturality of comedy has its own histrionic tradition and its own historical permutations. From the verisimilar come the extremes of litotes found in films such as those of Robert Bresson or Jean-Marie Straub and Danielle Huillet. Idiolects, such as the contextual gestures of the deadpan comic, cross the oppositional schema and are some indication that this opposition is less a division into mutually exclusive categories than a means of articulating elements that are differentially combined in various gestural praxes.

Familiarity with film history seems to me fundamental as background for analysis of the gestural in music video. One effect of early film was to influence the realm of the gestural and change its form and coding. In a circular process, early film influenced cultural gesture, assimilating gestures of various cultures and reifying some gestures as those most significant to contemporary identities.

Some early film theorists found various ways of expressing this process. Behind the claims of cinema as a "universal" language was a parallel consideration of its universalizing and homogenizing function as cultural form. More specifically, Louis Delluc's notion of "photogénie," the elusive magical properties of composition and tone in the filmic image, coupled with Bela Balasz's notion of film as revealing physiognomy as a terrain of expressive exploration, hint at the power of cinema simultaneously to reveal and construct gesture.

These antecedents are deployed implicitly by André Bazin in his appreciation of Jean Renoir's *Une Partie de compagne* (*A Day in the Country*, 1936), of which he writes:

> The love scene on the island is one of the most agonizing and most beautiful in all cinema. It owes its stunning effectiveness to a couple of gestures and a look from Sylvie Bataille, which have a wrenching emotional realism. In the space of a few frames she displays all the disenchantment, the pathetic sadness, that follows the act of love.

The isolation and highlighting by Bazin of "a couple of gestures and a look" in this passage is his acknowledgment of the internal framing of gesture and veneration of "photogénie" that Renoir, actress Sylvie Bataille, cameraperson, and editor accomplish. It is such filmic articulation "in the space of a few frames" that elicits such linguistic veneration as "stunning effectiveness" and "wrenching emotional realism." Those who know the scene will immediately remark that what Bazin neglects to mention is the frames preceding those that depict what he calls "the disenchantment, the pathetic sadness." Those frames constitute a rape, coded as seduction: male aggression, at first resisted, elicits female acquiescence, then passion in the briefest of intervals within the single long take. The "disenchantment" is therefore contextually far richer than Bazin indicates, as the range of regrets in Sylvie Bataille's gesture is multiple. It exceeds the notion of the sadness following "the act of love," though it might well include that. My point here is that gesture in those films renowned for their mastery of gestural expression is a complex mix of inscriptions, in which contextual elements operate as prefigurations and overlays, creating polyvalence and ambiguity.

Notably, immediately preceding the ending of the island love scene discussed above is a segment of crosscutting between the theatrically rendered and mythology-laced flirtation of Jacques Brunius and Jeanne Marken in a meadow and the verisimilar coding of gesture as Georges Darnoux and Sylvie Bataille make their way to the spot in which the rape-as-seduction occurs. Brunius's Pan persona leaps around a fluttering Marken with

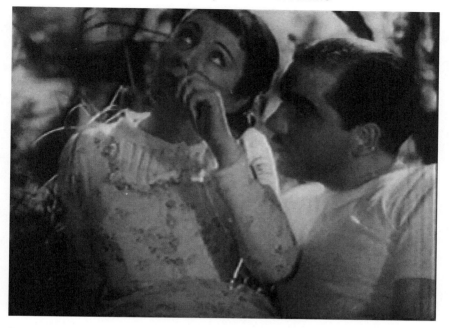

Sylvie Bataille as a young Parisienne about to be seduced responds to a bird's singing, her gesture of sensitive melancholy pervading the largely silent and traumatic sexual scene to follow, in Jean Renoir's *Une Partie de Compagne (A Day in the Country,* 1936). From this point through to the coda that ends the film, the aesthetic of the film suggests the dominance of gestural expression, recalling silent film and prefiguring music videos.

a visual lyricism underlined by the score. The contrast between this exaggerated theatricality and the far more subtle gestures of the Darnoux-Bataille encounter heightens the difference and specifics of each. The contrast may even disguise the brusque and melodramatic turbulence of Darnoux's grabbing gesture and Bataille's attempts to fight him off with fists pushing against his chest, and their nearly instantaneous conversion into a clutching passion; already positioned on the naturalist side of the opposition, the subsegment no longer fully displays its elements of melodrama, elements which reveal the exaggerated tendencies inherent in "naturalism."

Outtakes of Renoir's film, found as original negatives by the Cinémathèque Française and recently printed, compiled, and exhibited as a paradigmatic chronicle of the film's production, amply display the work that underlay the contrasts and blends of theatricality and somber realism that

137

so inflect the gestures in this film. One sees how both "styles" of gesture are produced as codes through equally intricate refinements of staging and careful processes of selection. The outtakes become a study in the "beats" and flow of a performance as inscribed across a take, so that gesture can be understood as elements constructed from the movement and stasis of bodies, in which abstracted structural components add tone and color.

If I have been arguing that filmic semiotics helps us understand music video, it is to insist that the methodology is not itself specific to a medium, to classical narrative or to aesthetic mastery. Narrative film is often seen as the opposite of music video, but often in much the same facile manner in which the novel is seen as the opposite of film. The segment discussed above from *Une Partie de compagne* shares a great deal with music video in the means through which montage figures, contrast is drawn and associations are made between fragmented elements, and emphatic gestures define characters and actions. In the interval which follows this segment, as the rain starts over the river and reeds bend to the wind, the gestural extends to include parts of nature. This reminds us that the camera itself partakes of a gestural poetics.

To summarize, as with film we can look at music video to address the ways in which gesture has become a mixture of reference to the supposedly "natural"—by which we mean variations of psycho-perceptual "universals," of specific cultural references, and of newly emerging gestures offered as an outgrowth of international exchange. Music video renews the filmic for a younger generation.

Music video denaturalizes the natural—performance, illustration, and montage override any narrative drive toward the incidental and the everyday. In fact montage is pervasive and rather astounding in music video, where images cut, interweave, superimpose, alternate angles, and present constantly interwoven textures in even the most banal of videos. Lately performance is deliberately broken by costume and set changes from line to line, creating a series of intervals. Michel Chion holds out hope that music video "frees" image in relationship to sound. "The music video has invented and borrowed a whole arsenal of devices; it's a joyous rhetoric of images. And this is the paradox of the television of optional images: it liberates the eye. Never is television as visual as during some moments of music video, even when the image is conspicuously attaching itself to some music that was sufficient in itself."[3]

I want to start with an example which, coming after Renoir, hardly makes a case for equivalent aesthetics, but has much to tell us about music video's associative female imagery. "The Power of Love," featuring Celine

Celine Dion's "Power of Love" video positions her in a number of suggestive poses, covering the erotic touching of the self with the gentility of lace, flowers, whispering pastel beiges, and soft lighting.

Dion, is a video that even more than most functions like a now nearly superannuated artifact: the LP record cover as a consumer emblem, an image that emblemizes the music inside with an image or design. This design not only intends to appeal at the point of purchase, but functions to guide or even lock the imagination of the consumer into a particular reception of the object. The CD insert, in its diminutive size, may be the miniature of the album cover, but perhaps it is too compact to fulfill this image-surround function without augmentation by the video clip.

Coming relatively early in Dion's conquest of the U.S. market and her climb toward superstar fame, the video dates from a time when choreographers working with the singer were trying to compensate for her still awkward stage presence. She had a tendency to arm gestures that were both wooden and overblown. Her French-Canadian heritage and her native Montreal, absent from the representation, are replaced by a romance-

139

novel setting, characterized by first a fireplace and thronelike chair, then by an image of her lounging on a bed. She is clothed alternately in a white angora sweater that looks fur-like and a white silk slip; her walking, stripping, and singing traverse space and multiply poses, presenting us the prototype of woman alone, available, on the brink of masturbation.

Why does this video, like so many involving women lately, bring us to the brink of witnessing masturbation without actually showing it? One obvious answer is the limit imposed by self-censorship, in compliance with the imperative of an industry aimed at adolescents that restricts itself from the directly pornographic so that it may capitalize on images and music that come as tantalizingly close as possible to pornography. If, in the pornographic pose, the woman on the brink of masturbation seems offered up to a male (or lesbian) audience as the enunciation of a readiness, willingness, and availability, these women on the brink offer the same accessibility, the invitation to sexual fantasies of possession.

Intriguingly, though, there is perhaps another cultural resonance to this flirtation with the brink, and it is for the part of the audience identifying with the woman within the representation, rather than longing for her; consider how Eve Sedgwick, in "Jane Austen and the Masturbating Girl," looks at masturbation in its indirect representation in the novel.

> If what defines "sexual identity" is the impaction of epistemological issues around the core of a particular genital possibility, then the compulsive attention paid by anti-onanist discourse to disorders of attention makes it a suitable point of inauguration for modern sexuality. Marianne Dashwood, though highly intelligent, exhibits the classic consciousness symptoms noted by Tissot in 1758, including "the impairment of memory and the senses," "inability to confine the attention," and "an air of distraction, embarrassment and stupidity." A surprising amount of the narrative tension of *Sense and Sensibility* comes from the bent bow of the absentation of Marianne's attention from wherever she is. "Great," at one characteristic moment, "was the perturbation of her spirits and her impatience to be gone"; once out on the urban scene, on the other hand, "her eyes were in constant inquiry; and in whatever shop the party were engaged, her mind was equally abstracted from every thing actually before them, from all that interested and occupied the others. Restless and dissatisfied every where . . . she received no pleasure from any thing; was only impatient to be at home again . . ." Yet when at home, "her agitation increased as the evening drew on. She could scarcely eat any dinner, and when they afterwards returned to the drawing room, seemed anxiously listening to the sound of every carriage."[4]

Let me suggest that Austen's depiction of an adolescent attention disorder and Sedgwick's deft connection of it to descriptions in medical anti-onanist tracts give us a new way of thinking about the rapidly shifting montage of these music videos. Rapid montage across disjunction places the spectator in the position of hungering for the next image, the next sound, as a cue to cut to something previously off-screen, another scene, more stimulus, an elsewhere.

Ironically, Dion's lyrics address the absent lover, with obeisance and the promise of perpetual support:

> I am your lady, you are my man
> Whenever you reach out to me
> I'll give you my hand

In some ways the images that accompany these lyrics recall soft-core pornography and display the ironic oscillation between polarities within the female repertoire of gestures of power versus powerlessness. The affirmation of an autonomous female world clashes with the slavishness of this fantasy once it is offered to a male viewer.

If we look to the romance novel as intertext and consider it in its appeal to a female audience, the solitary female fantasy dominates. This fantasy is augmented by the music and Dion's delivery, for her singing has emotional power, the high-voltage songstress belting lyrics in a long tradition of female pop vocalists, a tradition steeped in a cabaret chanteuse heritage. Then the final masturbatory gestures equally fit a double regime, intimating self-confirming release while safely ensconced in a male-oriented guarantee of availability, the pornographic invitation.

The sexual politics of power performance here contrasts with the videos of a more subversive songstress, Melissa Etheridge. The video of her song "I'm the Only One" is rooted in performance, with many shots devoted to the singer accompanying herself on guitar, backed by her group on stage, but this performance is set in a fictionalized club, a dive, whose walls, streaked and worn, perhaps underground, lend a backdrop to an audience dancing, sweating, though always chicly arrayed in the barely-dressed look of youth fashion. This audience becomes individualized as characters in a loose drama whose gestures both illustrate the lyrics and respond to Etheridge's delivery. Her delivery could be called "macho," as the montage fills in guitar and singing performance gestures which have become their own sexual ritual, as evidenced from their miming by nonsingers. Perhaps these gestures are not so much macho as "butch." For what is at stake in the lyrics and the narrative constellations attached to them by the montage are gender double-entendres.

Etheridge's lyrics suggest a lover's psychic trauma, the lover's refuge in another woman, and the singer's response. They do so in terms so fragmented, ambiguous, and disjunct that the narrative to which they seem to point is suggestively left open. "Go on and hold her till the screaming is gone / Go on believe her when she tells you nothing's wrong": the singer taunts the lover, sarcastically, in rhetorical flourishes that clarify their irony only after the fact, with repetition and substitution constituted by the second phrase—an anaclasis. Further, the screaming in question is suggestively ambiguous, indicating perhaps orgasm, perhaps a psychic cry, or both.

Against the imagined claim of the rival, the singer declares her counterargument in the chorus: "I'm the only one who'll walk across the fire for you / I'm the only one who'll drown in my desire for you." This enunciation doubles as pledge *and* threat. In it we hear Lacanian nuances of a speaker drowning in desire, with that drowning, that metaphorical death of the self, being offered as a sign of enduring trustworthiness, a paradoxically "undying" love. Similarly, the vow to "walk across the fire" serves as a pledge to withstand torture. It promises reliability, but simultaneously accuses the lover of staging and demanding such trials-by-fire. This is a love song that darkly insinuates the pledge of a slave (the role of the singer-persona) to a master. The slave suggests that she knows this master as one whose torments are internal, but that they become, as a consequence, performative. This master is tortured and therefore a torturer. The speaker's knowledge of the master's internal torments seems to assure her of ultimately gaining the upper hand, of regaining control. Pleas, despair, and promises of forgiveness offered by an abandoned lover in so many love songs in hope of reconciliation here become threatening and sarcastic, though at the same time a declaration of power. The singer's strength is her ability to withstand and absorb all inevitable onslaughts of pain.

The images of the bodies dancing introduce vignettes of bisexuality and of lesbianism, but these follow after a strangely truncated heterosexual gaze. A man is seen dressing to leave, his gaze seemingly retaining him as it fixes on an object—but which object is unclear. In the images crosscut with his looking, we see both Etheridge performing and brief, fragmented shots of women dancing or looking. Grinding hips or a caress, first between one pair of women, then between another, intercede in alternation with Etheridge's performance; then the man intervenes, comes between two women, and seems to seduce one into removing his recently redonned clothes: the sex is mobile, the couples permeable to a third party. This floating and transformational sexuality joins lyrics in which the pronouns "I," "she," and "you" likewise float; perhaps there are no males in the verbal

The gestures of a woman in a private, captive torment is crosscut with Melissa Etheridge's performance of her rock ballad "Come to My Window."

story, perhaps this song speaks of a lesbian triangle. Despite the male first seen looking at Etheridge singing, then seen as an undulating torso, perhaps the male as male is less significant here than is the male as double for Etheridge. Consider press interviews in which Etheridge discusses her idolatry of, and identification with, Bruce Springsteen for years before she achieved fame, so that their performance together became for her a dream come true. The male here is the Springsteen double, the self projected in its ideal and male form.

Of course this reading is only one of the ones available to audiences. Audiences for this video probably find different gender identifications possible in its montage of gestures. An underground version of this video re-edited for private viewing by video artist Adele Brown deletes all traces of the male character from the video, leaving only the suggestive lesbian imagery and therefore the lesbian reading of the lyrics as all that is possible. This re-editing is perhaps meant as a critique of Etheridge. It removes all ambiguity from Etheridge's identity and appropriates the lesbian performer from the mass-audience neutrality lent to her through her tape's appeals to bisexuality and heterosexuality.

Another view, however, might see her insinuation of lesbian fantasies into mainstream exhibition contexts, not as a play with bisexuality such as Madonna or David Bowie enacted, but as the turning of a heterosexual subtext on its edge to make it into a fantasy projection within a lesbian context. This view makes an implicit argument for a lesbianism that crosses gender lines and is able to assert male as well as female identifications.

Connections forged between dancing, sexuality, and writhing in pain are evoked in a different manner in Etheridge's "Come to My Window," in which Etheridge's performance of the song alternates with images of a fictional space in which an actress, Juliette Lewis, performs, apparently embodying the voice of the song. The narrative suggested by the lyrics alone is vague and ambiguous. As in "I'm the Only One," couplets and stanzas detach, separated from any larger coherent unity. The imagery internal to these fragments only connects to a larger story by means of various alternative readings.

> Come to my window
> Crawl inside, wait by the light of the moon
> Come to my window
> I'll be home soon

Heard apart from the video images, these lyrics treat "window" and "home soon" as ambiguous, perhaps sexual signifiers. Or perhaps they suggest a *Romeo and Juliet* balcony scene modernized to an urban or suburban window, a secret nighttime courtship.

The video's images fill in and supplement the lines, helping them cohere across the song. The window is fixed as one at the right of the image in a small cell-like room, a window with bars, or, to be more precise, an ornate iron grill. This suggests a fanciful, or perhaps exotically historical, image of a woman in prison or an asylum. We see within this space a woman alone, alternately on the bed and in the spaces immediately in front of the bed, performing gestures of masturbation, self-recrimination, and self-destruction, of writing on the wall and floor, then eventually dancing ecstatically. In this fragmented montage of recurring images, a child's drawing also comes to substitute for the set of the asylum room, a line drawing of a house, tree, sun.

The bars on the window and the bandages on the woman's wrists, along with lyrics of anguish and mental pain, come to suggest a mental asylum. The exhortation to come to the window then seems a fantasy speech to a friend or lover to visit a space that forbids visitation; the woman's dancing by the end of the clip prefigures or promises a later reunion.

There are three intertexts that, while perhaps never intended, still are suggestive in figuring the impact of such imagery. One is Chantal Ackerman's first film, *Je tu il elle,* which features an extended first scene of a character (played by Ackerman) alone in her bedroom, obsessively eating sugar from a brown paper bag as she writes page after page and strews them across the floor. The cell is also quite similar to the one in Kinoshita's *A Crazy Page* in which a former dancer incarcerated in a mental institution dances with her shadow, thrown on the wall by the light of the single window. In a less direct sense the video collapses images from German expressionism, such as those of *Nosferatu* (particularly the batting at invisible flies) and of *The Cabinet of Dr Caligari,* in which characters wait vulnerably or go crazy in cell-like rooms with single windows; the image is clearly one of an architectural figuration of the trapped soul, a psyche turned inward, but with only the most tenuous connection to the outside world. The slit wrists, the gaze turned only inward, or out to sea, is but the clinically depressed version of the masturbating girl; that is why the woman who seems to cure herself through song in the video "Come to my Window," who begins trapped but dances with abandon by the video's end, is the emblem of a cure authenticated by the masturbatory female gesture in video. The moral of these video stories seems to be that a self-awareness of sexual power, of self-fulfillment, is a prerequisite to any intercourse with the other, male or female, if the female self is to avoid being shattered. This is a moral that has affinities with Luce Irigaray's *Speculum of the Other Woman* (1994), with its positing of the necessity of sexual self-knowledge and its celebrating of female orgasm and pleasure as *jouissance.* Supplemental to that self-awareness may be a fantasy other, an invitation to another, but there is a striking solipsism at the root of these narratives and their gestures. In fact the gestures often transform a dialogue with the other in the verbal lyrics into something far more self- and body-centered in the image narrative.

Perhaps the most celebrated masturbating girl of all is Madonna. Of all female music video performers, Madonna is the most analyzed, so much so that there is a certain temptation to just indicate the provocative work already done on her song images.[5] Most adept at pastiche, at recycling images and gestures borrowed from the history of film and performance, Madonna provides vast raw material on which to base a theory of gestural

Madonna's videos create images focused on sexualized self-touching, illustrating here in "Secrets" a literal interpretation of "happiness lies in your own hand, it took me so long to understand."

reinscription. Not only does she redo the mise-en-scene of "Little Rock" from *Gentleman Prefer Blondes,* as acknowledgment of her general lifting of a myriad of Marilyn Monroe gestures, her imitations include a version of the Judy Garland waif who performs the "Born in a Trunk" number in *A Star Is Born,* for her video "Justify My Love," and she poses as Jimmy Dean, Maureen O'Sullivan, Marlene Dietrich, etc. Madonna's gestures toward film history help make my earlier point about music video's relation to cinema history and to filmic means of expression; rather than a different semiotics, we have self-conscious citations of a medium, cinema, whose own history includes the frequent reinscription of its own prior images.

Madonna's flirtation with a toreador, which forms the narrative of her "Take a Bow" video, certainly borrows from a wealth of classical Hollywood imagery. The video also draws on the more contemporaneous success of bullfight and seduction imagery in the films of Spanish filmmaker Carlos

Saura, an homage underlined by the decision to shoot the video in Spain. What I wish to draw attention to here, however, is another image included in this video, which I will call the "television masturbation" subsegment. It occurs after the singer, rebuffed by the toreador, returns to her bedroom and lies on her bed fondling her body. A television on the bed shows the toreador in the ring. As she pulls the sheet over the TV it becomes a source of white light, as well as her partner in orgasm. This is a meta-image that embeds within the video the relationship of the masturbating girl to television as fantasy relay. Metaphorically it suggests postmodern theories of the body as machine, or conversely, as a counterweight to the force machines exert in contemporary life.

The increasing prominence of racial themes and African American characters, or at least bodies, in Madonna's tapes raises the question of Madonna's pastiche of blackness, her search for some reference to the sexuality of historically black music idioms, such as rhythm and blues, soul, funk, hip-hop, and rap. In speaking of Madonna's setting her "Secrets" video in Harlem, *Entertainment Weekly* critic Amy Linden compares the video to works by black artists, proclaiming, "Madonna is behind the curve."[6] This proclamation describes Madonna's pastiche relationship to black singers and African American culture and resonates with an earlier video, "Vogue," which coupled its funk "Let your body move to the music" exhortation with more Marilyn poses, and its segment of breathless recitation of stars' names with images of African American male and Latino dancers. It recapitulates a complaint cultural critic Michelle Wallace has made that Madonna simply appropriates the overt gestures of black musicians such as Tina Turner and garners all the attention of feminist cultural critics, while her black predecessors are ignored. So let me note that there is a difference worth analyzing between Madonna's borrowing of gestures from Monroe and Garland and her borrowings that allude to a tradition of displayed sexuality in African American and Latino dance and performance. The difference is that race cannot be simply a citation in an industry in which racial divisions of artists and audiences have historically been a problem. In Madonna's case such gestural borrowings couple with musical and production contributions from African American artists, such as Kenny Edmonds, a.k.a. Babyface, who wrote and produced the recording of "Take a Bow." Before we can simply see this as a crossover integration of the industry, we must ask: how does the sexual gesture figure differently in the context of race?

It is ironic to note that the young African American singer Adina Howard sees "the curve" alluded to above from another perspective. "I want to be the black Madonna. Madonna is a businesswoman; she's very aggressive and she pushes everything to the limit." If a moment later Howard remembers some black superstars, adding, "I want to be as famous as her or Michael Jackson, or Prince or Janet," her phrase "black Madonna" is telling and is linked to a defensive posture. "There's nothing wrong with lust or being lusted after," Howard says, and it seems that the white superstar Madonna justifies Howard's dabbling in explicit sexual gestures; she complains in the same interview, "When you do something sexy, they say 'she's degrading, she doesn't respect herself'. But black females are sexual human beings, just like everyone else." When asked to clarify who "they" are, Howard responds "black females, . . . those closet freak females."[7]

This attitude is meant to promote Howard's video "Freak Like Me," which, like Nuttin' Nyce's "Froggy Style," is an extended sexual come-on, complete with directions to the male organ concerning particular movements. "Freak" is a multivalent slang term for intercourse, orgasm, and a person who desires sex, thus the lines "I wanna freak in the morning, freak in the evening, just like me" and "I've got a freaky secret." Howard gyrates in slow motion, straddles chairs, slides her hand between her legs, and sings of the "dog in me," a line accompanied by gestures that, across the bestiary, illustrate a posture that matches "froggy style."

In similar sexual gestures, TLC's "Red Light Special" (also written by Kenny Edmonds) links the lines "I let you touch it if you like to go down" and "I'll let you go further if you take the Southern route" with one member of the trio, T-Boz, spreading her legs and pointing to her genitals. The gesture is not subtle in its sexual meanings, but seems also to link with an urban gesture of spreading out the body so as to stake a claim on space—like the largeness of seated postures on New York subways, in which a male posture of spread knees, maximizing the body's bulk, has come to be used by both genders. Breakdancers with their street gyrations that fly out in space, and rappers with their ritual gestures that punch out time and space, seem to be conveying in gestural language the same powerful occupation of space, a demonstration of existence and significance.

Of the women, it is perhaps Queen Latifah and Salt n' Peppa who best translate these "in-your-face" demonstrative gestures to video images, gestures that serve to punctuate each line of furiously delivered lyrics, like the deliberate shaking of the head or the pointing of a finger, borrowed from the black Baptist sermon but often the gestural equivalent of the phrase "what's going down." These rap gestures command respect.

Rap gestures can help us place in context certain gestures so blatantly sexual and so apparently subservient to male fantasies—"bitches in heat"—

Strategic hand placement accents erogenous zones as TLC plays with nakedness and oversized environmental uniforms for some unspecified specialization. Black, hip, erotic, and high tech are the celebrated signifiers in such images, or as they put it, "Sexy, Crazy, Cool."

that they appear to some (Howard's "closet freak females") as self-degrading. The tension between "respect" gestures and "self-degrading" gestures may have collapsed as all such gestures have been annexed into a cultural gestural idiom. The focus of this gestural vocabulary is gestures that simply center on the self, on being a star, on having no shame about any gesture the body might make. In that sense, gesture here is ecstatic, in the religious sense of U.S. evangelism, and by itself evidence of a commitment not only

Des'ree's video uses contrasting black and white backgrounds and costumes to highlight her powerful gestures, and to create the effect of switching from positive to negative as in photography. One realizes the trick precisely by noticing her face and hand gestures as a constant.

to the music but to the audience, and perhaps to the self as goddess-star. In the context of Madonna—what she emblemizes and what she "gets away with" as a white superstar—these gestures seem to be part of a reclaiming of black power.

However, there are other black performers whose gestures dialogue with and perhaps critique such images of sexual display—certainly those of Queen Latifah, when her video takes her to a street corner to urge respect for black sisters, but also those of Des'ree. Des'ree's "You Gotta Be" video alternates black-and-white high-contrast images (some of which have black dominate, others white, as in negative and positive photography, though here the effect is entirely mise-en-scene). In this alternation, Des'ree's hand gestures surround her lyrics, extolling (an implicitly female) wisdom and strength with the mystic and exotic connotations she cultivates. The largeness and openness of her long arm gestures also suggest the multiple hands of Hindu religious statuary, as referenced in dance. This is part of a series of gestures that fluidly link the raised fist of black power movements to the gestures of 1960s girl groups, such as the Supremes and Gladys Knight and the Pips, where hand gestures illustrated in swaying rhythms the themes of each line of the lyrics. Though cut into a pattern of alternation, into which close-up profiles are also inserted, the match-on-movement editing of Des'ree's video creates a greater unity than the frenzied fragmentation typified in the other videos I've discussed.

Yet if I have concentrated on the rapid montage and on the sexual gesture in its relationship to masturbation in these music videos, it is not to highlight objects that realize the worst fears of the right-wing censors, but rather to suggest that these videos seek to gesture toward a female empowerment through decidedly various means. Each masturbatory gesture is in fact differently inscribed in a narrative that runs parallel to and sometimes merely expands, but at other times contradicts, a verbal and musical narration.

It is clear that this video gestural vocabulary and this type of image, juxtaposing gestures, is permeating the culture at large. It not only quickly disseminates new gestures as "cool" and "sexy," it will affect cinematic expression, and even opera, as is evidenced by recent works staged by Peter Sellars and John Adams. Though *Opera News* may decry this emphasis on a powerful and virtually autonomous image track, fragmenting and highlighting gestures and linking them to representations of gender, sex, and race seems to be a movement difficult to pause.

[9]

BOMBSHELL**STEPHANIE
A. SMITH**

Shocking, stunning, shattering: so a literal bombshell might be described. Low, vulgar, silly: these words, on the other hand, characterize a rather different sort of bombshell, that of the 1950s burlesque, va-va-voom! variety. American tabloid news reminded readers of these differences in December 1998, with headlines like the *New York Post*'s BOMBS AND BOMB-SHELLS.[1] Such headlines linked the bombing of Iraq to William Jefferson Clinton's presidential slouch toward impeachment; they also made former White House intern Monica Lewinsky's name a household word.

A bombshell, however, like a bomb, explodes—as Monica Lewinsky's image has, on the street, in the press, and on the Web, often juxtaposed to or superimposed upon that of another, more enduring version of this American type: Marilyn Monroe. Curiously, however, the bombshell seldom explodes to what many might call any "serious" effect. That is, although the word "bombshell" indicates potential violence, it also serves to ground a common sense about sex and violence according to which the former is life-affirming, while the latter is deadly. Connections between sex and violence continue to be popularly understood as criminal or aberrant, rather than as prevalent or constitutive. So although popular discourse continues to produce the idea of a cultural "war between the sexes," this war is usually treated as more of a joke than a problem, even if the conflict is frequently refracted through furious debates about domestic battery, rape, abortion, equal rights, gay/lesbian/transgender activism, and discrimination.[2] In the face of dispute, common sense maintains that sex, however potentially dangerous, is an insignificant "affair"—unless, of course, undertaken as the labor of reproducing the race. When compared, however, to the serious business of running America, sex is seen as a distraction.[3]

Therefore, although the 1998 visual joke of Moni-lyn (a mocking portrayal of Monica Lewinsky *as* Marilyn Monroe that was enacted pictorially on the Internet and on the steps of the State Capitol, February 11, 1998) was designed to inflame "serious" political opinion by pointing to how President Clinton has tried to cast himself in the role of another infamous John,[4] neither the present nor the former president are easily associated with the belittling frivolity that a Moni-lyn suggests. This is not to say that Clinton has escaped from his rather too public affair untouched; unlike the press in the 1960s, which shielded JFK's so-called personal peccadilloes from public scrutiny, newspapers in the 1990s did not hesitate to call Clinton a bimbo. Yet regardless of such invective, in the end, the bombshell remained the fool. In fact, common knowledge tells us what a Moni-lyn or a "Monroe"—and, by extension, a "bombshell"—must mean: "hussy," "kewpie doll," "a slatternly mother in a trailer camp," "zombie," "dingbat," "troublesome bitch."[5] The bombshell may be as volatile as "the bouquet of a fireworks display,"[6] may even be a gold mine of monetary profit or political currency, but she's also a joke.[7] Bill Clinton commits perjury and those "Bombshell Secret Files Even Congress Doesn't Want You to Read" might exist, but we all know a bombshell's just a "fat cheesy slut" because that's just plain old common sense.[8]

Bomb and bombshell: these words are linked. They are also dis-articulated from one another, so that the bomb in the bombshell betokens an explosive potentiality that lies dormant. The bombshell may locate a culturally designated site of concussive violence—she knocks your socks off, she knocks you off your feet, she knocks you for a loop, she can even knock you senseless. But a bombshell also, simultaneously, induces an enabling amnesia about that violence[9]—she's not likely, all references to bombs aside, to take you out permanently (or to knock you up, even if recent reproductive technologies make such an achievement at least theoretically possible).

Indeed, while I will argue that the bombshell, as a word and as a figure, is haunted by an underlying, traumatic knowledge of what Lacan calls the

Bombshell. Photo courtesy of AP/WIDE WORLD PHOTOS.

Real, a knowledge that leaves its trace in language, at the same time "bomb-shell" activates an amnesiac common sense that substitutes for that trau-matic knowledge. Using this description, one could also argue that the bombshell functions as a cultural fetish. Surely the seemingly endless com-modity-fetishization of Marilyn Monroe™ might be a symptom of such a

Moni-lyn and President Clinton. Photo courtesy of AP/WIDE WORLD PHOTOS.

claim: once you've entered "Marilyn Country" (Baty, 4) you'll find her on your lips and in your hair, on your tie or in your underwear. Like the figure of the vampire to which she once compared herself,[10] she is everywhere and nowhere, "a figurative effect of a modernist, rational, capital economy . . . and . . . a meet emblem of technologies of reproduction: of cinema, video and the internet."[11] And certainly a discussion of how "Marilyn Monroe" functions—as a cultural reference for the bombshell and as a site for both the creation and continuation of common-sense American narratives about sexuality, frivolity, and fatality—is of central importance to this argument. However, finally I am more interested in the word "bombshell" itself, because the continued circulation of this vernacular, arguably outdated, American word both reveals and reveils an ongoing common sense about sex, race, and violence. This is a common sense, I will argue, that remains necessary to the continuing composition of the United States as a democratic nation-state, a late-capitalist economy, and an "imagined community," the so-called promised land of the American dream.

Indeed, a word like "bombshell" helps to create the impression that common sense *itself* is natural and universal. And in the late twentieth century, this impression is perpetuated by both activist and reactionary discourse, inasmuch as demands that language become so "accessible" as to be stripped of ambiguity, so "common" as to be universally understood, or so "intimate" as to be transparent appeal to a most disabling and yet familiar form of humanist universalism: one that has the power to deny and forget both the sociopolitical history of political and cultural conflict in America and the key role that language plays in the split structure of the psyche. This common sense about common sense itself—i.e., the common sense that common sense is natural and universal and does not need to be learned or reinforced—grants not permanence but a certain recalcitrant endurance to long-standing modes of injustice and inequity, economic, legal, and social.

Furthermore, by constituting what will be considered commonly understood or useful as opposed to recondite or frivolous knowledge,[12] common sense also secures what will be understood as immediately recognizable knowledge *per se,* through which a primarily conservative balance of sociopolitical power in the capitalist democracy of the United States has been, at least since the mid-1970s, maintained. This does *not* mean that common sense is immutable. One can sketch out historical mutations. And yet common sense aids in the endurance of ideological "truths" that discourage the production of new knowledge, and retard anything like radical or even significant political alteration.

One can see the obstructive effects of common sense in how recent versions of historicism increasingly seem unable to address—at least in any politically meaningful way—the endurance of basic inequities that common sense so effectively sustains. Critical debates about cultural studies, or about history, or about the role of politics in the academy over the last three decades have produced, among other effects, what historian Lynn Hunt has termed a new positivism: a strenuously renewed faith in hard, reproducible, scientific or material fact. Versions of this "new positivism" may vary, but most contest the supposed relativism of poststructuralist and postmodernist modes of interpretation.[13]

I do not mean to quarrel about the value of researching, recounting, and interpreting historical change. Such historicism remains immensely valuable, and in this argument I rely upon the important archival work of others. But more often than not, "historical" arguments fail to grapple with the persistence of ideological vision that enduring modes of common sense can achieve. For example, given the increased visibility of sexual harassment cases, mustn't one ask why it is so easy for the popular press to dismiss Monica Lewinsky as a "bombshell"? Politics-as-usual is an easy answer—Lewinsky, one is told, was a pawn in the 1990s partisan conflict between a Democratic minority and a Republican majority. Meanwhile, history would tell us that the bombshell is really only a silly relic of the past, meant simply as a joking insult. But why does the bombshell remain at all, and remain as a common-sense joke? Why, despite the feminist activism of the late 1960s and 1970s, despite the so-called sexual revolution of those years, and despite later, ongoing critical attempts to alter or intervene in the repeated fetishization of "the" body as a biological site of indisputable verity—the contestation of the (supposedly) Freudian dictum that anatomy is destiny—does a commonplace like "bombshell" survive?

What the bombshell indicates, I will argue, is how "the" body remains a taken-for-granted source of inevitable and irreversible fact and therefore fate, not only through the modality of common-sense adage or fashion, but also through the tried-and-true wisdom of an ongoing, Cartesian duality that attempts to situate the body as a mere "object," one that bears little or no relation to the "mind." For example, we all know, don't we, that (well-endowed) blondes are just dumb? And that they have more fun because gentlemen, often to their own fatal disadvantage, prefer them? But wait, you might say, that's all very well for the typical blonde bombshell; however, Monica Lewinsky isn't a blonde and for all that she's a California girl by birth, she's not a Hollywood product. However, once called a "bombshell," any woman can be immediately associated with sex, with stupidity, and finally with at least the potential for criminal or negligent behavior. Indeed, by the prevailing anorectic standards of fashion in the 1990s, Lewinsky has been easily presented as a foolish, overweight nymphomaniac who threw herself at the President. Moreover, historical facts about Lewinsky that might be used to try to change her image do not explain why the word "bombshell" is still so potent a term.

One needs, of course, to remember that since at least the nineteenth century in the United States, anyone who is publicly associated with sex—or with a disciplinary practice of the body not linked to a sport traditionally understood as masculine and competitive—is swiftly characterized as empty-headed, loose, or dumb, as potentially dangerous (although this has been changing with the increased popularization of weightlifting for both men and women, and with the growing interest in televised professional wrestling).[14] Yet this association between sex and stupidity, too, is just history, is it not? Perhaps Lewinsky is simply a throwback. Surely we've "come a long way, baby" since the nineteenth century? Such a claim, however, still doesn't offer an answer as to why "bombshell" can circulate as shorthand for a plausible common sense about the narcissistic frivolity and deadly fatality of (female) sexuality.

In his essay on the conflicts in *Othello* that eventuate in the murder of Desdemona, Alan Sinfield writes that

> Ideology produces, makes plausible, concepts and systems to explain who we are, who the others are, how the world works. . . . the strength of ideology derives from the way it gets to be **common sense**. . . . The conditions of plausibility . . . govern our understandings of the world and how to live in it, thereby seeming to define the scope of feasible political change.[15]

Of course, such observations about the effect of ideology as "common sense" are hardly new. One thinks, as Sinfield did, of Gramsci. Yet, since the late 1980s, a significant renewal of a popular faith in both the efficacy and the benignity of common sense has taken place, along with a refusal, in many academic circles, of the concept of "ideology," as inflected by Marxist interpretation, and of post-Marxist thought *in toto*. For example, commenting upon this trend in her 1992 examination of the concept of ideology, *The Politics of Truth: From Marx to Foucault*, Michèlle Barrett concluded that it might be high time to abandon the attempt to modify or mobilize the Marxist term "ideology," because

> the definition of concepts, like the definition of *everyday words*, is partly a matter of usage: one cannot legislate against other people's uses of terms and one cannot with any confidence lay out a new meaning of a term and expect it to stick. . . . in some ways, the work undertaken by the concept of ideology is often too shallow and too easy, by virtue of the history of the usage of the concept. Better, perhaps, that we point with more accuracy

to an instance that might previously merely be labeled ideological: a partial truth, a naturalized understanding or a universalistic discourse, for example. Better, perhaps, that we oblige ourselves to think with new and more precise concepts, rather than mobilizing the dubious resonances of the old.[16]

Such a conclusion, however, begs the question: how can one point with "more accuracy to an instance that might previously merely be labeled ideological" without using "ideology"? Point, say, at the common-sense circulation of an everyday word—like bombshell? How does one enact a criticism that might intervene in the peculiarly stubborn effect of common sense? To put this differently: how can one make the bomb in the bombshell explode? And might such a detonation effect "a shift in the criteria of plausibility" (Sinfield, 822), and so begin to change what can be seen as politically feasible? Can a critical practice ever truly alter that which is too often taken for granted, that which "goes without saying"?

Words like "bombshell" both archive and vehiculate common sense; and they continue to have political effects—such as the easy production of a Moni-lyn. Even though a word like "bombshell" might explode the very common sense to which it is attached—i.e., this particular word could reveal how violence is inherent to the formation of gendered, racialized subjectivity in a capitalist democracy—it does not. But armed (as it were) with such an understanding, are we not better able to once again resume the challenge of Barrett's "perhaps" and oblige ourselves to think anew about the old?

FRIVOLITY AND FATALITY:
A BRIEF HISTORY OF THE BOMBSHELL

In the seventeenth century, the word "bombshell" was coined to name a new weaponry in a kind of warfare in which incendiary vessels fell from the sky. It quickly became idiomatic, used for any unexpected, upsetting event that befell one, most often news associated with a letter. During the Depression in the United States, "bombshell" also became slang for a dangerous woman, generally a blonde, as in one of its first recorded uses, according to the OED: "Bonnie Parker was a rootin', tootin', whiskey-drinking blonde bombshell" (1949). Hollywood soon took up the blonde bombshell, and then, from the late 1940s through the early 1960s, brunette, exotic, and ethnic (racist) versions—e.g., Jane Russell, Dorothy Dandridge, and Sophia Loren—were also cultivated as complements to, or as satellites of, the white standard of the blonde.[17] Thus, while the "bombshell" is part of a racist dynamic,[18] it also signifies another, more literal sort of female "figure": the full-bosomed, narrow-waisted, full-hipped 36-24-36 (or 38-24-36 or 40-22-35 and so on) hourglass which became a dominant standard for the fashionable female figure into the early 1960s.[19]

As Susan Bordo has argued, this "figure" can be read as both a relic of late Victorian standards of maternal femininity and a reaction against the social and economic extravagances that came to be signified by, and associated with, the flatter profile of the flapper-figure.[20] However, upon Marilyn Monroe's death in 1962 there was a historically significant, rather abrupt interruption in the popularity of the bombshell, blonde or otherwise. Although Hugh Hefner's *Playboy* bunnies keep large breasts visible as a sexual fetish during the 1960s, Hollywood film roles and televisual vehicles for actresses who either had been deliberate parodies of Monroe—like Jayne Mansfield—or had been groomed by the studio to take Monroe's place—e.g., Sheree North, Lee Remick, and Kim Novak—already on the wane, dried up entirely. Burlesque as a particular circuit of bombshell striptease stage performance began to vanish,[21] while models such as Twiggy and actresses such as Audrey Hepburn and Mia Farrow brought the gamin, the waifish, and a kind of slim elegance not seen as prevalent since the 1920s back into prominence (Brumberg, 119–21). Thus, although blondeness as a sign of racial purity did not disappear during the 1960s—one thinks, for example, of Grace Kelly—the popular fetishization of the ample hourglass figure that Monroe said would no doubt serve as her epitaph, "here lies Marilyn Monroe—38-23-36," (McCann, 171) went into a kind of remission.

Such waxing and waning of the fashionable female form, from hourglass ampleness to life-threatening anorexia, has often been read as a text for the economic cycles of boom and bust that have marked the United States throughout the twentieth century. Much has been written about the breast as a sexual fetish or as a maternal signifier, particularly for the boom of post–World War II culture in which Momism was blamed for every social ill under the sun, and no doubt much more could be said about the relation between economic cycles and bodily fixations. But again, what concerns me here is the curious endurance of the "bombshell" as a sign for both the excessive frivolity and the excessive fatality of (female) sexuality—witness the infamously "late" Marilyn Monroe's wry comments on her cultural status as "The Body," such as "'Everyone's just laughing at me. I hate it. Big breasts, big ass, big deal. Can't I be anything else?'" (McCann, 173), or her observation that her hourglass "numbers" would serve as a most "fitting" obituary.[22] Such statements have served as anecdotal evidence for the circulation of common-sense narratives about the plain dumb idiocy and yet the real, if alien, fatality of flesh *per se,* to the point where Monroe's name is shorthand not only for sex, but also for both frivolity and flesh, as evidenced by the following quotations taken from two quite different political contexts, the first from conservative critic Barry Sanders and the second from queer theorist Eve Kosofsky Sedgwick:

> The highly literate writer knows how to deconstruct real space and time and reconstruct an imaginary universe through casting counter-factuals: "If Marilyn Monroe were president of the United States." Counter-factuals speak of a supreme, human arrogance, a profane IF set against the intolerable IS of God's creation. But an IF has sufficient power to negate even the fact of Kennedy's presidency with the *delightfully frivolous* notion of Marilyn's. For a moment, Kennedy is placed in doubt, or vanishes altogether. History turns tail and hides; the writer has something better up his sleeve. In our mind's eye we see Marilyn occupying the Oval Office. At this level, language carries all the dynamic charge of good fiction.[23]

> The Sonnets present fair youth-as-ingenue, as the *prerational, premoral, essentially prehuman creature* that it is not possible to resist, to understand, or to blame. *Like Marilyn Monroe, the youth makes the man viewing him feel old,* vitiated, and responsible, even as the man luxuriates in the presence (the almost promise) of youth and self-possession.[24]

Frivolity on the one hand, an alien, prehuman, irresistible fatality on the other, Monroe is a delightful "doll" who came from "outer space" (Mills, 44), who was also cited for the genius of her flesh impact on film, an impact that was likened to light itself, to the radiance and sublime luminosity reported in descriptions of the first Trinity tests.

Marilyn Monroe was, of course, deliberately groomed to play (and helped to produce herself as) the quintessential comic-yet-dangerous blonde bombshell, even if she did ask, in her last interview, not to be made into a thing or a joke.[25] Rendered a commodity,[26] and remembered within that form, the "new blonde bombshell" of 1951 (Mills, 25) was the "it girl" of her time; she restaged Harlow, Dietrich, and Clara Bow;[27] she was "Mae West, Theda Bara and Bo Peep" (Monroe, 90), a sexual rocket-bomb for the Cold-War, atomic-bomb generation.[28] As photographer Cecil Beaton once enthused, Monroe was

> the wonder of the age . . . as spectacular as the silvery shower of a Vesuvius fountain . . . she had rocketed from obscurity to become our post-war sex symbol—the pin-up girl of an age. And whatever press agentry or manufactured illusion may have lit the fuse, it is her own weird genius that sustained her flight. . . . she's American and it's very clear that she is—she's very good that way; one has to be local to be universal. (Arnold, 32, 71)

161

Beaton's description pinpoints how Monroe was, as Richard Dyer notes, not only something like "a household word for sex" (Dyer, 23) but also an ambiguous, sometimes adored and often maligned emblem of America in the 1950s, that "blatant decade: cars grew fins; neon signs became an art form; pop music discovered the electric guitar and turned into rock and roll; the Yankees won the pennant year after year after year; and the Russians exploded record mega-tonnage of nuclear weapons" (Mills, 11). She was an American "Saint Marilyn," and yet a "cruel child tearing off butterfly wings . . . gay, mean, proud and inscrutable";[29] she kept whole film ensembles waiting, or, as Billy Wilder once quipped, "You can always figure a Monroe picture runs an extra few hundred thousand because she's coming later. It demoralizes the whole company. It's like trench warfare. You sit and sit, waiting for something to happen. When are the shells going to explode?" (Mills, 84).

Thus was Monroe positioned like the atomic bomb itself—"her very body was a white beam of truth"[30]—as the spectacular best and the spectacular worst the nation had to offer. Indeed, such descriptions of Monroe obsessively situate her as absurd, atomic, and American: absurd as a "frightened waitress in a diner" (Jack Paar), a "baby doll" (Jane Russell), all foam. Yet also dangerously Vesuvian, "a shimmering, molten wraith" (Eve Arnold) with an "electric something . . . she seemed to shine like the sun" (June Haver); "a flash of white" (Lena Pepitone) with "the face of a beautiful ghost" (Dame Edith Sitwell), who gave her attention to any information on how to improve one's body; long before jogging and weightlifting became regular activities for the healthy American woman, Monroe practiced both; she read whatever she could get her hands on about the body, from the work of the Renaissance anatomist Vesalius to Mabel Elsworth Todd's idiosyncratic book, *The Thinking Body* (recommended to her by one of her early drama coaches, Michael Chekhov) (Spoto, 190). She was also an All-American, linked, as she was, to baseball through her marriage to Joltin' Joe DiMaggio in 1954, and then to American high "art" when the Bombshell married the Brain,[31] playwright Arthur Miller, in 1956.[32] Photographer Eve Arnold's comments sum up such observations. Monroe, she claims, was regarded as an ordinary girl who became the "icon enshrined in the workman's toolbox" (Arnold, 20), a symbol of democracy. There was

> a glow about her: skin, fingernails, toenails are all translucently silvery. Everything about her becomes exaggerated. Finding that her nose photographs a bit long, she learns to drop her lip so that the shadow cast by her nose seems shorter. This gives her a slight tremor, a look of expectancy that adds to the sexiness. Later she will add the pursed lips, the open

mouth. This so affected her imitators that, going through fashion pictures of the '50s, you find yourself looking at so many open-mouthed models who seem to be gasping for breath that you wonder whether you've wandered into an aquarium. (Arnold, 17)

Monroe was as American as the atom bomb; she was considered absurd, mindless, and as alien as a fish—or a mermaid.[33] Her treatment as the bombshell of her time demonstrates that while the very stuff of reality itself is presumed to preside in "the" body—i.e., a reality so real that it "goes without saying,"[34] a reality often represented by that most absolute of realities, death—the body is also the site from which laughter is launched. Such laughter is the symptom of the knowingness of flesh, the "carnal knowledge" which film captures so well—because the "body" is not mindless; consciousness and flesh are interdependent and flesh does "know," it is articulate, it has impact—as jokes about men who think so much with the head below the belt indicate. The bombshell is a signifier of such knowledge and it participates in an anxious logic: it indexes a common-sense script about sex in which anyone primarily identified with flesh or sex will be located at the Cartesian ground zero of the supposedly mindless body, a fatal site at which, nevertheless, knowledge sits and from which hilarity— or joy—often erupts.

"She had no common sense . . ." (*Timebends*, 359)

As an emblem of both hilarity and fatality, then, Monroe exemplified the joyous, excessive plenty of the so-called American dream in the 1950s and the deadly price to be paid for it—or as Arthur Miller writes, "she knew she could roll into a party like a grenade and wreck complacent couples with a smile, and she enjoyed this power, but it also brought back the old sinister news that nothing whatsoever could last" (*Timebends*, 359). This statement remarks upon how Marilyn Monroe came to define—indeed inhabit—the word "bombshell" for the postwar, postatomic generation. At the same time, the statement situates her as part of a historically older, common-sense narrative about "the beautiful and the damned,"[35] a story of the inevitable demise of the beautiful or famous—which is, of course, a story about fate, usually the fate of Edgar Allen Poe's beautiful woman. The doom-of-fated-beauty story has served countless American novelists, dramatists, and filmmakers well, from the culturally "serious" domain of Hawthorne or James[36] to mass-culture versions endlessly repeated for a whole range of figures who have died, as the common saying goes, before their time, from Sylvia Plath, whom Jacqueline Rose calls the "Marilyn Monroe of the literati,"[37] to actor River Phoenix. And Monroe's demise did call forth a slew of popular elegies about "the beautiful and the torment-ed," as *Vogue* named her in Bert Stern's fashion-shoot turned memorial,[38] although up to that point the press had been increasingly hostile to her own attempts to remake herself as something other than the dumb blonde whom gentlemen preferred. Suddenly dead, however, she became the essence of a lost joy.[39] Once no more than a conniving idiot, she was made over into a "lively, intelligent woman" (McCann, 1) whose buoyancy about sex had had a "bracing candor" (*Timebends*, 381). In death she became the lovely child who never had the chance to grow up, a psychiatric mess who had needed help and hadn't gotten any.

Indeed, her death at the age of thirty-six from an overdose of barbiturates has been associated with dark conspiracy theories linking Hollywood, Ken-nedy, the CIA, the FBI, and the Mob. Repeated accusations that the LAPD's original investigation "had not been a marvel of thoroughness"[40] prompted a reinvestigation in the 1980s, and has provoked a morass of narratives about "what really happened" the night of August 4, 1962, a night recounted, dis-cussed, and dissected in popular texts such as Anthony Summer's 1985 *Marilyn Monroe: American Goddess* and Donald H. Wolfe's 1998 *The Last Days of Marilyn Monroe*. Still, the coroner's original legal finding of "probable suicide" stands. None of the nonfictional accounts constructed over the last thirty years— neither those that have quarreled with the story of Monroe's death as preor-dained, nor those that at-tempt to correct the image of "Little Miss Bubble-head" (Mills, 56)—have put much of a dent in the endurance of such common-sense stories about her, even when those stories are contradic-tory. No factual account has set the record straight once and for all, al-though gradually the various accounts have shifted the ground of com-mon sense about her, from the elegiac version of beauty lost to the more sinister version of beauty murdered.

But whether monster or angel, victim or vamp, Monroe remains prima-rily a "candle in the wind"[41] who might have had "a mind out of the ordi-nary"[42] but who didn't have the good sense to come in out of the rain; a basically intelligent woman who lacked that most basic American form of knowledge, common sense: "Many people commented on her quick wit and native intelligence, but no one ever accused her of having any com-mon sense" (Mills, 14). Yet, if she lacked common sense, not only has Monroe-as-bombshell produced *a* common sense, but her life's "story" has also given rise to—and continues to sustain—a lot of common sense. You can try, as Gloria Steinem did, to rescue the supposedly "real" Norma Jean from the objectification of The Body;[43] you can reprint forensic evidence about official discrepancies extant in the LAPD's investigation, FBI files, and coroner's reports, as *Crypt 33* and *The Last Days of Marilyn Monroe* do, or ransack archives, yet despite or perhaps *because of* these counter-narratives, both the script of fated, narcissistic doom and the force of Monroe-as-floozy—that giggling bombshell whose performances define the meaning of nonsense—remain stubbornly intact.

MAKE-UP

So while we might eventually learn to take some blondes seriously, this particular blonde is not a likely candidate[44]—which doesn't mean, however, that Monroe wasn't and isn't "taken," and quite seriously, if one means by this colloquialism that she's been exploited, dead and alive, for every ounce of flesh and every last dime and nickel. At the same time, it would seem that establishing a truth—whether it be an economic truth about the exploitation of her labor, buried in her bank statements; or a historical truth about her relations with the Kennedy family, buried in an archive; or even the so-called biological truth, still buried in a Westwood, California, cemetery crypt—isn't a particularly effective means of nailing down "the" truth. True-life, supposedly real narratives about "Norma Jean" don't impair the ability of the "Marilyn Monroe" bombshell to signify a common sense that says sex is just naturally frivolous.

As Richard Dyer persuasively demonstrates, Monroe's specific popularity resided in her ability to combine "naturalness *and* overt sexuality, notably in a series of gags that became known as Monroeisms" (Dyer, 35). The ground for the naturalization of sex as frivolous had been laid down much earlier than the 1950s, of course, and this naturalization has had a long life since. Significantly, Miller calls his wife a sweet and sheer force of nature, "the astonishing signal of liberation and its joys. Out of the muck, the flower" (*Timebends,* 381)—an observation that is at once couched in the terms of a yet-to-come 1960s sexual revolution and lifted almost verbatim from Stephen Crane's *Maggie: A Girl of the Streets*.[45] In fact, Monroe's endurance as a kind of cultural shorthand for the frivolity and fatality encoded in the word "bombshell" should be likened to the endurance of "sex as a political issue," to quote Foucault. Sex, like Monroe as a visual icon, remains too much with us, and if "we as a culture cannot forget Marilyn Monroe, so we make her up again and again" (Baty, 4), it seems that what matters is *not* the truth. What matters is the make-up.

Now, Monroe may be a rather obvious symbol of "make-up"—by which I mean to indicate both the process of production and a commodity product. But I think it is worth remembering that as cosmetic ad and studio-system product, Monroe was on, and of, the assembly line. Curiously, too, Antonio Gramsci once argued that the assembly line, a Fordist mode of labor, would require a "new type of man" in whom "the sexual instinct has been suitably regulated and rationalized." He also cautioned that "until women can attain not only a genuine independence in relation to men but also a new way of conceiving themselves and their role in sexual relations, the sexual question will remain."[46] Back in 1931, however, Gramsci was quite leery of any sexual regulation because, he said, it could "make way for unhealthy 'feministic' deviations of the worst sense of the word" (Gramsci, 298). Despite this statement, however, contemporary feminism might still find his observations about "genuine independence" rather bracing, given the global, ongoing "traffic in women"[47] as reflected by statistics on the rise in sex work, particularly in impoverished countries such as Thailand, or even given the ongoing traffic in Monroe as lucrative commodity.[48]

Yet I would caution that, as Karen Newman has argued, the feminist "reiteration and critique of the exchange paradigm is a disavowal of the object position and at the same time an over-valuing of subjectivity."[49] Using work by both Leo Bersani and Theodor Adorno, Newman demonstrates how feminist arguments that continue to decry the "objectification" of women—an objectification of which Monroe is often cited as an example—cannot see how the object position might be made to exert a seductive lure, a lure that could potentially shatter the sovereignty assumed to inhere in the subject position. Indeed, Newman's argument not only continues the work begun by Gayle Rubin's influential "The Traffic in Women," it also attempts to break the impasse of the once-fruitful "traffic" paradigm. What is crucial for feminism in Newman's argument, however, is more than simply a paradigm shift. What is at stake is veracity itself.

Why? To begin to explain this claim, I will start with a very bald example. In the legal game of "he said, she said," historically the "she" has had a harder time proving her case, no matter how much the "she" is legally granted the position of enunciating, sovereign subject. This is especially true when both sides of the conversation exert the force of a truth.[50] Such a case might be described, using Lyotard's term, as a *differend,* "a case of conflict between (at least) two parties, that *cannot be equitably resolved* for lack of a rule of judgment applicable to both arguments. One side's legitimacy does not imply the other's lack of legitimacy";[51] or, as Lyotard argues, a differend marks the site of a conflict wherein something true cannot, as yet, be put into words. "What is at stake," he continues, "in a literature, in a philosophy, in a politics perhaps, is to bear witness to differends by finding idioms for them" (*Differend,* xi). What the concept of the differend allows for here is the conceptualization of radical alteration whereby a different idiom for "new" truths might be forged and, in turn, disrupt the sediment of inequitable common sense in which a rule of judgment is mired. Or to return to Michèlle Barrett, if it might be "better, perhaps, that we oblige ourselves to think with new and more precise concepts, rather than mobilizing the dubious resonances of the old," then perhaps the differend, as a concept, along with Newman's argument, offers us a means to do so.

Indeed, one might even pause here to consider whether "second-wave feminism" wasn't a site of conflict from which a new idiom of sexual inequality arose in the face of what might have seemed a political differend. Although women had been granted the vote in 1921 (after at least a century of conflict) and thus granted, in the language of constitutional law, the legal status of full and equal citizens, by the mid-1960s it had become more than clear to many women that they did not enjoy, in fact, anything like "equal rights" in domains other than that of the Constitution. One might, then, see the conflicts enacted at the time between activists and those who opposed them as conflicts "between (at least) two parties" that could not, at the time, "*be equitably resolved* for lack of a rule of judgment applicable to both arguments." Feminism might be described, then, as a collection of oppositional idioms, all of which attempted to speak to existing states—economic, social, and cultural—of inequality, idioms of ongoing sexual exploitations and injustices, through which previously unvoiced or indeed unvoiceable grievances, grievances that could find no means of equitable address under the existing rule of Constitutional judgment, were increasingly voiced. Could it not be argued that the public feminism of the mid-1960s to late 1970s functioned as an aggregate of idioms wherein a prevailing common sense about sex—say, questions about economics or the common sense spelled out by bombshell-as-embodied-by-Monroe—was once disputed? At least for a time.

However, at the present moment, common sense tells us that feminist discourses—third wave or no—are not viable as idioms in which to voice oppositional politics. Much feminist terminology, indeed, has been incorporated into existing rules of judgment, to the extent that an understanding about sexual equality has been woven into the fabric of common sense. Title IX and the resulting rise in women's sports might be construed as a legal result of a new common-sense understanding about women. And yet, we are told, feminism *tout court* is old hat, it is too narrow, it is irredeemably classist and racist; oh, and by the way, Marxism, too, is moribund, especially "after the fall" of the Berlin Wall in 1988, and psychoanalysis, well, that's just as dead as poor old Sigmund himself. We don't need any of these "extreme" conceptual idioms anymore because plain old common sense about such matters now prevails.

Yet take note: in the historical context of these multiple invalidations, it is interesting just how often any claim to validity has had to dress itself up as a clearly identifiable "*body* of knowledge" or to offer hard, incontrovertible, and material evidence, as if in litigation—as in the controversies over whether Nobel Laureate Rigoberta Menchù or Binjimin Wilkomirski have lied in their widely acclaimed and prize-winning memoirs;[52] to appear unified, unambiguous, and objective, to pronounce itself the "real and only truth" as opposed to memory, illusion, or fantasy, even as there is an ever-increasing economic demand for the proliferation and dissemination of information-as-capital, one that requires endless amounts of novelty, of making-up.

But again and again, demands are made for the real, the true, the authentic (his)story (Marilyn *was* a bitch, wasn't she? She *was* abused, wasn't she? She said as much, didn't she?). Authority and security appear to reside in making these kinds of final judgments, particularly through the truth-claims of actual experience. But as critic Patricia Hill Collins notes, authenticity these days is a "hot commodity," and so "breaking silence by claiming the authority of experience has less oppositional impact than in the past"—particularly in the context of a capitalist political economy wherein a "synergistic relationship" exists between people and knowledge as commodities so that "knowledge becomes inseparable from the container in which it is packaged, namely, Black and White bodies."[53] Further, if "[r]eality," as Lyotard has claimed, "is not about what is 'given' to this or that 'subject,' it is a state of the referent (that about which one speaks) which results from the effectuation of establishment procedures defined by a unanimously agreed-upon protocol" (*Differend*, 4), then it would seem imperative to change the agreed-upon protocol in a sustained, *collective* fashion, rather than continuing to produce ever more authenticity to fill the needs of the market.

In other words, when reality becomes so utterly transparent as to be rendered only as an unquestionable given, or truth an object subject to no serious dispute, then it is confused with the referent and, as Lyotard notes, "so speaks positivism" (*Differend*, 28), a positivism that relies upon the essential universality of a common-sense truth—as if the violent breach opened up at the site of the formation of the subject through language might be defused by a utopic fusion whereby the referent is collapsed with the real. And one of the most significant problems posed by such a collapse of referent and reality—or, if you will, a problem posed by the substitution of a universalized common sense for new forms of knowledge—is how the status of "truth" will be determined. For example, the Holocaust, as Jacqueline Rose points out, has often been used as "the historical event which puts under greatest pressure—or is most readily available to put under such pressure—the concept of linguistic figuration." When "faced with the reality of the Holocaust, the idea that there is an irreducibly figurative dimension to all language is an evasion, or denial, of the reality of history itself" (Rose, 207). But paradoxically, as Lyotard observes, such a positivistic refusal to know the power of language can be, and has been, used to make the Holocaust itself seem illusory. For example, in 1981, Faurisson claimed that

> "I have tried in vain to find a single former deportee capable of proving to me that he had really seen, with his own eyes, a gas chamber" (Faurisson in Pierre Vidal-Naquet, 1981: 81). To have "really seen with his own eyes" a gas chamber would be the condition which gives one the authority to say that it exists and to persuade the unbeliever. Yet it is still necessary to prove that the gas chamber was used to kill at the time it was seen. The only acceptable proof that a gas chamber was used to kill is that one died from it. But if one is dead, one cannot testify that it is on account of the gas chamber—The plaintiff complains that he has been fooled about the existence of gas chambers, fooled that is, about the so-called Final Solution. His argument is: in order for a place to be identified as a gas chamber, the only eyewitness I will accept would be a victim of this gas chamber; now, according to my opponent, there is no victim that is not dead; otherwise this gas chamber would not be what he or she claims it to be. There is, therefore, no gas chamber. (*Differend*, 3–4)

That Faurisson's demand for authenticity along the most positivistic lines —to really see with one's own eyes—nevertheless provides evidence for the frightening power of language is, of course, part of Lyotard's point. History still is, after all, narrated—as conservative Barry Sanders clearly understands when he writes that one rousing good "if" and "[h]istory turns tail and hides; the writer has something better up his sleeve. In our mind's eye we see Marilyn occupying the Oval Office. At this level, language carries all the dynamic charge of good fiction" (Sanders, 56). In this light, fact is *always* a matter of idiom, despite those who devoutly wish otherwise, and so veracity, which depends on what is or will become a matter of fact, remains also a matter of whose history can fit established protocols of adjudication. To put this differently, Marilyn, having the legal rights accorded her by the Constitution, could have occupied the Oval Office. She was a citizen of the United States. But that was not her history, and so the picture is mere foolishness—isn't it? Or—?

Stephanie A. Smith

AFTER THE FALL: THE DRAMA

Positivist logic is, after all, a stubborn logic. And history—or experience or autobiography—is judged, especially in the popular press, by positivistic standards. The autobiographical "I," for example, must present an absolute historical veracity, a veracity that often depends upon the positivist logic of the true, authentic eyewitness, the victim of a proven trauma. Memory and illusion, fantasy and amnesia, these hold no legitimate place. As a result of such logic, however, history, in fiction or poetry, is viewed as "either dearth or surplus, either something missing . . . or something which shouldn't be there" (Rose, 206). While Jacqueline Rose may refer here specifically to those critiques of Sylvia Plath's poetry that have claimed the poet had no business speaking of Nazism, the same can be said about critiques of Arthur Miller's autobiographical play that isn't supposed to be autobiographical, *After the Fall*, because Miller is supposed to have both abused the real Marilyn Monroe by making her over into the likeness of sexpot songbird Maggie—a version of history as surplus—and to have trivialized both the atomic bomb and the Holocaust, by putting sex on stage against the backdrop of Hiroshima and the concentration camps— a version of history as dearth.

Almost more than anyone else who was associated with Monroe or who wrote about her, Arthur Miller has been condemned for telling both too, too much and too, too little. Any number of Monroe narratives—from the academic to the pornographic—exist, but Miller's 1962 stage play, *After the Fall*, is still often presumed to be the most tasteless display. So shameless was it considered at the time of its first performance that it was said James Baldwin "was seen stalking up the aisle and out of the theater before the end" (Weatherby, 221). Attacked repeatedly as "an exploitative exposé of Miller's relationship with Marilyn Monroe"[54] despite the playwright's protest that the play was not autobiographical,[55] *After the Fall* set off a firestorm of press in January 1964, in part because it cannot *not* be read as autobiography, even if it is also clearly a negotiation of "the distinction between autobiography and fiction" (Savran, 56).

To be reductive here: common sense insists that nonfiction *must* tell *the* truth, while fiction should, instead, merely ring true. Even in a publishing era that has seen the rise of a lucrative genre called "creative nonfiction"— a form that is, in part, the creation of two writers who took up Monroe as a subject, Truman Capote and Norman Mailer[56]—*After the Fall*, as a drama, still runs aground on the distinction between fact and fiction. I hasten to add here that I am not arguing for a complete breakdown of that distinction, particularly given the troubling ethics of historical truth. There remains a difference between fact and fiction; gas chambers did exist, Kosovar Albanians have been executed, Apollo 12 did land on the Moon; and autobiography is a genre that presumes to present a historical truth. Drama is presumed to be a performance only. And yet— Performance must also have truth, must it not, if it is to be respected or revered? But the autobiographical demands that have been made on *After the Fall* as a *drama* are very curious demands to make about a drama which, from the outset, "takes place in the mind, thought, and memory" of a retired lawyer, Quentin.[57] Staged as an internal, psychic "trial" of memory that shares its scene of interrogation with that of the "talking cure," the subject who speaks, Quentin, is split into multiple positions of enunciation; he investigates himself in an attempt to assimilate what he finds to be the unassimilable betrayals of history. He wants to understand his own political and personal history, as well as that of the Holocaust; he wishes to come to terms with traumatic events through which he has lived and after which, he believes, any prior concept of personal, sociopolitical, or cultural innocence has been rendered moot. For Quentin, the fact of the Holocaust and the fact of America's creation and deployment of the atomic bomb (it is significant that Miller regards both as central to this play's genesis [*Timebends,* 516]) divide a then from a now. Before Hiroshima and Nagasaki, before Auschwitz and Dachau, there were the illusions of progress, innocence, honor; afterward, nothing. The Fordism that saw a functional apogee in the Nazi concentration camps has left a blank for Quentin where there was once a meaningful (his)story.[58] As a lawyer, a proponent of rational discourse, Quentin treats Auschwitz as if ventriloquizing Adorno, who, as Lyotard remarks, "pointed out that 'Auschwitz' is an abyss in which the philosophical genre of Hegelian speculative discourse seems to disappear, because the name 'Auschwitz' invalidates the presupposition of that genre, namely that all that is real is rational, and all that is rational is real."[59]

Such devastation challenges any rational, universalist narrative of progress, and so challenges all narratives of causation. But while Quentin appears to know this, he also resists it. He can look "back at when there seemed to be a kind of plan," when everything seemed so simple, right and wrong, no confusions, as if it were "some kind of paradise," while simultaneously seeking a cure for the nothingness he knows is there. As he says, on the day we "stop becoming . . . the word 'Now' is like a bomb through the window, and it ticks" (*Fall,* 47). Quentin is referring, here, to the fact that he viewed his dead wife, Maggie, as the "Now" of being; she lacked common sense about causality, she lived "where nothing whatsoever is ordained" (*Fall*, 48). But his leap into her Now reveals to him how the immanence of being is as deadly as a bomb, because the "Now" denies the truth that humans are all separate, murderous beings "after the fall," and all of us are guilty.

Desire, or what Quentin calls the "truth" of "symmetrical, lovely skin, undeniable" (*Fall*, 48) as represented by Maggie—"Cause all I am," she says, " . . . is love. And sex" (*Fall*, 124)—becomes as lethal as a nuclear blast if untempered by an acknowledgment of universal guilt. As Quentin says to his terrified, suicidal wife, "If you could only say . . . I have been hurt by a long line of men but I have cooperated with my persecutors. . . . Do the hardest thing of all," he exhorts her—"see your own hatred, and live!" (*Fall*, 120).

In Miller's view, then, Maggie lacks a narrative of universal guilt after the fall and this is, finally, intolerable. Such fatalism is familiarly Biblical: Maggie is Eve and Quentin has fallen into the temptation to forget history—"to violate the past, and the past is holy and its horrors are holiest of all!" (*Fall*, 97). But as David Savran notes, when Quentin demands that Maggie understand herself as both the victim and the oppressor, he creates a problem, because "by demanding that oppressor and victim be telescoped into a single figure, *After the Fall* denies historical difference" so that "the concentration camp is simply a grotesque extension of the nuclear family" (Savran, 70) and historical time becomes the forever "Now" of sacred time. The play reasserts the necessity of a universalist narrative of (masculinized) wholeness (Savran, 71), and thus forecloses the possibility of other stories and different, perhaps as yet unarticulated idioms. The play would rather reassert a humanist, bourgeois subject, suitably chastened by his guilty contact with the abyss of "Now," than face the possibility of the "nothingness"[60] (as Quentin sees it) of being—or a Real—that is.

Suicide, in this context, is an outrage and immoral, not because Maggie has died but because Quentin has made Maggie (Marilyn) solely, sanely, individually *responsible* for her own death, and so guilty of both suicide and murder—or as Quentin claims, "A suicide kills two people, Maggie. . . . You've been setting me up for a murder" (*Fall*, 116–18). But if, as Michel Foucault has argued, "We . . . are in . . . a society 'with a sexuality'" that has an "insidious presence . . . everywhere an object of excitement and fear at the same time" (Foucault, 147–48), and therefore a society in which the deployment of sexuality makes suicide both "strange and yet so persistent and constant in its manifestations, and consequently so difficult to explain as being due to particular circumstances or individual accidents" (Foucault, 139), then suicide must be something other than an individual act—

as Maggie herself knows when she says, drunkenly, "Takes two to tango, kid" (*Fall*, 116). Indeed, as Foucault puts it, suicide is "one of the first astonishments of a society in which political power had assigned itself the task of administering life" (Foucault, 139). It *must* have as collective a dimension as genocide. Perhaps, then, Maggie/Marilyn's fatality should be read as a symptom of *collective* trauma in a society where sex, unless undertaken as a serious job of reproductive labor, has been naturalized as a mere frivolity?

AFTER THE FALL: THE BOMB

Indeed, despite the ways in which *After the Fall* bombed as a drama, the "blur [of] the distinction between the political and the domestic" (Savran, 61) that it accomplishes by working through the link between society and sexuality, between the Bomb and the Bombshell, might seem strategic: for one thing, the claim that "the personal is political," a radical statement about the frequently occluded relation between the domestic and the political, had yet to become a rallying cry in 1964. To force a visible, dramatic, even spectacular relation between the effects of the nuclear family and nuclear holocaust, long before Greenham Common, could be read, at this distance, as a necessary move. Given that the possibility of planetary annihilation is part of the narrative of nuclear holocaust, and that the atomic bomb has been represented as humanity's drive toward mass suicide, the connections become harder to disavow. And, as previously noted, Monroe was—and is, still—obsessively represented in descriptive terms that associate platinum with plutonium; her "whiter than white" radiance is the sublime beauty of an atomic blast. *After the Fall*'s attempt to force this association between the bomb and the bombshell to mean something "serious" as opposed to "silly" should therefore not go unremarked. In his psychic fusion of Bombshell with Bomb, Quentin wants to reveal, not only to himself but to those with whom he has lived and whom he has internalized as parts of himself, that the presumption of a white-clad innocence in a murderous world is finally more lethal than history itself.

Miller found, however, that this revelation could not unveil America's obsession with the blinding flash of its own treasured fantasy of political and cultural "pure" innocence, and so prove it deadly. Audience and critic alike in 1964 did not accept Miller's truth that innocence is—as Lyotard also notes—a nothing: "It is impossible to establish one's innocence, in and of itself. It is a nothingness" (Lyotard, 9). But Lyotard's use of the word "nothingness" and Miller's use of the concept are strikingly different, and this difference, I think, is crucial. Because to Miller—like Quentin—nothingness is a complete blank, a fake, the terrible absence of the "Now"; to Lyotard innocence is in and of itself nothing, *not* because it is a fatal blank, but because innocence must needs take meaning within a symbolic system. It does not exist as a universal given, outside a system of representation.

Now, according to Miller, his play's reception showed him that "it was impossible to seriously consider innocence lethal" (*Timebends,* 534). Instead, many asserted a "true" Marilyn Monroe over and against the character Maggie, both despite and because of the fact that Elia Kazan and Arthur Miller's staging of Barbara Loden as Maggie—their insistence, for example, that she wear a teased platinum wig—had made it, in fact, impossible to disassociate the historical blonde bombshell of 1951 from the lethal, fictional siren of the fatal "Now."[61] In this fusion of bomb with bombshell, *After the Fall* does attempt to reveal that the *jouissance* of sex is a serious matter. But the play also reveils that knowledge in a cloak of common sense. It installs a universal truth about being and "original sin" as a reality and invokes the seriousness of death in the form of a suicide in order to dispel the effect of the bombshell's frivolity. According to Quentin, then, a universal admission of human hatred must take the place of the innocence—in this case, Maggie's—which is a fatal delusion, a none, a nothing. And surely Marilyn Monroe had hated to be "taken" as a nothing, "a kind of joke taking herself seriously" (*Timebends,* 532); she wanted to be "taken" seriously. But, Miller says, "coming out of the forties and the fifties, she was proof that sexuality and seriousness could not coexist in America's psyche, were hostile, mutually rejecting opposites in fact. At the end, she had had to give way and go back to swimming naked in a pool in order to make a picture" (*Timebends,* 532). Even when "her life would be *taken* up by a writer whose stock-in-trade was the joining of sexuality and the serious . . . he could only describe what was fundamentally a merry young whore given to surprising bursts of classy wit" (*Timebends,* 532).

The professional jealousies and personal aspersions evident in Miller's remarks aside (he is speaking here of Norman Mailer), let us pause here a moment to ask some potentially frivolous questions. Why must one assume that swimming naked in a pool means that Monroe gave way to her status as a joke? What's wrong with being "merry" about sex? Why isn't laughter a serious matter—why must nothing be, well, *just* nothing, rather than an indication of that which has been socially, politically, and culturally designated as that which is silly and does not matter? We might do well to remember that "Philosophical style," as Derrida writes,

congenitally leads to frivolity. But the reason for this is logical, epistemological, ontological. If philosophical writing is frivolous, that is because
the philosopher cannot fulfill his statements. He knows nothing, he has
nothing to say, and he complicates, subtilizes, refines stylistic efforts to
mask his ignorance.[62]

Nothing—a space, a gap, a silence, a lack, a blank page, or the force of
laughter: surely all, as many feminists have repeatedly claimed, are something?

In *The Four Fundamental Concepts of Psycho-analysis*, Lacan reports a curious anecdote that he insists is "a true story"[63] about himself as a young
intellectual who wanted "desperately to get away, see something different,
throw myself into something practical, something physical, in the country
say, or at the sea" (Lacan, 95)—the philosopher throwing himself at nature
(or the brain throwing himself at the bombshell?).[64] One of the fishermen
with whom he sets sail, Petit-Jean,

> pointed out to me something floating on the surface of the waves. It was
> a small can, a sardine can. It floated there in the sun, a witness to the
> canning industry, which we, in fact, were supposed to supply. It glittered
> in the sun. And Petit-Jean said to me— "*You see that can? Do you see it? Well,
> it doesn't see you!*" (Lacan, 95)

Petit-Jean finds the glittering can's indifference funny because, as an intellectual, Lacan "appeared to those fellows who were earning their livings
with great difficulty, in the struggle with what for them was a pitiless nature
. . . like nothing on earth." Lacan proceeds, however, to show how the
"nothing" of the "I" (eye) illustrates the "relation of the subject with the
domain of vision," or as he says, "the picture, certainly, is in my eye. But I
am not in the picture." Indeed, the can *does* see, because

> that which is light looks at me, and by means of that light in the depths
> of my eye, something is painted . . . something that introduces was elided
> in the geometral relation—the depth of field, with all its ambiguity and
> variability, which is in no way mastered by me. It is rather it that grasps
> me, solicits me at every moment, makes the landscape something other
> than a landscape, something other than what I have called the picture.
>
> The correlative of the picture, to be situated in the same place as it,
> that is, outside, is the point of the gaze, while that which forms the
> mediation from the one to the other, that which is between the two, is
> something of another nature than geometrical, optical space, something
> that plays an exactly reverse role, which operates, not because it can be
> traversed, but on the contrary because it is opaque—I mean the screen.
> (Lacan, 96)

I quote Lacan at length here because both the anecdotal citation and his psychoanalytic exposition seem peculiarly apt when one recalls that Monroe's "weird genius" was essentially filmic: as a (screen) spectacle of pure light, like the diamond that became her trademark or like the silver-nitrate, later platinum, atomic whiteness of her presentation, she is luminosity itself, a necessary and indifferent light, that "space of light . . . that gleam of light" which lay at the "heart" of Lacan's story— "in short, the point of gaze always participates in the ambiguity of the jewel." And if the point of gaze is in the picture, says Lacan, it is always in the form of the screen—that which is opaque and cannot be traversed (Lacan, 95–97).

If we follow Lacan's logic, Monroe-as-atomic-bomb(shell) reads as a filter for how the object—as Karen Newman wishes to insist—and indeed objectification as a process are central to desire and thus to the formation of the "I." The iridescent sardine can—that "witness to the canning industry," that gleam of light—like the bombshell as a word and as a trope, both insists upon and studiously blinds us to the knowledge of the necessary flashpoint of objectification. This is not only because of the various pertinent historical implications for Americans—for example, any acknowledgment that people *are* also constructed things raises the spectre of race-slavery from the grave—but also because such an acknowledgment, though it is an understanding of the lack at the heart of signification, strikes at the unifying labor of the ego, and so also at the myth of American individualism. It points to how the sovereign subject, who is supposedly that "unique individual" of universal humanism, like the shining "star" or the serious artist, is always also and must be "taken" as an object. But in a relentless capitalist economy, where the object is always a commodity conceived as a product of exploited labor, it is difficult to know that you are always more a (no) "thing" than not.

Finally, then, I would argue that the vernacular usage of the bombshell to signify sex naturalized as frivolity both marks and deflects the trauma of the subject's entry into the Symbolic precisely because the common usage and continued circulation of the word *bombshell* serve to deflect an understanding of the bursting violence of jouissance at the heart of subjectivity: the necessary trauma that is the violent coming-into-signification formed around the kernel of the Real, in which (sexual) desire is shaped and from which it erupts, like laughter. In the bombshell, and in any attempt to come to terms with it, particularly as exemplified by my discussion of Marilyn Monroe, one finds condensed common sense about the mind and the body, the serious and the frivolous, the factual and the fictional, the lively and the fatal—and one sees how the distinctions between these pairings are constructed through reference to (female) sexuality, and, in fact, constitute in no small degree what is taken as that (female) sexuality. Thus the word "bombshell" both archives and vehiculates the common sense that produces a Moni-lyn in 1998, even as it might also explode that common sense. But the word will not perform this explosive labor *precisely* because common usage requires us to forget the violence that inheres in it, and so, indeed, to forget the shattering, structuring violence of language itself. Instead, the bombshell persists, to haunt the collective imagination—as Sammy Davis, Jr. once said, Monroe "hung like a bat in men's minds" (Mills, 37); or as S. Paige Baty claims, "Icon, American dream, dangerous passageway, corpse, goddess—she appears in all these forms and more. She radiates the stuff of history in our time, mass-mediated memory" (Baty, 179).

Oddly, however, Baty's concluding claim—as well as my own, if I should rest here—also seems to go without saying; it bears a curious and wearying *intellectual* stasis, as if in witness once again to how the radiant bombshell both gives evidence to, and yet also carries forward, a strenuous historical amnesia of the sort that American common sense now requires. And common sense will try to say that sex without "labor" is mere frivolity; that laughter is nothing, and history, although revered, is dead, while language must always be clear and useful; otherwise it is frivolous, in which case it is recondite. Such common-sense amnesia about the fact that common sense itself is a matter of history and language not only helps to produce universalist illusions, but is also necessary for a perpetuation of effects tied to the founding inequities—particularly but not exclusively economic—that subtend the trauma of the American dream at the close of the twentieth century.

Might it not be high time, then, to pay much closer attention to the rocket's red glare, to hear the bombs bursting in air, and wake up?

AFTERWORD: THE UNBROKEN CIRCLE OF ASSUMPTIONS TRUDIER HARRIS

Déjà vu. I am vacationing in Spain, returning to my hotel with bags of purchases in both hands. A man approaches me. He gestures that he will help me carry my bags. I say, "No thanks." He keeps walking beside me and insisting. He is speaking Spanish too quickly for me to comprehend his words, but his intentions become clear. He takes out his wallet, opens it, shows me money, points toward me and then back toward himself. I assume that my black female body has marked me as a prostitute—or at least as willing to become one. The man follows me for two more blocks to my hotel, constantly showing me his money and imploring my acquiescence. He scampers off quickly into the crowd when I ask the doorman to assist me in conveying that I am not the least bit interested.

Déjà vu. I am in line in the post office or grocery store or bank (take your pick), surrounded by a small sea of non-African American persons, and the clerk/cashier/teller announces that this particular line is closing. Sometimes it closes with me as the final customer and sometimes it closes just before me. My black body has again become the distinguishing marker for a point of separation. Whether it benefits me or causes me to wait longer, it is nonetheless the dividing marker.

Déjà vu. I am on a fellowship at a reputable research center with lots of other women, all of whom are European American except one. We routinely take breaks from our writing to share meals, play tennis, go to movies and plays, or otherwise entertain ourselves. My work is going well, and the breaks do not take away from it. A European American woman whose work is stalled is puzzled by and envious of my progress. She comes to my office almost every day to see what I have accomplished during the morning or afternoon. She remains puzzled that I can work and she cannot. Finally, perhaps in an effort to save her own presumed sense of superiority, she attributes my success to my blackness and what she sees as its accompanying strength. "You are a strong black woman," she essentially asserts in the paraphrase I am allowing her here, "and that's why you can play so hard and still keep writing." She does not seem capable of adding my intelligence into the equation, or my meticulously methodical work habits, or anything else that would attribute my progress to something more than the mere blackness of the skin I inhabit and the stereotypes that her culture has trained her to read into it.

Déjà vu. I am in an airport terminal restroom (or other public restroom). There are many women in front of me and even more behind, most of them usually European American. Finally, a door opens, and it is my turn to enter a stall. I enter. When I come out, the white woman next in line ignores the free stall that I have just vacated and that now has a conspicuously open door (the *only* open door), choosing instead to wait for a stall vacated by a white woman. The "she" of the moment apparently considers me dirty—by history, by present circumstances, and by my visibly black body. This has happened so frequently that I have come to expect it. Sadly, in one of the most recent occurrences of this phenomenon, it was a Latina woman who elected not to enter the stall I had just vacated.

Déjà vu. The list could go on. As the proverbial saying goes, if I had a dollar for every time my black body has elicited assumptions, or has been marked as deviant, or has been stereotyped, I probably could have retired to a small island in the Caribbean. Unfortunately, the impact of such assumptions can only be measured in intangible arenas, in new insights and a necessary transcendence, which ironically might approach the stereotype of the strength for which I have been repeatedly maligned, applauded, or erased. Yes, erased. It is easier for the frail white woman who plays tennis with me to attribute my level of play to excessive strength inherent

179

in the mystique of my supposed black genes than to conclude that her skills are simply inferior. Thus she effectively erases me from her mental field of further contemplation as far as tennis playing is concerned.

The brief journey through memory I have undertaken here is merely a fraction of the responses and reactions that this collection of essays elicited from me. The range of voices, writers, and issues that Debra Walker King has assembled in these pages is a powerful testament to how the world reads female bodies, how the owners of those bodies read themselves, and the psychological, physical, economic, and social consequences of such readings. These essays, which explore a mere fragment of the impact of body politics upon women, cry out for redress, reconstruction, revision, revolution. I felt Gloria Wade-Gayles's frustration and at times her anger at being categorized as a woman whom others judge to be too old to look as good as she does, too old to participate in certain activities, or too old to wear certain clothes or even to say certain things, and I celebrated the ways in which she has resolved those societally imposed issues of growing older. I found it noteworthy that one of the European American women included in the volume is openly lesbian and thereby slightly "other" to the hordes of white women who cause so much distress for brown and black women; her scientific research on women and her insistence that a gender factor operates in research isolated her in ways similar to those in which countless nonwhite women can be isolated in academia. I felt the humiliation that Asian and Latina women feel when they are the objects of sexual tourism, and I considered that black women constantly suffer those indignities as well—whether or not the males are "touring." I gained new insight into physical and linguistic victimization and containment from Stephanie A. Smith's extensive discussion of the Marilyn Monroe phenomenon in American culture. And I understood—and appreciated—the interpretive dynamics that African American and Japanese literature, treated by Debra Walker King, Maude Hines, and S. Yumiko Hulvey, enabled for furthering our understanding of how women have been represented through the ages and the current impacts of such representation.

This collection makes clear that the prohibitory or stereotypical markers that I so readily identify with blackness and African American women have their peculiar twists with almost all women of non-European origins (as well as with women of Spanish descent). Reading the collection supports an argument that browner women across races and cultures need to talk more to each other about these issues, rather than simply talking to the pages of the texts they create. I was somewhat surprised to discover, for example, that Coco Fusco and Nao Bustamante, the Latina artists whom

Rosemary Weatherston interviewed, respond to questions about their work as if Cuban and other Latina women are the primary objects of sexual tourism or of stereotypes of sexual promiscuity (though they do recognize the impact of the international sex trade on Asian women). As an African American woman saturated with at least a century of materials locating black women within such parameters of promiscuity, I wanted to see some intersection of the implications of transracial and cross-cultural stereotyping. What happens, for example, when an African American man goes to Cuba or Jamaica looking for the "hotblooded Latina" or the Caribbean woman of presumed easy virtue? Are the same sexual touristic dynamics operative, or do such men fall out of the picture because of presumed power and economic—not to mention racial—disadvantages? More immediately relevant to the positioning of women, what happens when an African American woman with sexual intentions goes to Cuba or Jamaica in an effort, à la Terry McMillan, to "get her groove back"? Do her race and nationality set her apart in Cuba, make her seem desperate in Jamaica?

Not only does the collection highlight the need for women of color—of all cultures and races—to talk with each other about how men stereotype them (and Debra Walker King cites one significant conference where such dialogue began), but it also raises an equally relevant, and much less discussed, issue: that of how women across these cultures where female bodies are politically maligned respond and react to each other. What fictions do Latina women perpetuate or create about African American, European American, or Asian female bodies? What fictions do African American women perpetuate or create about European American, Asian, or Latina female bodies? What fictions do Asian women perpetuate or create about Latina, African American, or European American female bodies? What fictions do European American women perpetuate or create about African American, Asian, or Latina female bodies? What fictions do straight women perpetuate or create about lesbian women, and what fictions do lesbian women perpetuate or create about nonlesbian women? One of the frequent stereotypes of women is that they keep other women in place for men. Is that the case here? Are women complicitous in ascribing certain traits to other women? For example, some nonblack women were tremendously annoyed with the publication of Toni Cade Bambara's *The Salt Eaters* (1980) and the discussion in it in which a group of black women assert that they can easily tell when black men have been "sleeping white," because "their rhythm is off." These particular black female characters thus stereotype white women as ineffectual sexual partners specifically for black men and perhaps for any men. In what ways do black, Hispanic,

Asian, and European American women perpetuate popular mythologies about their own bodies as well as about the bodies of one another?

I have just completed a book manuscript in which I address the issue of strong black female bodies and their representation in African American literature. In the historical background to that study, I discuss the ways in which black women are proud of the larger hips that mark so many of them, or of the physical strength that separates them from what they perceive to be fragile southern white women (especially in child-rearing and housekeeping responsibilities), or of the larger bodies that enable them to perform gospel songs with such force and power. This historical pattern is marked in the literature in countless ways, but it is most noteworthy in such characters as Toni Morrison's Sethe (who defies most human limitations by escaping from slavery six months pregnant and immediately after a whipping for an earlier escape attempt), Toni Cade Bambara's Velma Henry (who does the work of *seven* people before she is driven to attempt suicide) and Gloria Naylor's Mama Day (whose supernatural strength transcends her small body and enables her to kill those who would destroy her family). Are there comparable characters in Asian American literature— perhaps in Maxine Hong Kingston's *The Woman Warrior*? Or more of the type of the *yamauba* in Japanese folk tradition and literature? Does the pattern hold for Latina/o literature?

Given that representation of women is necessary in cultures that have only recently begun to define themselves extensively in print, it is sometimes difficult to distinguish between images of women that prove problematic outside the women's own cultures and images that do not present such difficulties. Without exception, African American women whom I have encountered while lecturing on strong black female characters applaud those characters even as they recognize the merits of my attempts to show the problematic components of such representation. "Why show weak black women?" they ask, and I understand the question. But I also stress the need for variety in strong black female representation—for those characters who can cry sometimes even as they take care of everybody else, for those who admit that they sometimes need a rest even as they keep on keeping on, for those who weigh one hundred twenty-five pounds instead of three hundred, for those who are just as strong in their humanity (with its attendant weakness to complement strength) as they are in their unwavering devotion to physical and moral strength.

It is understandable that women across browner cultures would want the best representations in literature, yet those representations can often be problematic. No less is that true in visual arts and performance. Coco

Fusco and Nao Bustamante walk tightropes at every one of their performances, for even as they encourage their audiences to view Latina women and Latino men with different eyes, they must simultaneously resort to the stereotypes that have created the distortions in the first place. Exaggeration as a medium of teaching in such performances perhaps makes clear the directions in which the artists prefer that their audiences respond. Nonetheless, there is a risk in such performances. That risk is equally obvious in the music videos on which Maureen Turim focuses. Women singers and artists who seek freedom of sexual representation in such videos nonetheless run the risk of reinscribing stereotypes. Of course it can be argued that such reinscription would work differently with Madonna than with Queen Latifah, but the projects themselves nonetheless make apparent that the artists must descend into the mud in order to clear the water, and they thereby run the risk of simply stirring up more mud. The politics of such representations, as Fusco realizes, is a form of activism that makes the artist's decision to perform inherently a political one.

But art and literature are contained forms. What of African American, European American, Asian, and Latina women in their social interactions with each other? What conclusions do we draw about each other? Thousands of Spanish-speaking people have relocated to my part of the United States in the 1990s. Do women like me look at those brown women and draw conclusions about their assumed need for social services, their seeming silence in following their men, their seeming inability to speak English? In a disco in Spain, a Spanish woman may be extremely proud of her dancing skills. That same woman removed to a disco in New York City might evoke, in the minds of other women, images of hot-blooded Spanish women who, just because of the way their bodies move on the dance floor, must be good in bed. Do we women join in the stereotyping of Asian female bodies as acquiescent, unassuming, or sexually superior?

Again and again, this collection invites further discussion even as it informs. It invites seminars, conferences, and conversations among the women who have conducted the research and produced these essays. It invites constant awareness that these patterns are not isolated within specific cultures. In short, it well presents Debra Walker King's intention: "The ultimate goal of this volume," she asserts, "is to suggest . . . the need for women's cross-cultural and cross-racial alliance building." Women who are members of the races and cultures represented here cannot afford to be chauvinistic about their exploitation or about the stereotyping that governs their lives. Such postures will only ensure that the circle of assumptions about all of us will remain securely intact. And while I am not naïve

183

enough to assume that the circle will be broken in my lifetime, I can hope that awareness minimizes the destructive potential of this endless process of drawing conclusions about women merely upon the evidence of female bodies, in all their color and variety, that present themselves before us.

In 1931, George S. Schuyler, an African American novelist, published *Black No More,* a narrative about the possibility of eliminating racial differences in America. In it, a scientist discovers a formula for turning black people white. There are some hilarious moments in the novel when black women pass up their weekly trips to beauty parlors and endure "nappy" hair because they are saving money for the ultimate treatment: the one that will turn them white. However, this attempt to eliminate racial discrimination based on body types finally proves futile. Some obsessively observant person discovers that the black folks scientifically turned white are whiter than the biological whites, so tanning becomes all the rage. Schuyler's point is ultimately discouraging: no matter the basis, human beings will find some reason to discriminate against other human beings exclusively because of their body types. Schuyler's take on body politics is instructive in reminding us that the progress we have made since 1931 is not appreciable. We cannot optimistically assert that discrimination based on body types will be eliminated from human cultures within a few lifetimes.

Schuyler joined Jean Toomer, another Harlem Renaissance writer, in positing that racial merger of one kind or another would perhaps end America's discriminatory practices. Toomer envisioned a new American, one who would be a blend of the streams of blackness and whiteness in America. Again, the theory was that if everyone *looked alike,* then no one would be discriminated against (of course that would not solve the problem of age discrimination, or discrimination against people with same-sex preferences). Toomer, like Schuyler, could not see the society in which he lived as capable of eliminating racial prejudice. Unfortunately, we have inherited precisely the landscape in which Toomer and Schuyler lived; therefore, the same problems persist. And though there has been much intermarriage across races, cultures, and ethnic groups since the 1920s, the possibility of racial amalgamation remains remote. The problem we have is the problem we have. No utopian vision will eliminate genotypic differences among us. We have no choice, therefore, but to learn to tolerate and respect differences.

Education and awareness remain the most viable combatants against visual prejudice on the basis of body types, but only world-wide economic equalization can bring about the redistribution of resources that would eliminate sexual tourism. But even that is a dream, as far-fetched as the vision of a common American or world-wide body type. So we continue to talk, to hold our conferences, to make each other aware, to write our essays, to sell our books, to conduct the projects that we hope will influence as many hearers, viewers, and readers as we can reach.

Realistically, I accept the fact that I live in a society and a world that carry presuppositions about my black female body. Realistically, I cannot contain those presuppositions or do very much to alter them. As vigorously as I can mount a campaign to say *what I am not,* those who believe otherwise can mount more vigorous, and more technologically sophisticated, campaigns to assert *what they think I am.* As long as history lives, there will be prejudice against my black female body.

So where does any power I have to combat the situation lie? How can I—and the authors of the essays in this volume—not merely end up striking out blindly, fighting the air? Many years ago, Michael Jackson composed "The Man in the Mirror," a song that places the onus on the individual to make change in his or her own small world. I take my example from him, and I feel even smaller in my ability to effect change. But I *can* make my own little social and work space a bit more aware and tolerant. I can refuse to stereotype women of other races and cultures. Or, when I find myself doing so, I can redirect my thoughts by remembering the conference on The Body Politic at Duke University in which I participated in November 1996 and by remembering the powerful issues, interpretations, and anecdotes presented in this volume. I can speak up when someone within my hearing "reads" a female body in a stereotypical way. I can remember that stereotypes confine and kill just as I remember that the word "nigger" confined and killed historically. I can remember that rejection is vicious and painful. I can remember that large black women are not always strong and thin white women not always weak. I can remember that I am a living, breathing creature who did not create herself and who, in the face of that grand mystery, has no right to question the value of other fantastic creations. I can remember that, in situations great and small, I have the power to hurt or to heal. And I can remember, finally, that, in the family tradition from which I spring, it is always humanly healthier to be counted among the healers.

NOTES

Introduction

1. Alice Walker, "Afterword," in *The Third Life of Grange Copeland* (New York: Harcourt Brace Jovanovich, 1970), 344.

2. Patricia Foster, ed., *Minding the Body: Women Writers on Body and Soul* (New York: Doubleday, 1994).

3. Robin West, "The Supreme Court 1989 Term—Forward: Taking Freedom Seriously," *Harvard Law Review* 43, no. 91 (1990).

2. When Body Politics of Partial Identifications Collide with Multiple Identities of Real Academics

1. Rosser, *Teaching Science and Health*, 24–25. Further references to this book appear in the text as *Teaching Science*.

2. See Yerkes, *Chimpanzees;* Lancaster, *Primate Behavior;* Leavitt, *Peaceable Primates and Gentle People;* Leibowitz, "Perspectives in the Evolution of Sex Differences"; and Rowell, "The Concept of Social Dominance."

3. See Gurwitz, Nananda, and Avorn, "Exclusion of the Elderly and Women"; and Rosser, *Women's Health*. Further references to the latter appear in the text as *Women's Health*.

4. See Rosser, *Feminism and Biology; Female-Friendly Science;* and *Teaching Science*.

5. See Rosser, *Re-engineering Female-Friendly Science* and "Next Millennium is Now Here."

6. See Dill, "Race, Class, and Gender."

7. Rich, "Compulsory Heterosexuality"; Ammer, *A to Z;* Vazquez-Calzadar, "La Esterilizacion Feminina"; Zimmerman et al., "People's Science"; Rodgers, "Rush to Surgery"; and Darty and Potter, "Lesbians and Contemporary Health."

8. See Campbell, "1 in 3 Lesbians."

9. Curran et al., "Epidemiology of HIV"; and Karl Schmidt, personal communication, 20 August 1998.

3. Body Language

1. Patricia Williams, *Race and Rights,* 45.

2. Paule Marshall, *Praisesong for the Widow* (New York: Plume, 1983); and Alice Walker, *Possessing the Secret of Joy* (New York: Pocket Books, 1992).

3. Naomi Zack, *Race and Mixed Race,* 171–72.

4. In the case of racism, imputed genetic association with black skin can replace actual skin color as a signifier.

5. Tashi's psychiatrist is none other than Carl Jung, whose presence in this novel is problematic. Not only is he helping Tashi grasp something that he doesn't even understand, he looks to her and Adam to find some strange primal self, "a self I have often felt was only halfway at home on the European continent. In my European skin. An ancient self that thirsts for knowledge of the experiences of its ancient kin" (86). Adam and Tashi are hardly "ancient"; in fact, Jung is several decades older than they are. Also, in a novel steeped in psychoanalytic symbolism, it seems very strange indeed that Jung wants to "ask Evelyn why she does not seem to fear *my turret/tower,* and what she would say to the gift of a very large bag of clay!" (87, Walker's italics). *Praisesong* presents a different problematic: Avey arrives as a tourist and departs as a part of Grenadian culture, although Marshall's emphasis on the physical, the simple, and even the primitive (Avey is reborn as a child on the island) points to a similarity between the use of Grenada in Marshall's text and the use of Africa, by Jung, in Walker's.

6. According to Sartre, "To know is to *realize* in both senses of the term. It is to cause being "to be there" while having to be the reflected negation of this being. We shall define transcendence as that inner and realizing negation which reveals the in-itself"—the object—"while determining the being of the for-itself"—the subject (Jean-Paul Sartre, *Being and Nothingness,* 249).

7. Simone de Beauvoir, *The Second Sex,* 303.

8. bell hooks, *Yearning,* 23; italics added.

9. She does so linguistically here; white people are the "other," a term which in postmodern discourse is used as a stand-in for a member of an oppressed group. See Leslie Roman, "White Is a Color!"

10. Like Esu Elegbara, Joseph limps and is a master of disguise. For more on this figure, see Henry Louis Gates, "The Blackness of Blackness," especially pages 286–87.

11. Another quality, usually described as intangible, is anthropomorphized in this book. Lebert Joseph's will, or spiritual presence, is described as "like a hand" (157), and is able to

> gently draw away the heat [on Avey's head] and slow down both her pulse and the whirling ring of harsh light behind her closed eyes. Finally, under its calming touch, the dizziness subsided enough for her to raise up and look around her. (159)

Lebert Joseph's will is able to leave his body. Avey's mind, too, is able to leave her body, a characteristic I will discuss later in this essay.

12. This imagery is ubiquitous in Walker's text. See, for example, pages 152, 159, 163, 224, and 231.

13. Note the similarity of the embodiment of the spirit in rum here, and the embodiment of the spirit in wine in Christian Communion.

14. The image of the shattered bowl is continued as Avey imagines her husband having an affair with a white woman while she imagines her own legs spread open on a hospital table as she delivers their baby: "there was the sound of glass on the verge of falling and shattering as she slammed the closet door and left the room" (101). The similarity between Avey's imaginings and Tashi's reality in *Possessing the Secret of Joy* is astonishing. Tashi, whose husband *is* having an affair with a white woman, hears the same sound as she is giving birth. She feels "as if there was a loud noise of something shattering on the hard floor, there between me and Adam and our baby and the doctor" (59).

15. Tashi's body is not only a racial text, but also a cultural one. Like all Olinkan women who have been "bathed," she has "the classic Olinka woman's walk, in which the feet appear to slide forward and are rarely raised above the ground" (66–67). M'lissa too has been especially marked; a gash through the tendon of her thigh and her resulting limp are "the mark, on my body, of my own mother's disobedience" (217). This corporeal text cannot be hidden; it is open at all times to the gaze of the reader.

16. Williams gives a similar reading of Tawana Brawley's eyes after her conversion to Islam ["Her eyes are *unreadable,* and her mouth is closed" (178, italics added)] and in her description of published pictures of Tawana following her rape: "Her body so open and public; her eyes closed, her face shuttered, her head turned always away from the cameras" (176).

17. My favorite example here is the subtitle of Werner Sollors's *Neither Black nor White yet Both: Thematic Explorations of Interracial Literature.* "Interracial Literature" is any literary text that concerns bi-racial characters—Twain's *Pudd'nhead Wilson,* for example.

18. John Guillory, *Cultural Capital,* vii–viii.

4. Writing in Red Ink

1. Karla F. C. Holloway, *Codes of Conduct,* 15.

2. Unless otherwise stated, Alice Walker's fiction is quoted from "Coming Apart," in *You Can't Keep a Good Woman Down* (New York: Harcourt Brace Jovanovich, 1971), that of Toni Morrison from *Beloved* (New York: Knopf, 1987) and *Sula* (New York: Knopf, 1973)—identified in parenthetical page citations where necessary as *Beloved* or *Sula,* and that of Gloria Naylor from *Linden Hills* (New York: Penguin Books, 1987). Hélène Cixous, "The Laugh of the Medusa."

3. Mae Henderson, "Toni Morrison's *Beloved,*" 71.

4. Hortense Spillers, "Mama's Baby, Papa's Maybe," 68.

5. Sherley Anne Williams, *Dessa Rose,* 189.

5. Myths and Monsters

1. Editor's note: Japanese names in this chapter are given with the family name first, and works by Japanese authors discussed here are listed accordingly in the

bibliography. Full documentation for works by Enchi Fumiko, Ōba Minako, Kurahashi Yumiko, and Tsushima Yūko may be found there.

2. Donald L. Philippi concurs with my view that the Japanese official mythology was compiled for political purposes, but he does not delve into the details behind the political agenda of the compilers of the *Kojiki* (*Record of Ancient Matters*, 712) and the *Nihongi* (also *Nihon Shoki, Chronicles of Japan*, ca. 720). On the other hand, Yoshida Atsuhiko, in *Mukashibanashi no Kōkogaku*, connects the yamauba topos to both the Japanese and the Great Mother creation myths and suggests that great mother worship was actively displaced by patriarchal society.

3. This study focuses exclusively on the folk version of the yamauba and does not consider the aesthetic yamanba found in the medieval Nō repertoire.

4. Meera Viswanathan, "In Pursuit of the Yamamba," 242.

5. Ōba Minako and Mizuta Noriko, "'Yamauba' Naru Mono O Megutte," in *Yamauba No Iru Fūkei* (Tokyo: Tabata Shoten, 1995).

6. Stone, *When God Was a Woman*, 4–5.

7. There are several parallels to the myth of Orpheus and Eurydice in the story of Izanagi and Izanami. Bereaved husbands travel to the underworld to retrieve their deceased wives, and in each case the male violates a prohibition against looking at females that negates the possibility of returning to the land of the living with their beloved wives. The underworld in both the Greek and Japanese myths is a place of death and darkness, above which the land of light and the living are situated. But perhaps the most interesting similarity is that of the Furies and the Shikome. The Furies (or *Erinyes*), whose office was to pursue and punish sinners, were called "those who walk in darkness" with writhing snakes for hair and eyes that weep tears of blood. The Shikome, the ugly females of the land of Yomi, were sent by Izanami to pursue Izanagi for having shamed her by looking at her body when she had expressly forbidden him to do so. Although the morals of the two myths differ, the similarities are striking. Edith Hamilton, *Mythology: Timeless Tales of Gods and Heroes* (New York: Mentor Books, 1942), 65.

8. Philippi, trans., *Kojiki*, 49–87.

9. Yoshida, *Mukashibanashi no Kōkogaku*, 64.

10. Ury, trans., "How a Woman."

11. Ury, trans., "How the Hunters' Mother."

12. Mayer, trans. and ed., *Yanagita Kunio*, 102–15.

13. Aston, trans., *Nihongi*, 25.

14. Mayer, 107–11, and Yoshida, 84–96, cite these variant versions.

15. Links to the great mother can be found in the food goddess, Ukemochi no Kami, from whose body valuable goods were produced, explaining the connection between yamauba and food, especially mochi. The *Nihongi* states that Amaterasu sent Tsukiyomi, the moon god, to ask after Ukemochi no Kami. When the food goddess served Tsukiyomi boiled rice, fish, and meat procured from her mouth, the moon god was offended and killed the food goddess with his sword. Thereafter, Amaterasu Ōmikami never wanted to see Tsukiyomi face to face again, which explains why the sun rules the day and the moon the night. The *Nihongi* variant, with its requisite ritual of slaying the food goddess, is associated with customs of ancient agricultural societies that believed that the ritual shedding of blood ensured bountiful crops.

16. Mayer, 110–11, and Kawai, "The Woman Who Eats Nothing," 28–30, propose the former version of the tale while Yoshida, 75–77, advances the latter.

17. Mayer, 110–14, and Yoshida, 73–80, collect variants that suggest the yamauba is repelled by irises and mugworts, but Kawai's variant, "The Woman Who Eats Nothing," 28–31, has the yamauba die from contact with these plants. In either case, these plants usually save men from being devoured or killed by yamauba.

18. Kawai suggests that the idea of storytelling as "spinning a yarn" comes from the image of a spider spinning her thread and equates the fabrication of fantastic stories with the action of spiders weaving their web. Women in the premodern period occupied themselves with the task of weaving cloth, so it is not surprising that the yamauba in some stories transforms into spiders. A related image is the mating ritual of black widow spiders, who devour their mates after coupling. Enchi Fumiko uses this motif along with vampire-like women who suck the life out of men to imbue her texts with eerie, macabre atmospheres. Kawai mentions the negative connotation of spiders in the Greek myth of Arachne, who transforms herself from a beautiful young girl into an old woman and is challenged to a spinning duel by Athena. When Arachne loses, Athena saves her life by transforming her into a spider who hangs in the air. So spiders sometimes represent the negative aspects of females. Kawai, "Woman Who Eats Nothing," 30–32.

19. Tonomura, "Positioning Amaterasu," 13.

20. Motoori Norinaga introduced the concept of the "impure fire of Yomi" when he noted that Izanami was unable to return to the land of the living when invited by Izanagi because she had "eaten at the hearth of Yomi," suggesting ritual defilement. Philippi cites folk customs that regard the fire of mourning families as impure. Matsumura Takeo supports this line of inquiry by stating that eating food cooked by impure fire taints the person who partakes of it because the food of the dead magically disqualifies a person from returning to his homeland, an idea that is also found in the Greek myth of Persephone. Philippi, *Kojiki,* 400–401.

21. Grappard, "Visions of Excess," 11.

6. Agency and Ambivalence

1. Coco Fusco and Nao Bustamante, performance script of *STUFF* (1997).

2. Coco Fusco is a Cuban American writer and performance artist. She has published a collection of essays titled *English Is Broken Here* (1995). Further references to this book appear in the text as *English Broken*. Visit Fusco's home page at http://www.favela.org/fusco/.

3. See Robert Rydell, *All the World's a Fair;* and Coco Fusco, "Other History" (further references to this article appear in the text as "History"). Also see Diana Taylor, "A Savage Performance."

4. Bhabha, "Other Question," in *Location of Culture,* 70. Further references to this chapter appear in the text as "Question."

5. hooks, "Eating the Other," in *Black Looks,* 23.

6. See Lippard, ed., *Partial Recall;* Edwards, ed., *Anthropology and Photography;* Lutz and Collins, *Reading National Geographic.*

7. Avgikos, "Kill All White People," 10.

8. Coco Fusco and Paula Heredita, *The Couple in the Cage: A Guatinaui Odyssey* (Authentic Documentary Productions, 1993), video.

9. Both of these essays are included in Bhabha's *Location of Culture.*

10. Bhabha, "Of Mimicry and Man," 86. Further references to this article appear in the text as "Mimicry."

11. For critiques addressing Bhabha see Parry, "Signs of Our Times"; Young, "Ambivalence of Bhabha," in *White Mythologies,* 141–56.

12. Bakhtin, *Rabelais and His World,* 5.

13. The artists displayed the actual work permits they had had to obtain in order to perform the piece.

14. Fusco, as quoted in Bailey, "Sentimental Necrophilia," 35.

15. Spivak, "Can the Subaltern Speak?"

16. Coco Fusco and Nao Bustamante, conversation with the author, Auckland, New Zealand, July 1997.

17. Cuxtamali is a fictitious, parodic figure invented by the artists. "Cuxtamali is a pun for 'cooks tamales'—which is what Indian women are supposed to be doing all the time, and during the Chicano civil rights movement many women activists complained that they were relegated to being the tamale makers for meetings. Tamales are pies wrapped in husks made of ground corn with meat, spice and vegetables and are a staple of many Latin diets." Coco Fusco, E-mail to the author, 5 November 1998.

18. Bakhtin, "Epic and Novel," in *Dialogic Imagination,* 23.

19. Foucault, *Archeology of Knowledge,* 7.

20. The word *text* is derived from the Latin *textus,* meaning "tissue" or "texture" (that which is woven). See Barthes, *Image, Music, Text.*

7. Performing Bodies, Performing Culture

1. Quoted from Nao Bustamante's bio sheet.

2. Fusco, Introduction to *English Is Broken Here,* x.

3. Ibid., 50.

8. Women Singing, Women Gesturing

1. Fiske, *Television,* 240.

2. See Kaplin, *Rocking around the Clock.* See also Lisa Lewis, *Gender Politics and MTV: Voicing the Difference* (Philadelphia: Temple University Press, 1990).

3. Chion, *Audio-vision,* 166.

4. Sedgwick, "Jane Austen and the Masturbating Girl," 119.

5. See Schwichtenberg, ed., *The Madonna Connection.*

6. VH1 Round Table discussion.

7. *Four on the Floor,* December 1994. Birch, "Wanna Get Freaky," 26.

9. Bombshell

1. *New York Post,* 18 December 1998. The *Daily News* ran an editorial the same day titled "Of Bombs and Bombshells."

2. Despite political activism about and cultural flirtations with androgyny, drag, unisex, bisexuality, and transgendering, traditional heterosexual arrangements

remain dominant and privileged—as evident in most social arrangements, in advertising, law, medicine. Take, for example, the persistence of the term "the opposite sex." Or the popular book that has become a board game in the late 1990s, *Men Are from Mars, Women Are from Venus.* See also Michael Warner, *Fear of a Queer Planet: Queer Politics and Social Theory* (Minneapolis: University of Minnesota Press, 1993); Pat Califia, *Public Sex: The Culture of Radical Sex* (San Francisco: Cleis Press, 1994); and Cindy Patton, *Fatal Advice: How Safe-Sex Education Went Wrong* (Durham: Duke University Press, 1996).

3. Common sense often also insists that sex is better left a private matter, although how it can be considered a private matter at all is questionable, given the numerous public legalities, political restrictions, religious disciplines, and discursive practices about sex that are continually produced (hourly, if you are on the Internet), as Michel Foucault was at pains to demonstrate in *The History of Sexuality.* Further references to this book appear in the text as Foucault.

4. Although whether such an association with JFK hurts or helps Clinton's "image" remains debatable.

5. All of these descriptions were given of Monroe at one time or another by those to whom she was close or with whom she worked, including her husband Arthur Miller, Laurence Olivier, Lauren Bacall, Jane Russell, Billy Wilder, Nunally Johnson, and Jack Paar, among others. See Mills, *Marilyn on Location.*

6. Photographer Cecil Beaton, as quoted by Eve Arnold in *Marilyn Monroe: An Appreciation,* 32. Further references to this book appear in the text as Arnold.

7. It's worth remembering, for example, that Monroe was one of the few people Nikita Krushchev requested to meet on his goodwill tour of the U.S. in 1959; later, in 1992, photographs from this meeting were used by tabloid newspapers to prove that Monroe was a spy for the KGB. For the most reliable biographical information on Monroe, see McCann, *Marilyn Monroe;* Spoto, *Marilyn Monroe: The Biography;* Leming, *Marilyn Monroe;* and Baty, *American Monroe.*

8. *The Star,* 20 October 1998.

9. See also Cathy Caruth, *Unclaimed Experience: Trauma, Narrative and History* (Baltimore: Johns Hopkins University Press, 1996).

10. Marilyn Monroe, *My Story,* 27. Further references to this book appear in the text as Monroe.

11. Stephanie A. Smith, "Suckers," *differences* 10, no. 1 (1998): 183.

12. As John Murchek reminds me, French has two terms that can be translated as "knowledge": "savoir" and "connaissance." English makes no such distinction.

13. One thinks of the Sokol-Ross debates.

14. See Miller, *Technologies of Truth*

15. Sinfield, "Cultural Materialism, *Othello,* and the Politics of Plausibility," 806. Further references to this article appear in the text as Sinfield.

16. Barrett, *The Politics of Truth,* 168, italics added.

17. A pattern of the Light Lady/Dark Lady literary pairing, inherited from the nineteenth century. See also my argument in Smith, *Conceived by Liberty,* 11.

18. See Dyer, "Monroe and Sexuality," 42–44.

19. See Brumberg, *The Body Project.* Further references to this book appear in the text as Brumberg.

20. Bordo, *Unbearable Weight,* 208.

21. See Sullivan, *Bombshells;* and *Va Va Voom! Bombshells, Pin-Ups, Sexpots, and Glamour Girls* (New York: St. Martin Griffin, 1996).

22. Or the famous statement in *My Story:* "Yes, there was something special about me, and I knew what it was. I was the kind of girl they found dead in a hall bedroom with an empty bottle of sleeping pills in her hand" (66).

23. Sanders, *A is for Ox,* 55–56, italics added. Further references to this book appear in the text as Sanders.

24. Sedgwick, *Between Men,* 43, italics added.

25. *Life Magazine,* July 1962, Richard Meryman's interview.

26. Marilyn Monroe's name is multiply trademarked by her estate as Marilyn™, Marilyn Monroe™, and Marilyn Monroe (signature) ™.

27. See Richard Avedon's sequence of Monroe stills in *Life Magazine,* 11 December 1958.

28. See, for example, a popular novel of the 1960s, Alvah Bessie's *The Symbol* (New York: Random House, 1966), which is a fictionalized account of Monroe's life. Here, she is called the S-X Bomb. Indeed, in the novel, "Sometimes her picture was superimposed over the mushroom cloud itself, and the montage provoked editorial writers on the Worker and the West Coast People's World to mild paroxyms of rage at this display of vulgar and corrupt capitalist ideology, which Spectacular executives thought quite amusing until the San Francisco Chronicle wrote: To couple the blatant exploitation of sex with the horror of the bomb that destroyed Hiroshima and Nagasaki—as a Hollywood movie company is doing in advance advertisements for a forthcoming feature film—strikes us as the height of mindless vulgarity" (169).

29. Carl E. Rollyson, Jr., *Marilyn Monroe: A Life of the Actress* (Ann Arbor, Mich.: UMI Research Press, 1986), 66.

30. Arthur Miller, *Timebends,* 370. Further references to this book appear in the text as *Timebends.*

31. Variations on this theme of the incongruence between the Bombshell and the Brain fascinated the popular press and imagination at the time; Fox studios considered floating a story that linked Jayne Mansfield to Charles Van Doren as a publicity stunt, and the rumor that Monroe once slept with Albert Einstein continues to circulate. That brains and bodily attributes are opposite continues to run as a topos through contemporary popular forms, as in Nicholas Roeg's film *Insignificance,* in which the Monroe-DiMaggio marriage is triangulated through Albert Einstein and the creation of the theory of relativity. The film attempts to link sex and violence through the invocation of the atomic bomb, although it also manages to suggest that the Monroe figure deserves to be blown away, for reasons that remain obscure.

32. Famously, although Miller was targeted by the House Un-American Committee, it was the announcement of his upcoming marriage, made publicly to the press on the steps of the Senate even before he'd proposed, that helped to defang the committee's prosecution. The marriage revised Miller's public persona so that the left-wing, Jewish, one-time Communist intellectual vanished in the bright flash-bulb light of his new role as famous, presumably virile husband. Thus the potential version of Miller as an alien, a Communist, or a national traitor was replaced by a version of Miller as a heroic national treasure, both artistic and moral:

a very different public fate than the one Miller's friend, director and one-time Monroe bedmate Elia Kazan, faced after his testimony (Leming, *Marilyn Monroe,* 9–11, 77).

33. See also Dorothy Dinnerstein's *The Mermaid and Minotaur* (New York: Harper Colophon Books, 1977).

34. One thinks, for example, of Governor Jesse "The Body" Ventura's popular voter appeal as someone who was more "real" than most politicians.

35. Recalling F. Scott Fitzgerald's *The Beautiful and the Damned,* a narrative of doomed beauty. Biographies of F. Scott Fitzgerald himself often fall into such a narrative, as if he had become his own *Great Gatsby.*

36. Curiously, one of the caretakers of the child Norma Jean Baker repeatedly likened her to Henry James's *Princess Cassimassima,* Christina Light.

37. Rose, *Haunting of Sylvia Plath,* 26.

38. *Vogue,* 15 September 1962.

39. Or a valiant "victim of . . . a society that professes dedication to the relief of the suffering, but kills the joyous," as Ayn Rand wrote in the *L.A. Times,* 19 August 1962.

40. Weatherby, *Conversations with Marilyn,* 225.

41. Elton John and Bernie Taupin, "Candle in the Wind," 1974. The song was revised in August 1997 as an elegy and tribute to Lady Diana Spencer, Princess of Wales.

42. Carl Sandburg, "Tribute to Marilyn," *Look Magazine,* September 1962, 90–94.

43. See Gloria Steinem, *Marilyn/Norma Jeane.*

44. With apologies and thanks to my colleague Susan Hegeman ("Taking *Blondes* Seriously," *American Literary History* 7, no. 3 [1995]). Critics have taken the *idea* of the blonde seriously—particularly with regard to questions about race—but Monroe herself is often featured as the site of a breakdown in anything like serious significance. For example, in *The Chronicle of Higher Education,* January 14, 2000, an article titled "The Bombshell Ponders Cather" makes it clear that Monroe is still "considered the bombshell, the sex symbol," nothing more.

45. Steven Crane, *Maggie: A Girl of the Streets* (New York: Fawcett, 1960), 29: "The girl, Maggie, blossomed in a mud-puddle."

46. Gramsci, *Selections,* 294–98.

47. A brief comment here: it is worth remembering that Emma Goldstein, in her article "The Traffic in Women" (in *Feminism: The Essential Historical Writings,* ed. Miriam Schneir [New York: Vintage, 1972], 308–17) was writing about marriage as a form of prostitution, a thematic that Gayle Rubin did not lose sight of in writing her oft-cited and more theoretical exploration of the topic.

48. Prostitution, of course, is not gender-specific. See also Wendy Chapkis, *Live Sex Acts: Women Performing Erotic Labor* (New York: Routledge, 1997).

49. Karen Newman, "Directing Traffic: Subjects, Objects and the Politics of Exchange," *differences: A Journal of Feminist Cultural Studies* 2, no. 2 (1990): 50.

50. The conflicting testimonies of Anita Hill and Clarence Thomas regarding his sexual harassment are a case in point, given the reluctance of the all-male Senate Committee to accord any credibility to Anita Hill.

51. Lyotard, *The Differend.* Further references to this book appear in the text as *Differend.*

52. See Philip Gourevitch, "The Memory Thief," *New Yorker,* 14 June 1999, 48–

68; James Poniewozik, "Rigoberta Menchù Meets the Press," in *Salon Magazine,* at http://www.salonmagazine.com/news/1999/02/12newsa.html.

53. Collins, *Fighting Words,* 48–56.

54. Savran, *Communists,* 56.

55. Miller has insistently and repeatedly claimed that the play was not autobiographical. See also Savran, *Communists,* 57; and Miller, *Timebends,* 532.

56. Capote's *In Cold Blood* is often cited as the first best-selling creative nonfiction; Capote wrote *Breakfast at Tiffany's* with Monroe in mind and was reputedly furious when Audrey Hepburn was given the film role. Mailer's *Executioner's Song* is also considered to have furthered this genre, although one might also call his book *Marilyn,* as well as his *On the Elegance of Women* and his stage play *Strawhead,* versions of "creative nonfiction." On Mailer's writing about Monroe, see also Miller, *Timebends,* 532–33.

57. Arthur Miller, *After the Fall.* Further references to this book appear in the text as *Fall.*

58. It is well known that Adolf Hitler admired Henry Ford. And as Michel Foucault writes about Nazism, it was "doubtless the most cunning and the most naïve . . . combination of the fantasies of blood and the paroxysms of a disciplinary power" (Foucault, 149).

59. Lyotard, "The Sign of History," 162.

60. Maggie gives herself the pseudonym Sarah None, and to make sure the audience understands the significance of this, Quentin spells out N-u-n only to be corrected, although from a feminist perspective the homonym is revealing.

61. It is also interesting to note that the failure of this play ended an attempt to form a collective *national* theater under the rubric of Lincoln Center.

62. Jacques Derrida, *Archeology,* 125.

63. Jacques Lacan, *Four Fundamental Concepts of Psycho-analysis.* Further references to this book appear in the text as Lacan.

64. I make this connection, too, through Dyer's argument in "Monroe and Sexuality" that Monroe was being used to locate a "new" understanding of female sexuality that arose in the 1950s—the concept of the vaginal vs. clitoral orgasm, represented as "oceanic."

SELECTED BIBLIOGRAPHY

Allen, Blaine. "Music Television." In *Television: Critical Methods and Applications,* ed. Jeremy Butler. Belmont, Calif.: Wadsworth, 1994.

Ammer, C. *The A to Z of Women's Health.* New York: Everest House, 1983.

Arnold, Eve. *Marilyn Monroe: An Appreciation by Eve Arnold.* New York: Alfred A. Knopf, 1987.

Aston, W. G., trans. *Nihongi: Chronicles of Japan from the Earliest Times to A.D. 697.* Tokyo: Tuttle, 1972.

Avgikos, Jan. "Kill All White People." *Art Forum International,* May 1993: 10.

Bailey, Cameron. "Sentimental Necrophilia: Coco Fusco Asks Why the Only Loved Latina Is a Dead Latina." *Mix: The Magazine of Artist-Run. Culture* 23 (summer 1997): 35–38.

Bakhtin, Mikhail. *The Dialogic Imagination.* Ed. Michael Holquist, trans. Caryl Emerson and Michael Holquist. Austin: University of Texas Press, 1981.

———. *Rabelais and His World.* Trans. Helene Iswolsky. Cambridge, Mass.: MIT Press, 1968.

Barrett, Michèlle. *The Politics of Truth: From Marx to Foucault.* Stanford, Calif.: Stanford University Press, 1991.

Barthes, Roland. *Image, Music, Text.* Trans. Stephen Heath. London: Fontana Press, 1977.

Baty, S. Paige. *American Monroe: The Making of a Body Politic.* Berkeley and Los Angeles: University of California Press, 1995.

Beauvoir, Simone de. *The Second Sex.* New York: Random House, 1974.

Bhabha, Homi K. *The Location of Culture.* London: Routledge, 1994.

————. "Of Mimicry and Man: The Ambivalence of Colonial Discourse." *October* 28 (spring 1994): 125–33.

Birch, H. "Wanna Get Freaky with Me? Adina Howard Wants to Set Black Women Free, Sexually." *The Independent,* 28 April 1995: 26.

Bordo, Susan. *Unbearable Weight: Feminism, Western Culture and the Body.* Berkeley: University of California Press, 1993.

Brecht, Bertolt. *Brecht on Theatre: The Development of an Aesthetic.* 6th ed. Trans. John Willett. London: Methuen, 1987.

Brumberg, Joan Jacobs. *The Body Project: An Intimate History of American Girls.* New York: Random House, First Vintage, 1998.

Calbris, Genevieve. *The Semiotics of French Gestures.* Trans. Owen Doyle. Bloomington: Indiana University Press, 1990.

Campbell, Kristina. "1 in 3 Lesbians May Get Breast Cancer, Expert Theorizes." *The Washington Blade* (2 October 1992): 1–23.

Chion, Michel. *Audio-vision: Sound on Screen.* Trans. Claudia Gorbman. New York: Columbia University Press, 1994.

Cixous, Hélène. "The Laugh of the Medusa." In *Feminisms,* ed. Robyn R. Warhol and Diane Price Herndl, 334–49. New Brunswick, N.J.: Rutgers University Press, 1993.

Collins, Patricia Hill. *Fighting Words: Black Women and the Search for Justice.* Minneapolis: University of Minnesota Press, 1998.

Curran, J. W., et al. "Epidemiology of HIV Infection and AIDS in the United States." *Science* 239 (1988): 610–16.

Darty, T., and S. Potter. "Lesbians and Contemporary Health Care Systems: Oppression and Opportunity." In *Women Identified Women,* ed. T. Darty and S. Potter. Palo Alto, Calif.: Mayfield Publishing Company, 1984.

Derrida, Jacques. *The Archeology of the Frivolous: Reading Condillac.* Trans. John P. Leavey, Jr. Lincoln: University of Nebraska Press, 1980.

Dill, B. T. "Race, Class, and Gender: Prospects for an All-Inclusive Sisterhood." *Feminist Studies* 9, no. 1 (1983).

Dyer, Richard. "Monroe and Sexuality." In *Heavenly Bodies: Film Stars and Society,* 35. Cinema, BFI series. New York: St. Martin, 1986.

Edwards, Elizabeth. *Anthropology and Photography: 1860–1920.* New Haven: Yale University Press, 1992.

Enchi Fumiko. "Haru no Uta." In *Enchi Fumiko Zenshū,* vol. 5, 253–65. Tokyo: Shinchōsha, 1977.

————. *Saimu.* In *Enchi Fumiko Zenshū,* vol. 13, 215–429. Tokyo: Shinchōsha, 1977.

Fanon, Franz. *Black Skins White Masks.* Trans. Charles Lam Markmann. New York: Grove Weidenfeld, 1967.

Fiske, John. *Television Culture.* London: Methuen, 1987.

Foucault, Michel. *The Archeology of Knowledge and the Discourse on Language.* Trans. A. M. Sheridan Smith. New York: Pantheon Books, 1972.

————. *The History of Sexuality: Volume I—An Introduction.* New York: Vintage, 1980.

Fusco, Coco. *English Is Broken Here: Notes on Cultural Fusion in the Americas.* New York: New Press, 1995.

————. "The Other History of Intercultural Performance." *The Drama Review* 38, no. T141 (spring 1994): 143–67.

Gates, Henry Louis, Jr. "The Blackness of Blackness: A Critique of the Sign and the Signifying Monkey." In *Black Literature and Literary Theory,* ed. Henry Louis Gates, Jr. New York: Methuen, 1984.

Goodwin, Andrew. *Dancing in the Distraction Factory: Music Television and Popular Culture.* Minneapolis: University of Minnesota Press, 1992.

Gramsci, Antonio. *Selections from the Prison Notebooks.* Ed. Quintin Hoare and Geoffrey Nowell Smith. New York: International Publishers, 1995.

Grappard, Allan G. "Visions of Excess and Excesses of Vision: Women and Transgression in Japanese Myth." *Japanese Journal of Religious Studies* 18, no. 1 (1991): 11.

Guillory, John. *Cultural Capital: The Problem of Literary Canon Formation.* Chicago: University of Chicago Press, 1993.

Gurwitz, Jerry H., F. Colonel Nananda, and Jerry Avorn. "The Exclusion of the Elderly and Women from Clinical Trials in Acute Myocardial Infection." *Journal of the American Medical Association* 268, no. 2 (1992): 1417–22.

Henderson, Mae. "Toni Morrison's *Beloved:* Re-Membering the Body as Historical Text." In *Comparative American Identities: Race, Sex, and Nationality in the Modern Text,* ed. Hortense J. Spillers, 62–86. New York: Routledge, 1991.

Hezekaih, Gabrielle. "Ethnic Talent for Export: Mexarcane International." *Fuse Magazine* 18 (spring 1995): 37–39.

Hochegger, Hermann. *Le Langage gestuel en Afrique Centrale.* St. Augustin: Steyler Verlag, 1978.

Holloway, Karla F. C. *Codes of Conduct: Race, Ethics, and the Color of Our Character.* New Brunswick, N.J.: Rutgers University Press, 1995.

hooks, bell. *Black Looks: Race and Representation.* Boston: South End Press, 1992.

———. *Yearning: Race, Gender, and Cultural Politics.* Boston: South End Press, 1990.

Irigaray, L. *Speculum of the Other Woman.* Trans. Gillian C. Gill. Ithaca: Cornell University Press, 1985.

Jones, Gayl. *Eva's Man.* Boston: Beacon Press, 1976.

Kaplin, E. Ann. *Rocking around the Clock: Music Television, Postmodernism and Consumer Culture.* New York: Methuen, 1987.

Kawai, Hayao. "The Woman Who Eats Nothing." In *The Japanese Psyche: Major Motifs in the Fairy Tales of Japan,* trans. Hayao Kawai and Sachiko Reece, 27–45. Dallas: Spring Publications, 1988.

Kojiki. *Nihon Koten Bungaka Zenshū.* Vol. 1, 43–367. Tokyo: Shogakukan, 1973.

Kurahashi Yumiko. "Haru no Yo no Yume." In Kurahashi, *Yume no Kayoiji,* 184–95. Tokyo: Kōdansha, 1989.

———. "The Long Passage of Dreams" [Nagai Yumeji, 1968]. In *The Woman with the Flying Head and Other Stories by Kurahashi Yumiko,* trans. and ed. Atsuko Sakaki, 105–55. Armonk, N.Y.: M. E. Sharpe, 1998.

———. "Spring Night Dreams." In *The Woman with the Flying Head and Other Stories by Kurahashi Yumiko,* trans. and ed. Atsuko Sakaki, 67–76. Armonk, New York: M. E. Sharpe, 1998.

Lacan, Jacques. *The Four Fundamental Concepts of Psycho-analysis.* New York and London: W. W. Norton, 1981.

Lancaster, J. *Primate Behavior and the Emergence of Human Culture.* New York: Holt, Rinehart and Winston, 1975.

Leavitt, R. R. *Peaceable Primates and Gentle People: Anthropological Approaches to Women's Studies*. New York: Harper and Row, 1975.

Leibowitz, L. "Perspectives in the Evolution of Sex Differences." In *Toward an Anthropology of Women*, ed. R. Reiter. New York: Monthly Review Press, 1975.

Leming, Barbara. *Marilyn Monroe*. New York: Crown, 1998.

Lewis, Lisa A. *Gender Politics and MTV: Voicing the Difference*. Philadelphia: Temple University, 1990.

Lippard, Lucy. *Mixed Blessings: New Art in a Multicultural America*. New York: Pantheon Books, 1990.

———, ed. *Partial Recall: Photographs of Native North Americans*. New York: New Press, 1992.

Lutz, Catherine, A., and Jane L. Collins. *Reading National Geographic*. Chicago: University of Chicago Press, 1992.

Lyotard, Jean François. *The Differend: Phrases in Dispute*. Minneapolis: University of Minnesota Press, 1988.

———. "The Sign of History." In *Post-Structuralism and the Question of History*, ed. Derek Attridge, Geoff Bennington, and Robert Young. Cambridge, England: Cambridge University Press, 1987.

Marshall, Paule. *Praisesong for the Widow*. New York: Plume, 1983.

Mayer, Fannie Hagin, trans. and ed., *The Yanagita Kunio Guide to the Japanese Folk Tale*. Bloomington: Indiana University Press, 1986.

McCann, Graham. *Marilyn Monroe*. New Brunswick, N.J.: Rutgers University Press, 1987.

Miller, Arthur. *After the Fall: A Play by Arthur Miller*. New York: Viking Press, 1964.

———. *Timebends*. New York: Grove Press, 1987.

Miller, Toby. *Technologies of Truth: Cultural Citizenship and the Popular Media*. Minneapolis: University of Minnesota Press, 1998.

Mills, Bart. *Marilyn on Location*. London: Sidgwick and Jackson, 1989.

Monroe, Marilyn. *My Story*. New York: Stein and Day, 1974.

Morrison, Toni. *Beloved*. New York: Knopf, 1987.

———. *Sula*. New York: Knopf, 1973.

Murphy, Ellen W. Goellner, and Jacqueline Shea, eds. *Bodies of the Text: Dance as Theory, Literature as Dance*. New Brunswick, N.J.: Rutgers University Press, 1995.

Naylor, Gloria. *Linden Hills*. 1985. New York: Penguin Books, 1987.

Newmann, Erich. *The Origins and History of Consciousness*. Bollingen Series. Princeton, N.J.: Princeton University Press, 1954.

Ōba Minako. "Candlefish." In *Unmapped Territories: New Women's Fiction from Japan*, ed. Yukiko Tanaka, 18–38. Seattle, Wash.: Women in Translation, 1991.

———. "The Smile of the Mountain Witch." In *Stories by Contemporary Japanese Women Writers*, trans. and ed. Noriko Mizuta Lippit and Kyoko Iriye Selden, 182–96. Armonk, N.Y.: M. E. Sharpe, 1982.

Parry, Benita. "Signs of Our Times: A Discussion of Homi Bhahba's *The Location of Culture*." *Third Text* 28/29 (autumn/winter 1994): 5–24.

Pearson, Roberta. *Eloquent Gestures*. Berkeley: University of California Press, 1992.

Philippi, Donald L., trans. *Kojiki*. Tokyo: University of Tokyo Press, 1969.

Rich, A. "Compulsory Heterosexuality and Lesbian Existence." *Signs: Journal of Women in Culture and Society* 5 (summer 1980): 631–60.

Rodgers. J. "Rush to Surgery." *The New York Times Magazine*, 21 September 1973: 34.

Roman, Leslie. "White Is a Color! White Defensiveness, Postmodernism, and Anti-racist Pedagogy." In *Race Identity and Representation in Education*, ed. Cameron McCarthy, Warren Crichlow, et al. New York: Routledge, 1993.

Rose, Jacqueline. *The Haunting of Sylvia Plath*. Cambridge, Mass.: Harvard University Press, 1992.

Rosser, Sue V. *Female-Friendly Science: Applying Women's Studies Methods and Theories to Attract Students to Science*. New York: Pergamon Press, 1990.

———. *Feminism and Biology*. New York: Twayne, MacMillan, 1992.

———. "The Next Millennium is Now Here: Women's Studies Perspectives on Diotechnics and Reproductive Technologies." In *New Perspectives in Gender Studies: Research in the Fields of Economics, Culture and Life Sciences*, ed. Boel Berner, 7–35. Stockholm, Sweden: Almquist and Wilosell International, 1998.

———. *Re-engineering Female-Friendly Science*. New York: Teachers College Press, Columbia University, 1997.

———. *Teaching Science and Health from a Feminist Perspective: A Practical Guide*. New York: Pergamon Press, 1986.

———. *Women's Health—Missing from U.S. Medicine*. Bloomington: Indiana University Press, 1994.

Rowell, Thelma. "The Concept of Social Dominance." *Behavioral Biology* 4 (1974): 131–54.

Rydell, Robert. *All the World's a Fair: Visions of Empire at American International Exhibitions, 1876–1916*. Chicago: University of Chicago Press, 1984.

Sanders, Barry. *A Is for Ox: The Collapse of Literacy and the Rise of Violence in an Electronic Age*. New York: Random House, Vintage Books, 1995.

Sartre, Jean Paul. *Being and Nothingness*. 1956. New York: Washington Square Press, 1966.

Savran, David. *Communists, Cowboys, and Queers: The Politics of Masculinity in the Work of Arthur Miller and Tennessee Williams*. Minneapolis: University of Minnesota Press, 1992.

Schwichtenberg, Cathy, ed. *The Madonna Connection: Representational Politics, Subcultural Identities, and Cultural Theory*. Boulder and San Francisco: Westview, 1993.

Sedgwick, Eve Kosofsky. *Between Men: English Literature and Male Homosocial Desire*. New York: Columbia University Press, 1985.

———. "Jane Austen and the Masturbating Girl." In Sedgwick, *Tendencies*. Durham, N.C.: Duke University Press, 1993.

Sinfield, Alan. "Cultural Materialism, *Othello*, and the Politics of Plausibility." In *Literary Theory: An Anthology*, ed. Julie Rivkin and Michael Ryan. New York: Blackwell, 1998.

Smith, Stephanie. *Conceived by Liberty: Maternal Figures and Nineteenth-Century American Literature*. Ithaca, N.Y.: Cornell, 1995.

Sollors, Werner. *Neither Black nor White yet Both: Thematic Explorations of Interracial Literature*. New York: Oxford University Press, 1997.

Spillers, Hortense. "Mama's Baby, Papa's Maybe: An American Grammar Book." *Diacritics* (summer 1987): 65–81.

Spivak, Gayatri Chakravorty. "Can the Subaltern Speak?" In *Colonial Discourse and*

Postcolonial Theory: A Reader, ed. Patrick Williams and Laura Chisman, 66–111. New York: Columbia University Press, 1994.

Spoto, Donald. *Marilyn Monroe: The Biography.* New York: Harper Collins, 1993.

Steinem, Gloria. *Marilyn: Norma Jean.* Photos by George Barris. New York: Signet, 1986.

Stone, Merlin. *When God Was a Woman.* New York: Harcourt Brace Jovanovich, 1976.

Sullivan, Steve. *Bombshells: Glamour Girls of a Lifetime.* New York: St. Martin's, Griffin, 1998.

Tanabe Seiko. *Tanabe Seiko no Kojiki.* Tokyo: Shūeisha, 1991.

Taylor, Diana. "A Savage Performance: Guillermo Gómez-Peña and Coco Fusco's *The Couple in the Cage.*" With a response by Barbara Kirshenblatt-Gimblett. *The Drama Review* 42, no. T158 (summer 1998): 160–80.

Tonomura, Hitomi. "Positioning Amaterasu: A Reading of the Kojiki." *The Japan Foundation Newsletter* 22, no. 2 (July 1994): 12–17.

Tsushima Yūko. "Maboroshi." In Tsushima, *Danmari Ichi,* 42–61. Tokyo: Shin-chōsha, 1984.

———. "Yume no Michi." In Tsushima, *Danmari Ichi,* 24–39. Tokyo: Shinchōsha, 1984.

Ury, Marian, trans. "How a Woman Who Was Bearing a Child Went to South Yamashina, Encountered an Oni, and Escaped." In Ury, trans. and ed., *Tales of Times Now Past: Sixty-two Stories from a Medieval Japanese Collection,* 161–63. Berkeley: University of California Press, 1979.

———. "How the Hunters' Mother Became an Oni and Tried to Devour Her Children." In *Tales of Times Now Past: Sixty-two Stories from a Medieval Japanese Collection,* 163–65. Berkeley: University of California Press, 1979.

Vazquez-Calzadar, J. "La Esterilizacion Feminina en Puerto Rico." *Revista de Ciencias Sociales* 17 (San Juan, Puerto Rico, September 1973): 128–308.

Viswanathan, Meera. "In Pursuit of the Yamamba: The Question of Female Resistance." In *The Woman's Hand: Gender and Theory in Japanese Women's Writing,* ed. Paul Gordon and Janet A. Walker, 239–61. Stanford, Calif.: Stanford University Press, 1996.

Walker, Alice. "Coming Apart." In *You Can't Keep a Good Woman Down.* New York: Harcourt, Brace, Jovanovich, Harvest, 1971.

———. *Possessing the Secret of Joy.* New York: Pocket Books, 1992.

Weatherby, W. J. *Conversations with Marilyn.* New York: Mason, Charter, 1976.

Williams, Patricia. *The Alchemy of Race and Rights.* Cambridge, Mass.: Harvard University Press, 1991.

Williams, Sherley Anne. *Dessa Rose.* New York: William Morrow, 1986.

Yerkees, Robert M. *Chimpanzees.* New Haven, Conn.: Yale University Press, 1943.

Yoshida Atsuhiko. *Mukashibanashi no Kōkogaku: Yamauba to Jomon no Joshin* [Archeology of folk tales: Yamauba and Jōmon goddesses]. Tokyo: Chūō Kōronsha, 1992.

Young, Robert. *White Mythologies: Writing, History and the West.* London: Routledge, 1990.

Zack, Naomi. *Race and Mixed Race.* Philadelphia: Temple University Press, 1993.

Zimmerman, B., et al. "People's Science." In *Science and Liberation,* ed. R. Arditti, P. Brennan, and S. Cavrak, 299–319. Boston: South End Press, 1980.

CONTRIBUTORS

TRUDIER HARRIS
is J. Carlyle Sitterson Professor of English at the University of North Carolina at Chapel Hill. She is author of *Exorcising Blackness: Historical and Literary Lynching and Burning Rituals* (1984), *Black Women in the Fiction of James Baldwin* (1985), and *Fiction and Folklore: The Novels of Toni Morrison* (1991), among other works. She is also editor of *New Essays on Baldwin's "Go Tell It on the Mountain"* (1996) and co-editor of *The Oxford Companion to African American Literature* (1997), *Call and Response: The Riverside Anthology of the African American Literary Tradition* (1998), and *The Literature of the American South: A Norton Anthology* (1998).

MAUDE HINES
is Assistant Professor of English at the University of Florida where she teaches American literature, children's literature, and cultural studies. Her article "Missionary Positions: Taming the Savage Girl in Louisa May Alcott's *Jack and Jill*" appears in *The Lion and the Unicorn* (vol. 23.2, September 1999).

S. YUMIKO HULVEY
is Associate Professor of Japanese Literature at the University of Florida. Her essays appear in several collections, including *Japanese Women Writers:*

A Bio-Critical Sourcebook (1994), *Japan in Traditional and Postmodern Perspectives* (1995), and *Medieval Japanese Writers* in the Dictionary of Literary Biography series (1999), and in journals such as *Monumenta Nipponica, Japan Studies Review*, and *Manoa: A Pacific Journal of International Writing.*

DEBRA WALKER KING
is Associate Professor of English at the University of Florida. She is author of *Deep Talk: Reading African American Literary Names* (1998) and articles and reviews appearing in *Names: The Journal of the American Name Society; Philosophy and Rhetoric;* and *African American Review.* She also contributed essays to the *Oxford Companion to African American Literature* (1997) and *Recovered Writers/Recovered Texts,* edited by Dolan Hubbard (1997).

SUE V. ROSSER
is Professor of History, Technology, and Science and Dean of the Ivan Allen College, the Liberal Arts College of Georgia Institute of Technology. She has edited collections and written approximately eighty journal articles on the theoretical and applied problems of women and science and on women's health. She is author of *Teaching Science and Health from a Feminist Perspective: A Practical Guide* (1986), *Feminism within the Science and Health Care Professions: Overcoming Resistance* (1988), *Female-Friendly Science* (1990), *Feminism and Biology: A Dynamic Interaction* (1992), *Women's Health—Missing from U.S. Medicine* (1994), *Teaching the Majority* (1995), *Re-engineering Female-Friendly Science* (1997), and *The Crucial Union for the Millennium* (forthcoming). Rosser also served as the Latin and North American co-editor of the Women's Studies International Forum from 1989 to 1993.

STEPHANIE A. SMITH
is Associate Professor of English at the University of Florida. She is author of *Conceived by Liberty: Maternal Figures and Nineteenth-Century American Literature* (1995) and essays in several collections, including *Harriet Jacobs and Incidents in the Life of a Slave Girl: New Critical Essays* (1995), and in journals such as *American Literature; Criticism; Genders;* and *differences: A Journal of Feminist Cultural Studies.* She is also author of three novels: *Snow-Eyes* (1985), *The Boy-Who-Was-Thrown-Away* (1987), and *Other Nature* (1996).

MAUREEN TURIM
is Professor of English and Film Studies at the University of Florida. She is author of *Abstraction in Avant-Garde Films* (1985), *Flashbacks in Film: Memory and History* (1989), and *The Films of Oshima: Images of a Japanese Iconoclast* (1998).

She has also published more than fifty essays in anthologies and journals on a wide range of theoretical, historical, and aesthetic issues in cinema and video, art, cultural studies, feminist and psychoanalytic theory, and comparative literature, and written catalogue essays for museum exhibitions.

CAROLINE VERCOE
is a lecturer in the Art History Department at Auckland University, New Zealand, where she teaches Pacific art history and postcolonial theory. She has completed major research projects on Samoan body adornment and published essays on the fiction and agency of postcard images taken in the Pacific and on contemporary artists who rethink colonial strategies of cultural representation. She is currently completing her dissertation, which focuses on postcolonial and semiotic theories in a reading of works by Pacific artists.

GLORIA WADE-GAYLES
is a poet, essayist, and literary critic, and the RosaMary Eminent Scholar's Chair in Humanities/Fine Arts at Dillard College in New Orleans, Louisiana. She is author of *No Crystal Stair: Visions of Race and Sex in Black Women's Fiction* (1984), *Anointed to Fly* (1991), *Pushed Back to Strength* (1993), and *Rooted against the Wind* (1996), among other books, as well as chapters in edited collections. She is also editor of *My Soul Is a Witness: African-American Women's Spirituality* (1995) and *Father Songs: Testimonies by African-American Sons and Daughters* (1997).

ROSEMARY WEATHERSTON
is a doctoral candidate in English at the University of Southern California, where she is completing her dissertation, "Turning the Informant: Administrations and Negotiations of Difference in Twentieth-Century Literature and Culture." She is author of articles, reviews, and book chapters appearing in *Theatre Journal; Discourse; Journal for Theoretical Studies in Media and Culture;* and *Post Identity;* and co-editor of *Queer Frontiers: Politics, Polemics and Possibilities for the Millennium* (forthcoming).